The Possibility of Satan

The Possibility of Satan

A Case for Reformulating the Catholic Church's Teachings on the Devil

ALAN McGILL

◆PICKWICK *Publications* · Eugene, Oregon

THE POSSIBILITY OF SATAN
A Case for Reformulating the Catholic Church's Teachings on the Devil

Copyright © 2021 Alan McGill. All rights reserved. Except for brief quotations in critical publications or reviews, no part of this book may be reproduced in any manner without prior written permission from the publisher. Write: Permissions, Wipf and Stock Publishers, 199 W. 8th Ave., Suite 3, Eugene, OR 97401.

Biblical quotations are from the New Revised Standard Version, unless otherwise noted.

Pickwick Publications
An Imprint of Wipf and Stock Publishers
199 W. 8th Ave., Suite 3
Eugene, OR 97401

www.wipfandstock.com

PAPERBACK ISBN: 978-1-7252-6665-0
HARDCOVER ISBN: 978-1-7252-6666-7
EBOOK ISBN: 978-1-7252-6667-4

Cataloguing-in-Publication data:

Names: McGill, Alan M., author

Title: The possibility of Satan : a case for reformulating the Catholic Church's teachings on the devil / Alan McGill.

Description: Eugene, OR: Pickwick Publications, 2021 | Includes bibliographical references.

Identifiers: ISBN 978-1-7252-6665-0 (paperback) | ISBN 978-1-7252-6666-7 (hardcover) | ISBN 978-1-7252-6667-4 (ebook)

Subjects: LCSH: Devil | Demonology | Devil—Christianity | Catholic Church—Doctrines | Good and evil

Classification: BX1746 M34 2021 (paperback) | BX1746 (ebook)

04/01/21

For the inhuman creatures whose ontological existence I more readily accept—the pets who have been for me sacraments of God's love.

Contents

Introduction		1
1	Personalizing Satan by Historicizing Myth	9
2	Satan: A Hybrid Born of Cross-Pollinating Myths	28
3	Can the Existence of Satan Be Demonstrated without Recourse to Myth?	45
4	The "Modernist Crisis": A Refusal to Benefit from the Insights of Modernity	60
5	Vatican II and the Case for the Ongoing Development of Doctrine	69
6	Why Doctrinal Formulations Should Respect the Genre of Biblical Texts	87
7	What Is Myth and What Kind of Truth Does It Express within the Bible?	98
8	The Doctrine of Satan Entangled in a Conflict about Magisterial Authority	114
9	Pope Francis on the Devil, Discernment, and Interpretations of Doctrine	134
10	What Did Jesus and the New Testament Authors Teach About Satan?	148
11	Interpreting Gospel References to Demons	163
12	Towards a Less Dualistic Approach to Possession and Exorcism	175

13	Zeal for the Damnation of the Enemy versus Enemy Love and Forgiveness	187
14	A Proposed Reformulation of the Doctrine of Satan	203
15	The Satan of Satanism: Validating Doctrine through Behavior	219

Bibliography   233

Introduction

What are educated, twenty-first-century people supposed to make of the Catholic Church's teachings on the existence of Satan as a disembodied being, an eternally damned person, and, specifically, a fallen angel? The 1992 Catechism of the Catholic Church presents Satan in just such terms, rejecting an interpretation of the motif as a figurative personification. In response, the present work will argue that this insistence upon the existence of Satan as a supernatural creature is rooted in a literalization of myth that runs contrary to the Church's own teachings on biblical interpretation. The implications of this hermeneutical error are then compounded by dualistic speculations, particularly the assumption that we can know with certainty that any being is damned so as to be eternally separated from God, with no possibility of reconciliation. This matters deeply for the Catholic faith since its current account of the doctrine of Satan undermines its credibility and contradicts its most central claims about God and the world.

Clearly, no human has witnessed a battle in heaven and the Fall of rebellious angels, or for that matter, observed the temptation of Adam and Eve by the devil masquerading as a snake. Myth conveys truth—truth of a kind that is best expressed through story—but the truth in question is not historical truth. It does not record the antics of particular persons, whether human or supernatural. Rather, it explores the tension between possibilities and the existential limitations that confront every free-willed, mortal person. It is hence ludicrous to think of the battle in heaven as one might think of the Battle of Hastings and of mythical personages as though they signify disembodied spirits.

The Adamic myth does not reveal the existence, choices, and acts of a particular snake, or a particular angel any more than it relates the fate of a particular piece of fruit. By presenting this narrative in a historicized manner, the Catechism's account of Satan ignores seventy years of Church teaching that scripture should be interpreted in light of its literary genres and authorial contexts. The Catechism, in its references to the devil, seems oblivious to an approach to biblical interpretation, long accepted by the Catholic Church, that reads myth as myth, not pretending that it is history. This selective imperviousness to responsible exegesis does nothing for the credibility and viability of the Catholic faith. It would present no threat to the faith to present myth as myth, allowing the genre to serve as a powerful medium of metaphysical truth and, from a perspective of faith, divine revelation. Indeed, by resisting the overwhelming thrust of modern scholarship on the interpretation of myth, the magisterium undermines its own stated vision for a dialogical relationship between the Church and the modern world.

The Second Vatican Council in 1965 mandated the Church to seriously consider insights derived from modern scholarship, proposing, "The experience of past ages, the progress of the sciences, and the treasures hidden in the various forms of human culture, by all of which the nature of man himself is more clearly revealed and new roads to truth are opened, these profit the Church too."[1] The Council would recognize that the "progress of the sciences" can help to uncover and convey the "experience of past ages," rediscovering and developing the wisdom of antiquity.[2] This book is impelled by modern scholarship that does exactly this, rediscovering and developing the wisdom conveyed by ancient motifs of Satan.

Pope Francis, writing in 2018, epitomizes the spirit of Vatican II when he recognizes the value of modern insights for the expression of Catholic doctrine, remarking that "the questions of our people, their suffering, their struggles, their dreams, their trials and their worries, all possess an interpretational value that we cannot ignore if we want to take the principle of the incarnation seriously. Their wondering helps us to wonder, their questions question us."[3] Francis posits that doctrinal formulae, as attempts to express eternal truths in human words, should be open to development in light of the questions of modern people, proposing, "In effect, doctrine, or better, our understanding and expression of it, is not a closed system, devoid of the dynamic capacity to pose questions, doubts, inquiries."[4]

Vatican II particularly recognized that the methods and insights of modern biblical scholarship could contribute towards the continuing

---

1. Paul VI, *"Gaudium et Spes"* 44.
2. Lindbeck, "How a Lutheran Saw It," 16.
3. Francis, *"Gaudete et Exsultate"* 44.
4. Francis, *"Gaudete et Exsultate"* 44.

development of doctrine.⁵ Indeed, since 1943, the Church has urged exegetes to adopt the best interpretative methods at their disposal, explicating in 1964 that the fruit of such inquiry should contribute towards the "continued progress of sacred doctrine."⁶ Fifty years later, in 1993, the Pontifical Biblical Commission explicitly promoted the historical-critical method as "indispensable" for the interpretation of scripture.⁷ An integral concern of this method is its attention to the implications of the literary genres.⁸ One such genre through which the Word of God is mediated in human words is that of myth.

An approach to myth associated with Paul Ricoeur regards the genre as the symbolic expression of ubiquitous actualities and possibilities that characterize the experience of being human in any time and place. These existential realities and potentialities cannot be explained in an equivalent way by means of other genres—they are truths best told through fiction.⁹ As such, Ricoeur ideates a form of demythologization that does not seek to replace the symbolic language of myth with some other register of language, but rather to liberate myth from the misguided expectation that it affirms particular historical events, and delivers causal explanations.¹⁰

Ricoeur's model of myth, envisaging the genre as concerned with universal, supra-historical rather than historical truth, has been largely embraced within contemporary Catholic biblical exegesis. John McKenzie, in *The New Jerome Biblical Commentary*, which bears the *imprimatur* and *nihil obstat*, affirms an understanding of myth as conveying universal rather than historical truth, stating, "Myth is couched in narrative, but the narrative is not historical. The event of myth is not the singular event located in time and space, but the recurring event of the eternal now."¹¹ McKenzie distinguishes between the symbols contained within the narrative arc of myth and particular entities in the world beyond. "It does not pretend that the symbol is the reality, but it proposes the symbol as that which affords an insight into a reality beyond understanding."¹²

In contrast with the model of myth advanced by Ricoeur and adopted by a swathe of Catholic exegetes within the pages of ecclesiastically approved

5. Paul VI, "*Dei Verbum*" 12; CDF, *Catechism of the Catholic Church* 109.
6. Pius XII, "*Divino Afflante Spiritu*" 37; PBC, "*Sancta Mater Ecclesiae*."
7. PBC, "Interpretation of the Bible in the Church" 34.
8. PBC, "Interpretation of the Bible in the Church" 1.
9. Ricoeur, "Preface to Bultmann," 60.
10. Olson, "Mythic Language of the Demonic," 12.
11. McKenzie, "Aspects of Old Testament Thought," 1289.
12. McKenzie, "Aspects of Old Testament Thought," 1289.

commentaries, the Catechism historicizes the mythical motif of the Fall of the angels and the Adamic narrative of Genesis 3 so as to regard Satan as a particular person who exercised agency through specific historical deeds.[13] This insistence on Satan's existence as a particular person stands in tension with the positions of notable Catholic theologians including Joseph Ratzinger, Walter Kasper, and Hans Urs von Balthasar who have denied that Satan exists as a person.[14]

While myth does not in itself provide an authoritative basis from which to argue the existence of the devil as a particular person, it might be asked whether its language serves as a figurative means through which to express an ontological reality the existence of which can be affirmed philosophically through reason and life experience. The short answer is no. This book will argue that no amount of inductive reflection upon the experience of evil provides a reasonable basis for belief in the ontological reality of the Satan profiled in the Catechism. The doctrine, as currently formulated, lacks a basis in either scripture or natural theology. It is the doctrinal equivalent of the long-defunct altar rails that no parish priest has had the courage to remove—a throwback to the pre-Vatican II Church, and a bone thrown to those who resent the vision of the Council.

All this said, this book does not deny the possibility that malevolent disembodied entities, demons, that is, might exist in some sense. Such a claim is beyond its scope and perhaps unfalsifiable. The book is not the theological equivalent of an attempt to debunk the existence of Sasquatch. Rather than denying the existence of some entity in the universe, it challenges, on hermeneutical and theological grounds, the particular identikit of Satan as promoted by the Catechism and other magisterial sources. Until the invention of the telescope in the seventeenth century, humanity lived in ignorance of the existence of micro-organisms, and who knows what may dwell in the dark recesses of the universe—or of ourselves? What this book debunks is not the existence of a creature that may or may not lurk menacingly in the shadows, but an alleged snapshot of the creature—a supposed representation of reality.

And yet the book does not find the doctrine of Satan to be entirely obsolete and meaningless, detecting in it profound theological truth, the expression of which can be further developed. It proposes that Satan exists in the mode of possibility rather than actuality. Myth, as noted by Paul Ricoeur, serves as the "bearer of possible worlds" and it is through the

---

13. CDF, *Catechism of the Catholic Church* 390–421, 2851, 2852; McKenzie, "Aspects of Old Testament Thought," 1289.

14. Kasper and Lehmann, *Teufel, Dämonen*, 173.

interpretation of myth that the religious imagination discovers Satan.[15] The mythic motif of Satan serves as a probe into possibilities in the Creator-creature relationship.[16] However, when the language of myth is transposed into doctrinal formulations, there is an apparent tendency to lose sight of the mode of truth mediated by myth and to speak in terms of certainties rather than possibilities. This misplaced certainty invites either fundamentalism or incredulity—and arguably, most often the latter, losing credibility for a Catholic-Christian worldview and even for religion more generally.

Ultimately, I suggest but one soteriological and eschatological possibility expressed in the mythic motif of Satan. Even if a person were to finally and irrevocably reject God so as to choose the privation of evil, opting for nonbeing instead of being, God, the ground of all being, would continue to sustain that person in being.[17] The doctrine of Satan envisages that God does not destroy being, or allow it to be subsumed by nothingness. As such, the doctrine is a powerful statement of God's unconditional commitment to creation and to enemy love. Understood thus, the doctrine of Satan is but a footnote in support of Catholicism's sacramental vision of the universe whereby the omnipresent God is understood to exist in and through all things. The doctrine of Satan serves to emphasize that "all" things means all things—that there is nothing in and through which God does not exist—not even the enemy or the most reviled component of creation.

Since the Church no longer insists that we can know with certainty that any particular human person has finally and irrevocably rejected God so as to experience the state of hell, it is fitting that the narrative of Satan presents this possibility with reference to an inhuman person who exists within the narrative arc of myth.[18] If, however, the doctrine of Satan is presented in a manner that historicizes the mythical narratives upon which it is based, then the universal is presented as though it were the particular. A dynamic, evolving tradition is arbitrarily freeze-framed so as to pander to an apocalyptic investment in the exclusion of the demonized Other.

A note may be appropriate regarding the portions of this book that read as something approaching literature reviews, surveying and summarizing teachings of the Church and the work of scripture scholars and theologians. It may seem as though a parade of witnesses is called to take the stand—and such is necessary in this hotly disputed case. The curators of

---

15. Kearney, "Myth as the Bearer of Possible Worlds," 112–18; Bell, *Deliver us from Evil*, 173.

16. Kearney, "Myth as the Bearer of Possible Worlds," 112–18.

17. Tillich, *Systematic Theology*, 1:238.

18. McBrien, *Catholicism*, 1152; Balthasar, *Dare We Hope That All Men Be Saved?*, 65–68.

the doctrinal museum within which formulae are zealously guarded from any prospect of development will employ arguments the refutation of which requires a succession of testimonies.

The book argues from within the Catholic theological tradition, and from within Judeo-Christian scholarship more broadly, for a reformulation of prevalent accounts of the devil that stand at odds with the broader thrust of the tradition itself. Its detractors, however, may contend that its arguments are "modernist," an imposition of modern perspectives contrary to the Catholic tradition. They may decry, downplay, or even deny the Church's endorsement of the historical-critical method in biblical interpretation, misrepresenting the method by conflating it with reductionist philosophies that do indeed stand in counterpoint to a view of scripture as the Word of God.

Detractors may reject the argument that the Second Vatican Council called the Church to genuine dialogue with modernity, dismissing such dialogue as an unwarranted compromise on divinely revealed truth. So too, they may dismiss the book's claim that doctrinal formulae can and must develop. Much depends, as we shall see, on what one means by "doctrine" and by "develop." As was the case at the Second Vatican Council, the postconciliar Church includes a vocal minority that is deeply suspicious of any prospect of doctrinal development, sometimes equating the doctrinal formulae with the eternal truth itself. Hence, some of the ground covered in this book is not directly related to Satan so much as the evolution of Catholic doctrine and biblical interpretation. This is the terrain upon which the case for the development of any doctrine must be fought.

All that said, why does it matter how the Church presents the doctrine of Satan—a teaching that is hardly likely to impinge upon the workaday existence of most of her members and might easily be spared theological scrutiny as has largely been the case for other pious speculations involving supernatural beings such as angels and archangels? Is this project as redundant as arguing that the sea-monsters of the Old Testament, Rahab and Leviathan, do not exist as ontological realities but as literary motifs? Far from it. The existence of Satan as a particular, intelligent being is affirmed by the 1992 Catechism of the Catholic Church that, wisely or otherwise, is routinely placed in the hands of Catholics and catechumens as a systematic presentation of the Catholic faith, and in its online form offers an obvious point of reference for anyone who is curious about Catholic doctrine. It is a position regularly affirmed in the homilies and writings of Pope Francis. The doctrine has been invoked through the centuries so as to demonize the perceived enemies of orthodoxy, insist upon the actuality of final damnation, and reinforce the assumptions of cosmic dualism. The figure of Satan has gathered considerably more theological significance than has any other mythological denizen of scripture or tradition. Its cost is, however, too great to bear.

What we say about Satan holds implications for who we say our God is. How can an assertion of God's infinite mercy, unconditional love, and omnipresence in and through all creatures be reconciled with the eternal damnation of a creature who now has no opportunity to recant? A dogged insistence upon the existence of Satan as a particular eternally damned being loses credibility for belief in the God who is the animator and sustainer of all being. Such an account of Satan is more suggestive of a model of God as the greatest being among many who rejects some lesser beings as irreconcilable enemies.

What we say about Satan holds implications for what we say our Church is. Is the Church the Pilgrim People of God journeying together towards a richer insight into truth—or is the Church a refrigerator for the preservation of a doctrinal status quo that must remain uncontaminated by new insights?

What we say about Satan holds implications for our beliefs about the Bible. Is the Bible the Word of God in human words, to be interpreted using God-given intelligence and evolving insights into the ancient texts—or is the Bible a who's who of other-worldly entities, knowledge about which was supernaturally imposed upon human authors whose intelligence and life-experience played no role in their writings and that should be read at face value in its myriad translations and versions?

What we say about Satan holds implications for what we say doctrine is. Is doctrine the endeavor to express eternal truths in human words as completely and as effectively as possible in the realization that the words always fall short of the eternal truth itself? Or are the words identical with the eternal truth so that any tampering with the verbiage is necessarily a dilution of the truth? And if one formula is reworded, does this risk toppling the entire house of cards and hence endangering the salvation of souls?

What we say about Satan holds implications for our understanding of faith. Is faith a blind obedience to speculative, metaphysical propositions—or is it a search for truth that has enough trust in the One who bestows us with reason to courageously follow questions wherever they may lead, secure in a conviction that truth should never be suppressed to preserve the doctrinal status quo—for God is truth.

What we say about Satan holds implications for who we are. Are we free-willed persons, albeit subject to environmental, genetic, and deep psychological forces that can orient us towards evil as well as towards the good—or are our thoughts, moods, and choices insidiously manipulated by a malicious supernatural being and his minions?

What we say about Satan holds implications for our disposition towards those who oppose us. Is the enemy another beloved creature of God to whom we are mandated to extend oxymoronic enemy-love—or is the enemy irreconcilable, irredeemable, and damned for all eternity? And should we ever resignedly accept that such is the fate of any creature?

In short, the cost of maintaining the Church's current formulation of the doctrine of Satan is too great to bear as it implicitly compromises more foundational teachings. The doctrine of Satan as currently presented by the Church sabotages the Catholic vision of God and of creation. It is an embarrassing caveat that siphons power and significance from the sacramental vision.

1

Personalizing Satan by Historicizing Myth

SATAN AND THE FALL OF HUMANITY: THE CATECHISM'S HISTORICIZED INTERPRETATION

In a subsection entitled, "How to read the account of the fall," the 1992 Catechism of the Catholic Church interprets the Adam and Eve narrative as recounting a historical event and, by extension, the agency of particular persons, including that of a fallen angel called Satan.

> Behind the disobedient choice of our first parents lurks a seductive voice, opposed to God, which makes them fall into death out of envy. Scripture and the Church's Tradition see in this being a fallen angel, called "Satan" or the "devil."[1]

Whereas the Genesis narrative of Adam and Eve can be dated to the fifth century BC, St. Justin Martyr, writing in the mid-second century AD, is widely regarded as the first on record to identify the snake of Eden as Satan.[2]

---

1. CDF, *Catechism of the Catholic Church* 391.
2. Kelly, *Satan*, 176–79; "Adam Citings before the Intrusion of Satan," 13; Tertullian, *Adversus Marcionem* IV; Almond, *Devil*, 34.

Satan's classification as a fallen angel may be accredited to Justin Martyr's contemporary, Tertullian. This designation of Satan as an angel turned rogue was in time affirmed by Church Councils at Braga I (561 AD) and Lateran IV (1213 AD).³

The Catechism alleges that the fallen angel, Satan, facilitated the fall of humanity in what it regards as a particular "event" or "deed" in history: "The account of the fall in *Genesis* 3 uses figurative language, but affirms a primeval event, a deed that took place *at the beginning of the history of man*."⁴ The Catechism's acknowledgement of the use of figurative language concedes that not every detail in the narrative is to be read as history in the modern sense. So while the designation of figurative language may extend to the motif of the talking snake as an imaginative representation of Satan, the Catechism still regards the Fall itself as a historical event rather than a figurative way of speaking about the difference between the world as we find it and the world we might imagine a loving God would want it to be. Historical events involve particular persons rather than "everyman" characters. The Catechism hence suggests that, while the language of the narrative may be figurative, its characters correspond to particular personages such as a historical Adam and Eve, and in some form, a historical manifestation of Satan. Such is the nature of "events" and "deeds."

The interpretation of the Adamic myth as recounting a historic event and the designation of Satan as a particular person might be entirely consistent with a tradition that espouses biblical literalism. However, it poses a major contradiction to the Catholic Church's teachings on biblical interpretation. The 1992 Catechism's exposition on the interpretation of scripture reflect some fifty years of Church teaching, endorsing the implementation of the methods of modern biblical scholarship.⁵ The same Catechism exhorts readers of the Bible to be sensitive to questions of authorial context and literary genre. "In Sacred Scripture, God speaks to man in a human way. To interpret Scripture correctly, the reader must be attentive to what the human authors truly wanted to affirm, and to what God wanted to reveal to us by their words."⁶ This statement suggests that one cannot circumvent the intentions of the human authors so as to gain direct access to God's intended message.

The Catechism's teachings on the interpretation of scripture reflect the position of the Second Vatican Council, specifically *Dei Verbum* 12, in

---

3. Kelly, "Adam Citings before the Intrusion of Satan," 34.
4. CDF, *Catechism of the Catholic Church* 390.
5. CDF, *Catechism of the Catholic Church* 109–12.
6. CDF, *Catechism of the Catholic Church* 109.

recognizing the distinctive manner in which each literary genre mediates truth. "For the fact is that truth is differently presented and expressed in the various types of historical writing, in prophetical and poetical texts, and in other forms of literary expression."[7] Granted, the precise wording of this statement is curious in its suggestion that "truth is differently presented and expressed" through various genres, rather than saying that the different genres present different kinds of truth such as, for example, historical truth, theological truth, and moral truth. The implication might be drawn that different genres are alternative ways to express the same kind of truth through different means. If this were simply the case, however, the purpose of the injunction in *Dei Verbum* 12 would be moot. If, for example, poetry was simply another means through which to convey historical truth, then the question would arise as to why it is important to be attentive to the genres. They would simply be various routes to the same end.

Catholic biblical scholars Raymond Brown and Sandra Schneiders remark, "We approach forms of literature with different expectations and we profit from them differently. A history or a novel may treat the same person or event, but we expect different degrees of fact or fiction from them."[8] These authors contend that one genre can sometimes convey a form of truth that the others cannot and, with reference to poetic language, "the issue of fact and fiction is irrelevant."[9] Truths expressed in poetry and myth do not depend upon historical facticity.

The Catechism's historicist interpretation of the Adamic narrative to some extent reflects Pope Pius XII's approach to the first eleven chapters of Genesis as conveyed in his 1950 encyclical, *Humanae Generis*, but does so selectively, failing to reflect the nuance and openness to future development present in the 1950 statement. In *Humanae Generis*, Pius XII insisted that the first eleven chapters of Genesis convey history, though not history in the classical sense, implying that the history in question is not a matter of reconstructing events.[10] Notably, Pius had seven years earlier published *Divino Afflante Spiritu* in which he mandated that exegetes should use the best possible interpretative methods at their disposal, censoring them that it would be neglectful not to do so.[11] Consistent with this mandate, the pontiff recognized that it remained for the exegetes to determine precisely what

---

7. CDF, *Catechism of the Catholic Church* 109–12.
8. Brown and Schneiders, "Hermeneutics," 1151.
9. Brown and Schneiders, "Hermeneutics," 1151.
10. Pius XII, "*Humani Generis*" 38.
11. Pius XII, "*Divino Afflante Spiritu*" 37.

form of history is at stake.[12] Forty-two years later, however, the Catechism reflects Pius's assertion that Genesis 3 reflects history, but ignores the pontiff's caveat regarding different forms of history, and ignores the exegetical progress encouraged by Pius that had since transpired.

MODELS OF HISTORY

Extending hermeneutical charity, the possibility might be considered that the authors of the Catechism invoke the term "history" in relation to the Fall in a more nuanced sense than so as to refer to a chronology of events and their significance. Theologians, after all, speak of "salvation history," a narrative that is primarily concerned with God's relationship with Israel and the world rather than with cold, hard facts. James Barr notes that there may be less agreement than supposed as to what theologians routinely mean by the term "history," from *Gehschichte* to *Heilgeschichte*, from *Weltgeshcichte* to *Urgeshschichte*, from *Historie* to *Sage*, Barr suggests that models of history are often constructed to serve the theological purpose at hand.[13] On a similar note, Luke Timothy Johnson points to the sense in which the term "history" can denote something other than recounting sequences of events.

> The term, *history* cannot be used simply for "the past" or "what happened in the past" any more than *historical* can be used simply as a synonym for "what was real about the past." History is, rather the product of human intelligence and imagination. It is one of the ways in which human beings negotiate their present experience and understanding with reference to group and individual memory.[14]

While conceding that the term "history," especially in relation to the Bible and theology, may suggest an interpretative narrative that goes well beyond chronology, the Catechism's references to history in relation to the Fall of humanity are still problematically historicist. In contrast with the nuanced views of history invoked by Johnson, the Catechism interprets the Adamic narrative as recounting, albeit in figurative terms, an event that transpired in the past, drawing sharp distinction between the prelapsarian and postlapsarian conditions.[15]

---

12. Pius XII, "*Humani Generis*" 38.
13. Barr, "Revelation in the Old Testament," 68.
14. Johnson, *Real Jesus*, 81–82.
15. CDF, *Catechism of the Catholic Church* 390.

Paul Ricoeur offers an nuanced perspective on the relationship between history and myth when he suggests that the process of writing history passes through a documentary stage of gathering evidence, a comprehensive stage of seeking to understand and explain what the sources reveal, and a literary stage at which point, facticity and meaning-making can become vexingly intertwined.[16] Whereas, Ricoeur argues vehemently that myth is not history, he recognizes that historical narrative can be infused with mythical symbolism. To detect the emergence of a mythical register of language within historical narrative, however, is a different matter than to argue that mythical narrative is a figurative way of recounting history. To illustrate the distinction, it would be one thing to argue that the retelling of history almost unavoidably incorporates symbolic language such as the "Dark Ages," "Renaissance," "Cold War," "Great Depression," "Axis of Evil," and "Celtic Tiger," and quite another to argue the "Fall" belongs in this list.

Whereas, historical narrative may be replete with symbolic references, cultural memes, and apocryphal anecdotes, if the term "history" is to be employed so broadly as to denote interpretations of experience that do not to some extent reflect particular events, then the distinction between historical narrative and other narrative forms, including myth, becomes distorted. Having blurred such distinctions, the importance of acknowledging literary form in the interpretation of the biblical text would then be questionable.

THE FALL AS AN EVENT INSTIGATED BY THE DEVIL

Based upon its historicized reading of Genesis 3, the Catechism attributes to the devil responsibility for the temptation of humanity. "Man, tempted by the devil, let his trust in his Creator die in his heart and, abusing his freedom, disobeyed God's command."[17] This indictment of Satan as responsible for facilitating the Fall of humanity helps to establish the being's singular identikit, a rap-sheet that distinguishes Satan from the other fallen angels.

Granted, it might be argued that even if the Genesis authors lacked a fully developed concept of the devil as known to modern interpreters, ultimately all temptation, including the temptation of prototypal humans, figuratively represented by Adam and Eve, might be indirectly attributed to the devil, in whatever sense the devil exists. Pope Francis, in his homilies and writings, regularly attributes the temptation of contemporary people to the devil—even with regard to such seemingly mundane moral issues as

---

16. Ricoeur, "Humanities between Science and Art."
17. CDF, *Catechism of the Catholic Church* 397.

gossiping nuns.[18] In that sense, could it not be argued that the Catechism simply assumes that all temptation is, to some degree, instigated by the devil, and is not claiming some unique and direct involvement by the devil in the sin of a historical Adam and Eve? The Catechism is, however, emphatic in insisting upon the Fall of humanity as a particular, catastrophic event that ended a period of Original Justice.

> The harmony in which they had found themselves, thanks to original justice, is now destroyed: the control of the soul's spiritual faculties over the body is shattered; the union of man and woman becomes subject to tensions, their relations henceforth marked by lust and domination. Harmony with creation is broken: visible creation has become alien and hostile to man. Because of man, creation is now subject "to its bondage to decay."[19]

In counterpoint to our argument that the Catechism presents the Fall as a particular event, it might be ventured that this litany of broken relationships signifies the ubiquitous reality of humanity's alienation from one another and the wider environment and that the Catechism might hence be presenting the Fall as an existential reality rather than a historical event. However, it should be noted that the Catechism's authors do not view the broken relationships among humans, between humans and God, and between humans and the wider environment as themselves constituting the Fall but, rather, as the consequences of a "Fall event," a first act of disobedience at the dawn of history: "Scripture portrays the tragic consequences of this first disobedience."[20]

HISTORICISM REINFORCED BY THE IMPLICATION OF PRIMAEVAL IMMORTALITY

Reinforcing its historicized view of the Fall as a particular event that rendered creation subject to decay, the Catechism suggests that death entered the world at a particular point, early in human history, as though humans would not otherwise have died. "Finally, the consequence explicitly foretold for this disobedience will come true: man will 'return to the ground,' for out of it he was taken. *Death makes its entrance into human history.*"[21] The implication is that, were it not for the historical deed of disobedience,

---

18. Francis, *"Gaudete et Exsultate"* 160–61, 166, 170.
19. CDF, *Catechism of the Catholic Church* 400.
20. CDF, *Catechism of the Catholic Church* 399.
21. CDF, *Catechism of the Catholic Church* 399.

humans would be immortal and the wider creation would be spared the reality of "decay," implying finitude. Furthermore, the Catechism teaches that a personal Satan facilitated the introduction of death: "Through him sin and death entered the world and by his definitive defeat all creation will be 'freed from the corruption of sin and death.'"[22] This implication of a pre-Fall era when there was no sin or death in the world, heightens the historicism with which the Catechism interprets the Adamic myth as recounting the disaster behind all disasters, and the crushing culpability it attributes to the agency of particular characters, assuming Satan to number among them.

Once again extending hermeneutical charity, it might be asked whether the Catechism's reference to death as a consequence of the Fall could be interpreted as something other than the encroachment of physical death upon the human condition. Such a claim is, after all, difficult to reconcile with the Church's broad acceptance of the theory of evolution which involves death on a mass-scale.[23] It is a tall order to suggest that death and decay were unknown in the physical creation until prototypal humans committed a misdeed. Rather, any immortality implied in the Adamic narrative rings of the mythic trope of wistful craving after that which never was, rather than an actuality that has been lost.

The Catechism's historicist interpretation of the Adamic myth reflects St. Paul's assertion in Romans 6:23 that "the wages of sin are death." Joseph Fitzmyer posits that "Paul is certainly thinking of the story of the fall in Genesis 1—3 but he prescinds it from all its dramatic details to utilize the theological truth of the enslavement of all men because of sin."[24] Fitzmyer recognizes that Paul seeks to extrapolate a theological proposition from the "drama" of the narrative, endeavoring a transposition from mythical to doctrinal language. Fitzmyer contrasts the symbolic intentions of the authors of the Adamic myth with St. Paul's historicist interpretation: "Paul treats Adam as a historical human being, humanity's first parent and contrasts him with the historical Jesus Christ. But in Genesis itself, Adam is a symbolic figure, denoting humanity."[25] Fitzmyer's observations suggest that, while the Adamic narrative was composed as a myth, a historicist interpretation is included in the very canon of scripture.

Offering a nuanced account of the sense in which death might be considered the "wages of sin," N. T. Wright suggests that the fall of humanity

---

22. CDF, *Catechism of the Catholic Church* 2852.

23. John Paul II, "Message to the Pontifical Academy of Sciences." See also Chardin, *Phenomenon of Man*, 218, 220, 223, 227, 228, 277.

24. Fitzmyer, "Romans," 407.

25. Fitzmyer, "Romans," 407.

gave rise to a spiritual death that is distinct from physical death and decay which the author regards as integral to God's creation. "There is nothing wrong with the tree dropping its leaves in the autumn. There is nothing wrong with the sunset fading into darkness. Evil consists in none of these things. Indeed, it is precisely the transience of the good creation that serves as a pointer to its wider purpose."[26] Wright's position implies that what is good for the leaf and for daylight is also good for the human person, who too is a part of the good creation. Wright argues that sin has knocked the cosmos "out of joint" so that humanity no longer experiences death as a "pointer to its wider purpose" and as the moment when the transcendent becomes undeniable.[27] Wright suggests, "The result is that death, which has always been a part of the natural transience of the good creation, gains a second dimension, which the bible sometimes calls 'spiritual death.'"[28] Hence Wright views not biological death, but rather a corrupted perspective on death, as a consequence of sin. It might hence be argued that the fear of death per se, as opposed to the fear of tragic, violent, and painful death, is symptomatic of a loss of trust in God and hence a postlapsarian reality. While the Catechism itself suggests that death is a consequence of a Fall event and the subterfuge of the personal Satan, it is crucial that more nuanced readings are proposed when presenting the text to audiences of any age so as to maintain some modicum of credibility.

THE CATECHISM'S IDENTIKIT OF SATAN

In its reflections upon the Fall of the angels, the Fall of humanity, and the seventh petition of the Our Father, the Catechism conveys the identikit of Satan that is critiqued in the present study. It is not the purpose of this book to deny a first-order truth claim, disputing the ontological existence of demons, that is, disembodied evil spirits in general. Neither does it deny that some such spirit might be called "Satan," insofar as such beings might have names constructed from human language. Rather, our central thesis denies the capacity of the Church's account of the doctrine of Satan, hinged upon a framework of mythic motifs, to convincingly affirm the ontological existence of a particular being that fits the identikit cited in the Catechism, and further asserts that the doctrine as currently formulated is preserved at too great a cost to the sacramental view of God and of the world.

---

26. Wright, *Surprised by Hope*, 94–95.
27. Wright, *Surprised by Hope*, 94–95.
28. Wright, *Surprised by Hope*, 94–95.

The Satan identified in the Catechism is a fallen angel, a free-willed, intelligent being who personally interacted with a prototypal human couple, influencing them to commit the Original Sin, and by doing so, personally facilitated the entrance of death and decay into the human experience, so as to be damned beyond any hope of reconciliation with God.[29] While it would be impossible to completely discount any degree of correspondence between the Catechism's account of Satan and some malign, incorporeal being or beings, the Catechism's historicized interpretation of myth does not provide a credible basis upon which to insist upon such a correspondence.

CONTEMPORARY EXEGESIS OF THE ADAMIC MYTH

In 1993, the Pontifical Biblical Commission stated that the interpretation of scripture must take account of the context and intentions of the ancient authors and of the literary forms in which they wrote.[30] It has also mandated exegetes to use the best modern methods at their disposal so as to contribute to the continued development of doctrine.[31] Therefore, it would not seem consistent for the Church's presentation of doctrine to ignore the broad thrust of exegetical opinion. With this in mind, what follows is an overview of contemporary biblical scholarship on the historicity and genre of the Adamic narrative, including the insights of exegetes who have published in Catholic commentaries bearing the *Imprimatur* and *Nihil Obstat*.[32]

Daniel Harlow asserts that the overwhelming thrust of biblical scholarship regards the first eleven chapters of Genesis as "story" rather than history:

> The vast majority of interpreters take the narratives in these chapters as story, not history, because their portrait of protohistory from creation to flood to Babel looks very stylized—with sequences, events, and characters that look more symbolic than "real" events and characters in "normal" history.[33]

Harlow's use of scare quotes with reference to the term "real" evokes the sense in which modern readers of the Genesis narrative may tend to glibly equate reality with historical facticity.

---

29. CDF, *Catechism of the Catholic Church* 391, 2851–52.
30. Pius XII, "*Divino Afflante Spiritu*" 37; PBC, "Interpretation of the Bible in the Church" 34.
31. Pius XII, "*Divino Afflante Spiritu*"; PBC, "*Sancta Mater Ecclesiae*."
32. McGill, "Tensions between the Catechism's Teachings," 51–68.
33. Harlow, "After Adam," 179–95.

The Adamic narrative of Genesis 2 and 3 exhibits the literary hallmarks of myth. Lévi-Strauss detects in the narrative a tension between binary forces that is characteristic of the genre, in this case a tension between obedience and disobedience, innocence and knowledge, life and death.[34] Kapelrud posits the influence of the Gilgamesh and Adapa myths, all three addressing the theme of finitude.[35] Lyn Bechtel notes the prevalence of "trees of life" in Ancient Near Eastern Myths.[36] Within the narrative, God acts as a potter and surgeon who walks in a garden, a snake speaks, and a cherubim with a flaming sword is appointed to sentry duty. The literary characteristics of the text suggest that the authors of the Adam and Eve narrative wrote in a genre that moderns and postmoderns most closely approximate as "myth."

Eugene Maly, writing in the *Jerome Biblical Commentary,* states, "No scholar today would hold that Gn [sic] presents history in the modern sense of that term."[37] Maly's remark implies the equivocal sense in which the term "history" can be invoked, the point made by Barr when he cites multiple German terms that correspond to the English word."[38] Michael Guinan posits, "The overall narrative of Genesis 2—11 reflects a 'creation-flood story' that was well known in the Ancient Near East; several examples have come down to us from Mesopotamia."[39] Guinan proceeds to explicitly deny the historicity of the narrative, "The biblical authors used this familiar (to them) story to teach their own distinctive view of God, the world and human beings. In other words, to read the story of Adam and Eve as a historical account is to misinterpret the text. Like a parable, it teaches a profound truth."[40] Guinan hence decouples the truthfulness of the text from the question of historicity, implying that "profound truth" need not be historical truth, in the modern sense of "historical."

Monika Hellwig asserts with reference to the Adamic myth, "It has become more generally acknowledged that the original story-tellers, scribes and compilers of the Book of Genesis were not relating the story of two people in the dim distance of pre-history but were interpreting the human situation in which each of us is placed."[41] Hellwig's remarks acknowledge the

---

34. Lévi-Strauss, *Naked Man,* 556.
35. Kapelrud, "You Shall Surely Not Die," 50–61.
36. Bechtel, "Rethinking the Interpretation of Genesis 2:4," 87.
37. Maly, "Genesis," 40.
38. Barr, "Revelation through History," 67–68.
39. Guinan, "Adam, Eve and Original Sin," 1.
40. Guinan, "Adam, Eve and Original Sin,"1.
41. Hellwig, *What Are the Theologians Saying Now?,* 101.

prevalent tendency on the part of modern exegetes to interpret the text as pointing to universal truths concerning the human condition.

James Connor detects in the Adamic myth a didactic intention to explain the universality of sin in ancient Israel.[42] The sin in question included pandering to the serpentine idols of the fertility cult, essentially phallic symbols. Connor regards the narrative as a "symbolic and imaginative account, in which Adam, the talking serpent, the tree of life, and the four rivers are all of a piece."[43] While focusing upon the narrative's significance for Israel, Connor notes that the name, "Adam" means "man" and does not reject more universal significance for the human condition.[44]

Raymond Brown regards the purpose of the Adam and Eve story as to teach that humanity is endowed by God with the breath of life, that humanity was created good, and humanity's tendency towards corruption does not come from God.[45] Brown's interpretation is hence attentive to a theodicist function served by the narrative, exonerating God of direct responsibility for evil.

Gabriel Daly warns that the Catechism's insistence upon a historicized interpretation of the Adamic narrative may well lose credibility for the doctrine of Original Sin so that the doctrinal formulations in question become an embarrassment to the preacher and the catechist. In reference to Original Sin, Daly remarks, "As long as the doctrine continues to be expressed in the language of a dead anthropology, and a fundamentalist reading of sacred scripture, a vitally important truth of Christian revelation will go by default in many pulpits and classrooms."[46] A historicized interpretation of the myth may hold similar implications for the credibility of the doctrine of Satan.

Daly does not wield the term "fundamentalist" in a loose or pejorative fashion in this context. Rather, several of the pamphlets entitled *The Fundamentals*, from which the term "fundamentalism" is derived, refute the insights of the historical-critical method and propose a historicist reading of the Adamic narrative as though the text witnesses to the Fall as a historical event. These include Dyson Hague's essay on "The Doctrinal Value of the First Chapters of Genesis" and James Orr's essay on "The Early Narratives of Genesis."[47] Orr asserts, "It is clear that the narratives of Creation, the

---

42. Connor, "Original Sin," 215.

43. Connor, "Original Sin," 215.

44. Connor, "Original Sin," 217.

45. Brown, *Responses to 101 Questions on the Bible*, 34.

46. Daly, "Creation and Original Sin," 97.

47. Orr, "Early Narratives of Genesis"; Hague, "Doctrinal Value of the First Chapters of Genesis."

Fall, the Flood, are not myths, but narratives enshrining the knowledge or memory of real transactions."[48] Orr concedes, as the Catechism does, that the language employed by the Genesis texts may be figurative rather than objectively factual in a modern sense. "The language used was not that of modern science, but, under divine guidance, the sacred writer gives a broad, general picture which conveys a true idea of the order of the divine working in creation. Man's fall was likewise a tremendous fact, with universal consequences in sin and death to the race."[49] The Catechism's insistence upon the Fall as a "deed" or "event" and its concession that the narrative used figurative language, is reminiscent of Orr's insistence upon a "fact," related in the past tense so as to underscore its historical particularity rather than the timeless ubiquity associated with more existential models of the Fall.

Offering further support for Daly's charge that the Catechism's reading of Genesis 3 is rooted in a fundamentalist perspective, its interpretation suggests dispensationalism, a defining characteristic of Christian fundamentalism. Dispensationalism views history in terms of a series of epochs, each of which descends into moral degeneration and ends in catastrophe. The dispensationalist may hence depict the expulsion of Adam and Eve from Eden, the destruction of the Tower of Babel, or the Great Flood on a chronological timeline, in the extreme, surmising dates.

Paul Ricoeur refutes a historicist interpretation of the Adamic myth that he believes to have caused undue spiritual angst for the faithful. "The harm that has been done to souls, during the centuries of Christianity, first by literal interpretation of the story of Adam, and then by the confusion of this myth, treated as history, with later speculations, principally Augustinian, about original sin, will never be adequately told."[50] Ricoeur's remarks lament the conflation of the biblical text itself with its reception history, rather than allowing the text to speak on its own terms. The reception history in question is largely one of historicization.

RETROSPECTIVELY DISCOVERING SATAN IN MYTH

Noting the absence of the Satan motif from the Adamic narrative in Genesis, Pauline Viviano notes that "nowhere in this text is the serpent identified as the devil; this interpretation does not come about until the first century BCE."[51] Richard Clifford and Roland Murphy concur, stating, "The snake

48. Hague, "Doctrinal Value of the First Chapters of Genesis."
49. Orr, "Early Narratives of Genesis."
50. Ricoeur, *Symbolism of Evil*, 239.
51. Viviano, "Genesis," 43.

is not Satan, though later traditions so interpreted it."[52] With reference to the conflation of later speculation with the biblical text itself, Henry Ansgar Kelly asserts, "When we look at the beginning of Genesis with unblinkered eyes, we see that there is no creation or fall of angels, but only a very clever talking serpent."[53] Kelly regards the tendency to detect a devil in the Genesis narrative as "retro-fitting of past data with later ideas."[54] Maly regards the serpent as evocative of the idolatrous fertility cults that posed a competitive threat to Israelite religion.[55] Viviano suggests that the source of evil in the world is, in the Adamic myth, left a mystery.[56] The designation of the snake as *arum*, translated as "cunning," does not necessarily imply the diabolical undertones later asserted in the reception history of the text.

It is post-biblical speculation, epitomized by Justin-Martyr, that regarded the talking snake as a manifestation of Satan. This is not of course to say that the motif of the snake has never before been invoked to symbolize evil. In a case in point, ancient Egyptian mythology envisaged the serpent Apophis or Apep as the enemy of the sun god Ra.[57] Apophis is perhaps the most infamous of many snake motifs in Egyptian mythology. The *Pyramid Texts* of Unas are crawling with serpentine entities that might within a Christian framework be retrospectively classified as demonic.[58] To assume, however, that the portrayal of a cunning, talking snake in the Adamic narrative must have been inspired by the more ancient Egyptian motifs would be akin to assuming that all vulpine motifs in Western literature are inspired by the motif of the werewolf. In worlds wherein corporeal snakes or wolves lurked in the thicket, the stark realities of everyday life may be more than adequate to explain the invocation of the animal imagery in question.

Sinister snake motifs arising from diverse ancient cultures are not evidence that ancient peoples believed in the existence of a supernatural Satan as later imagined by Christians, and in no way bolster the credibility of such a doctrine. If Christian commentators seize ancient Egyptian motifs as evidence of Satan's ubiquitous existence and fetish for snakeskin, they will hardly be as eager to affirm the ontological reality of a sun-god or the other supernatural denizens of Egyptian mythology so that their appeals to the ancient texts are highly selective.

52. Clifford and Murphy, "Genesis," 12.
53. Kelly, *Satan*, 3.
54. Kelly, *Satan*, 3.
55. Maly, "Genesis," 40.
56. Viviano, "Genesis," 44–45; McGill, "Vassal's Lament," 112.
57. Mark, *Set*.
58. Allen, *Ancient Egyptian Pyramid Texts*, 65–67, 81, 98,324, 355.

While evil supernatural snake-beings feature with some frequency in ancient Egyptian mythology, they do not abound in the Hebrew Bible which in Numbers 21:4–9 invokes the serpent as a symbol of healing when God instructs Moses to fashion a bronze serpent that would mediate the healing of serpent bites. This raises the question as to whether Justin Martyr and later interpreters legitimately uncovered a layer of significance to the snake of Eden, not accessible to earlier readers, especially those who lacked access to the New Testament. Is it possible that such Christian readers validly detected reference to a particular ontological Satan, where earlier audiences saw a symbol of the fertility cult and a general warning against forsaking covenant with YWHW?

It might be suggested that the New Testament is awash with motifs that first arise in the Hebrew Bible but are attributed new layers of significance by the Christian imagination. The *Ruach*/Holy Spirit, the Suffering Servant, the practice of baptism, the observance of Passover, and the ancient motif of the Messiah may be cases in point. While the Church has indeed held up the historical-critical method as an indispensable tool for the interpretation of scripture, it has also regarded this method as one that can and should be used in concert with other methods, as the PBC notes, it "may even in some respect be corrected by other approaches."[59] We turn now to the question as to whether a theological interpretation of myth in the context of the entire Bible, can disclose the kind of truth that affirms historical events and personages that cannot be detected through a historical-critical exegesis of the myth on its own terms.

THE SENSUS PLENIOR AND THE HISTORICIZATION OF MYTH

Through the application of canonical exegesis, that is, interpreting a text in the context of the Bible as a whole, the "fuller" sense or *sensus plenior* of the text may be discerned beyond what might be uncovered through a close reading of that text in isolation. This could mean reading an Old Testament text in light of something we know from the New Testament which was unknown to the Old Testament author. Raymond Brown defines the *sensus plenior* as "the deeper meaning intended by God but not clearly intended by the human author that is seen to exist in the words of scripture when they are studied in the light of further revelation or of development in the understanding of revelation."[60] By definition, meaning of this kind cannot

---

59. PBC, "Interpretation of the Bible in the Church" 81.
60. Brown, "Hermeneutics," 616.

be uncovered by the application of the historical-critical method to a given text in isolation since it goes beyond the intention of the author and requires attention to the canon as a whole.

The Catechism defends its interpretation of the Adamic narrative as a case of the *sensus plenior* that can only be detected in light of the gospel:

> With the progress of Revelation, the reality of sin is also illuminated. Although to some extent the People of God in the Old Testament had tried to understand the pathos of the human condition in the light of the history of the fall narrated in Genesis, they could not grasp this story's ultimate meaning, which is revealed only in the light of the death and Resurrection of Jesus Christ.[61]

Perhaps in an attempt to explain the apparent absence of the doctrines of the Fall and Original Sin in ancient Israelite religion and the Jewish faith, the Catechism asserts that the authors of the Hebrew Scriptures did not know the ultimate meaning of that which they wrote. As Daniel Harrington observes, there is surprisingly little reference in the Old Testament to the sin of Adam.[62] This could appear problematic if Adam's sin constituted a historical event with such catastrophic implications for all of human history. The Catechism's response is that, without the benefit of the Christ event, the implications of a historical Fall were not understood. "We must know Christ as the source of grace in order to know Adam as the source of sin."[63]

Maly distinguishes the likely intention of the Genesis authors from the later Christian interpretations of the serpent in Genesis 3.[64] The ancient authors may have intended the serpent to imply a polemic against the fertility cults which posed a competitive threat to Israelite monolatry, that is, the worship of only one god while believing in the existence of others, but, as Maly notes, "later revelation will go far beyond this."[65] Maly's reference to later revelation, suggests the development of the Christian understanding of Satan and its association with the snake in the Adamic myth.

In support of Maly's point that later revelation may reveal significance in a text beyond the historical author's intent, the Catechism exhorts the reader to be attentive to the "analogy of faith," that is, to the manner in which truths of the faith are interrelated and systematically cohesive.[66] This

61. CDF, *Catechism of the Catholic Church* 388.
62. Harrington, "Paul's Use of the Old Testament in Romans."
63. CDF, *Catechism of the Catholic Church* 388.
64. Maly, "Genesis," 12.
65. Maly, "Genesis," 12.
66. CDF, *Catechism of the Catholic Church* 114.

implies that early formulations may be profitably read in light of later ones. Through the application of canonical exegesis, interpreting a text in the full canon of scripture and tradition, the *sensus plenior* of the text may be discerned. The *sensus plenior* could hence include theological truths that develop the intentions of the sacred authors.

The question arises as to what constitutes legitimate development as opposed to downright misinterpretation.[67] So, one might ask, does it constitute development or discontinuous change to segue from the motif of a smooth-talking animal to the Christian Satan? Once it is clear that we are speaking of the evolution of a mythical motif, I must for two reasons concede that this may be a case of legitimate development as opposed to misinterpretation or corruption. First, the development from cunning snake to Satan may not be as drastic as it first appears if one is mindful that Satan in the Christian tradition, however sinister and distanced from God's good graces, remains a mere creature, and is not an evil equivalent of God. The *De Trinitate* attributed to Eusebius of Vercelli states the orthodox position with canonical candor, "If anyone professes that in the nature in which he was made the apostate angel is not the work of God, but that he exists of himself, going so far as to attribute to him his own beginning, let him be anathema."[68] The association of the talking snake with Satan helps to underscore that Satan is not an evil god.

Second, the development of the concept of Satan is no more radical or arguably discontinuous than is the development of the concept of God in the Judeo-Christian heritage. The canon of scripture reflects images of God that are henotheistic and not far removed from polytheism, that is, believing in the existence of multiple gods and choosing one to worship. Other images of God are monist, suggesting that evil as well as good proceeds from the will of God. While such ancient images of God are far removed from a Christian one, we view this contrast in terms of development.[69] We consider the God of Exodus, portrayed as commanding exclusive worship in the midst of other gods, or the God depicted as violently massacring the enemies of ancient Israel as a culturally-conditioned allusion to the same God that Jesus came to reveal. This may provide a fair precedent for drastic developments in the understanding of biblical motifs far less central than that of God. However, while dramatic development in the symbolic significance of the snake of Eden may legitimately reflect the *sensus plenior* uncovered through canonical exegesis, the historicization of myth, and the

---

67. Benedict XVI, "To the Roman Curia"; Vincent of Lerins, *Commonitory*, 26–28.
68. Eusebius, *De Trinitate*, VI, 17, 1–3; CDF, "Christian Faith and Demonology."
69. Cook, "Can God Take Responsibility?"

literalization of its motifs, cannot be justified in this manner. The interpretation of a text in light of later revelation or later-breaking tradition cannot change its genre, somehow transposing myth into history or biography.

THE LIMITS OF THE SENSUS PLENIOR: RESPECT FOR LITERARY FORM

Raymond Brown notes the objection of J. M. Robinson that the *sensus plenior* could be abused to justify doctrines that have no basis in scripture, and adamantly concludes that Church authority is a mediator but not the originator of revelation.[70] Brown contends that the *sensus plenior* is not a license by which the Church can justify claims that have no basis in the literal sense of the biblical text.[71] Rather, the *sensus plenior* must be "a development of what the human author wanted to say."[72]

If the *sensus plenior* is a level of significance that was inaccessible to the author and original audience of a scriptural text, could it be that Fall stories, contrary to the intentions of their pre-Christian authors, actually refer to particular, historical events? James Kelly suggests not, arguing that "metaphysical interpretations must respect the historical data, and cannot create or change them."[73] By extension, I propose that interpretations must also respect the literary data. In a sense, the fact that the biblical author wrote with recourse to a particular genre and worldview is itself a historical datum. If Jesus told a parable or the Yahwist authors crafted a narrative that reflects the hallmarks of what we would now call myth, these are historical facts that cannot be retrospectively altered by later interpretation.

The recognition of the genre of a text as intended by its authors is a matter that lies firmly within the competence of the historical-critical method rather than canonical exegesis.[74] *Dei Verbum* makes clear that in order to detect what God wants to reveal, the interpreter of scripture must read a text in light of the literary genre in question, not for example, supposing allegorical correspondence where none was intended.[75] If the human authors were seized by the Holy Spirit as a quill, serving as unconscious instruments rather than as thinking beings, their intentions would be non-existent or

70. Robinson, "Scripture and Theological Method," 6–27; Brown, "Hermeneutics," 617.

71. Brown, "Hermeneutics," 616.

72. Brown, "Hermeneutics," 617.

73. Kelly, "Hermeneutical Debate Within Modernism," 288.

74. PBC, "Interpretation of the Bible in the Church."

75. Paul VI, *Dei Verbum* 12.

irrelevant. *De Fontibus*, the draft constitution on revelation rejected by the vast majority of Council Fathers at Vatican II, had proposed a model of literal revelation that largely dismissed the agency of the human authors in cooperating with the Holy Spirit. Joseph Ratzinger, a *peritus* at the Council, eloquently declaimed the curia's stance on the matter.[76] Ratzinger argued that the sacred authors are inspired by God and are not primarily the collective voice of their community. Equally well, Ratzinger decried the position that the human author and his thoughts are completely overwhelmed by God, a theory derived from Middle Platonic mysticism that St. Augustine, to some extent, accepted. Ratzinger argues that the historical consciousness of the human author is maintained since God seeks to reveal precisely in the context of human history.[77]

History is always the context, if somewhat rarely the genre of biblical texts. While the *sensus plenior* can be rightfully evoked to justify developments in the perceived theological significance of the Adamic narrative in light of the Christ event, it cannot justify the historicization of mythical narrative or the literalization of mythical motifs. No amount of theologizing can transform a literary persona into an ontological person who exists beyond the narrative arc of myth. No number of theological Geppettos can turn a mythical demon into a "real" demon—though the poignant image of Geppetto bearing a lantern and searching in the darkest of places for the prodigal Pinocchio may, as we shall later see, be deeply evocative of truths concerning Satan and God.

CONCLUSION

The 1992 Catechism of the Catholic Church historicizes the Adamic myth and literalizes the mythic motif of the talking snake so as to assert the agency of Satan as a particular, supernatural person. That said, concepts of Satan that have developed in the Judeo-Christian tradition are not necessarily inauthentic because they add new layers of significance to more ancient ones. Canonical exegesis can legitimately develop the theological significance of a text beyond the intentions of its authors. However, canonical exegesis, and the *sensus plenior* to which it gives rise, cannot legitimately contradict the findings of the historical-critical method in the identification of literary genre. Otherwise the counsel of *Dei Verbum* 12, reiterated in the Catechism 109–10 regarding the implications of literary form, would be redundant.[78]

76. Wicks, "Six Texts by Prof. Joseph Ratzinger," 278.
77. See Wicks, "Six Texts by Prof. Joseph Ratzinger."
78. Paul VI, "*Dei Verbum*" 12; CDF, *Catechism of the Catholic Church* 109–12.

Canonical exegesis cannot transform a myth into an historical account, or a mythical persona into a historical character, a particular being exercising their free will in the events of history. This does not discount similarities between the personas of myth and ontological persons, including disembodied persons should they exist. However, to assert a direct correspondence between a mythical motif and some particular personage, embodied or otherwise, is to obfuscate the applicability of the mythical motif to all people in all times and places.

2

Satan: A Hybrid Born of Cross-Pollinating Myths

The fact that we have hitherto referred to Satan and the devil interchangeably offers just an inkling as to the litany of terms that may be invoked to denote the same supposed entity, and the nuance involved in deciding what does and does not count as another name for Satan or the devil. A constellation of motifs drawn from diverse religions, cultures, and languages have contributed towards the evolution of our central construct. Christian versions of Satan have evolved over the centuries from the cross-pollination of mythical narratives and motifs, some of which predate ethical monotheism and challenge its key suppositions about a benign Deity, instead reflecting polytheistic, henotheistic, or monist images of God.

Upon the emergence of ethical monotheism in the Judeo-Christian tradition, the doctrine of Satan continued to develop as a byproduct of evolving perspectives on divinity. Given this history of development, driven by ongoing exploration of the mystery of God, there is no compelling reason to fossilize one expression of the motif of Satan as though its truth could never be more effectively or more completely conveyed. This is even more the case when an anachronistic presentation of the doctrine contradicts the tradition's beliefs about God.

FROM LITERARY TO LITERAL PERSONIFICATION

The Christian imagination discovers Satan through its interpretation of myth—a literary genre that does not verify the existence or deeds of particular beings.[1] Myth, rather, is concerned with the relationship between all human beings and the world, with life, death, freedom, evil, and the existential experiences that confront humans across cultures and millennia. As Almut-Barbara Renger observes, "myth thematises the relationship between a human being and superhuman powers."[2] From a Judeo-Christian perspective, myth explores the relationship between God and creation, in particular, humanity.

We have noted that the Catechism of the Catholic Church, informed by the mythical narrative of the battle in heaven, refers to Satan as a fallen angel. This classification of Satan as an angel occasions an excursus into the biblical motif of the angel, and the question as to whether the biblical authors intended their references to angels to signify the ontological reality of particular supernatural beings.

The angels of the Hebrew Bible, that is to say, the motif translated into English as "angel," are a very different proposition to the angels about which St. Thomas Aquinas speculated in the thirteenth century. So too, they bear little resemblance to the winged babies of Renaissance art, while children praying by their bedside to their guardian angel probably do not have in mind the fiery-sword bearing cherubim of Eden.

Indeed, it is debatable as to whether the ancient authors of the Hebrew Bible intended their references to angels to denote distinct beings as opposed to manifestations of the divine in a form with which humans could interact.[3] References to angels in the Hebrew Bible, it might be argued, reflect the belief that humans cannot look directly upon the face of God and live, so God interacts with humanity under the guise of an avatar, the "Angel" of the Lord.[4]

The Hagar narrative of Genesis 16 offers a case in point. When Abram and Sarai cannot conceive a son, the couple agree that the slave girl, Hagar, is to be impregnated by Abram (Gen 16:3). This endeavor proves fruitful and tension flairs in the camp as Sarai grows to resent Hagar who flees into the wilderness to escape the wrath of her mistress. The run-away Hagar encounters the Angel of the Lord who urges her to return to her irascible

---

1. Bell, *Deliver Us from Evil*, 173.
2. Renger, "Ambiguity of Judas," 8.
3. Viviano, "Genesis," 56.
4. Wolpe, "Angels in Jewish Tradition."

mistress and to submit to her. The text as we have it is quite clear that Hagar's encounter has been with the Angel of the Lord so that when Hagar later asks, "Have I really seen God and remained alive after seeing him?" the reader might exclaim "No! What you encountered was an angel!," or else ask, "Have I missed something?" The disconnect in the text seems to reflect the work of an editor who has inserted the motif of the angel so as to place Hagar at a degree of remove from the Deity.

The Yahwist strand of tradition in the Hebrew Bible is marked by a tendency to refer to God in an anthropomorphic and relatively familiar manner. It is the Yahwist authors who depict YHWH strolling in the Garden of Eden, engaging in conversation with the naked Adam and Eve, and may have had no difficulty with a narrative whereby Hagar encountered God in the desert. Later strands of biblical tradition, however, resisted such anthropomorphic depictions of the Deity chatting with humans. These authors imagined God in more transcendent terms and, the textual evidence suggests, replaced an earlier account of Hagar's encounter with God with an encounter with the Angel of the Lord.[5] Still, they leave Hagar asking a question as to whether she has encountered God, thus sustaining a degree of ambiguity. Within the Hagar narrative, the Angel of the Lord is not definitively distinguished from God and seems to be a mediated form of divine presence. The point is that it cannot be assumed that the biblical authors, by their invocation of mythical personas, asserted the existence or agency of beings.

The insidious dynamic whereby mythical personas have been interpreted as directly corresponding to beings that exist beyond the narrative arc is a form of euhemerism, an approach to the interpretation of myth named after the fourth-century BC Greek mythographer Euhemerus.[6] Euhemerism is a perspective that attributes historical existence to mythological characters, or one might say, invents a supposed history. It includes attempts to bestow historical status upon the deities of ancient religions. In a case in point, the third-century mythographer Porphyry claimed that the tomb of Zeus had been discovered.[7] It might thus be argued that the transposition of mythical motifs of the angel, the demon, or for that matter, Satan, into an alleged ontological reality is a spiritualized form of euhemerism. While, in these cases, the mythical personas are not attributed a bodily historical existence, they are imagined to exist as ontological realities beyond the narrative world of the myth, and to have intervened in the history of humanity.

---

5. Maly, "Book of Genesis," 20; Brown, "Genesis 16."
6. Spyridakis, "Zeus Is Dead," 38; Brown, "Euhemerus and the Historians," 259–74.
7. Harrison, "Epilegomena to the Study of Greek Religions," 57.

SATAN AS A BY-PRODUCT OF ETHICAL MONOTHEISM

If the motif of the Angel of the Lord serves as a literary device to mediate human encounters with the divine, the same may be said of the motif of Satan. The trope of Satan emerged in large part as a by-product of the evolution of ethical monotheism as evil was gradually construed as contrary to the will of God and an imaginative void ensued as to who or what is responsible for malice and misery.

Contemporary Christians might wrongly assume that Israelite religion has always been defined by the view that there is only one God and God is love. However, emerging from the mists of polytheism, a henotheistic worldview espoused faithfulness to one god among the plurality of deities. It took seriously the existence of enemy gods and envisaged strife between the gods of warring tribes. From this henotheistic perspective, the gods were quite willing to smite those outside their tribal fold (and quite possibly those within it should they transgress their covenant)

To employ a rather boorish analogy, the tribal deities were akin to the mascots of warring hordes of soccer fans. Horns, with all of their menacing and arguably diabolical connotations, were regarded as a sign of divinity, as evidenced by the horned altars excavated in the Ancient Near East.[8] The tribal god might, within such a worldview, be imagined to punish breaches of covenant by handing its errant devotees over to the whims of foreign gods. This served as a means through which to explain military defeat, exile, and plague without calling into question the sovereignty of the tribal or national god. When catastrophe struck, this mindset looked for a sin that deserved abandonment by God and justified the consequent misfortune.

With the demise of henotheism and the emergence of monotheism, foreign gods could no longer be blamed for the nation's afflictions and misfortune seemed to originate from the will of the one true God. Hence, the backdrop against which much of the Hebrew Bible was authored, envisaged both good and evil proceeding from the Deity.[9] YHWH was once regarded as possessing a "demonic" dimension.[10] This is not quite the oxymoron that it may seem when we consider the logic that the Creator of all things must, according to a certain train of thought, have created unpleasant things as well as the more delightful features of creation. Also, in imagining that YHWH possessed a demonic dimension, the term "demonic" need not denote evil spirits in the sense of ontological beings so much as a more amorphous

---

8. Puthussery, *Days of Man and God's Day*, 148; Obbink, "Horns of the Altar," 43–49.
9. Nielson, *Satan*, 55.
10. Volz, *Das Daimonische in Jahwe*; Nielson, *Satan*, 55.

reference to wrath and hostility. This view of a somewhat capricious God is evident in lament literature and the wheedling of Old Testament authors as they prevail upon the Deity to avert is anger and be merciful.

First Samuel 16:14 offers a pertinent example of the demonic side of YHWH who is depicted as sending an evil spirit to trouble Saul. In a worldview that did not yet assume a "fall of the angels" whereby evil spirits had been handed their walking papers by the celestial HR department, it made sense to imagine even evil spirits as servants of God. Long before the emergence of a divine command ethic that assumes God's will to be inherently good, no matter what God wills, the inscrutable whims of the Deity might be experienced as evil.

As is the case with the Angel of the Lord, it is far from certain that the author of First Samuel intended the reference to an evil "spirit" to denote a particular being. Nowhere in the Bible are spirits or demons ascribed individuality and personality. Neither, as we shall see, do references to Satan in the Hebrew Bible denote a three-dimensional character and it is even debatable as to whether "Satan" should be translated as though it signifies a name.

"SATAN" AS A ROLE RATHER THAN A NAME

Old Testament passages conventionally translated as references to "Satan" may relate to a role rather than to a being, and could be regarded as a common noun, sometimes denoted as *ha-satan*.[11] The role is that of adversary, enemy, or obstructionist, and includes in its remit tempting, testing, and, upon occasion, torture.

There is little to suggest that the satans of the Hebrew Bible pursue their own agenda as distinct from a divine mandate. As is the case with the Angel of the Lord, the satan functions as a device to mediate God's dealings with humanity—particularly dealings of a more acrimonious nature. In a case in point, the author of 1 Chronicles 21:1 asserts that the satan incited King David to conduct a census. This was essentially a military draft, implying hawkish intent on the part of David and heralding nothing but trouble for Israel. The narrative suggests that, because David took the census, God inflicted upon Israel a plague that kills seventy thousand people (1 Chr 21:14). However, in an earlier account of the census debacle, 2 Samuel 24:1 suggests that it was God that directly incited David to take the census. It might hence be argued that God is depicted in the role of a satan, tempting, testing, and tormenting. It would appear that the insertion of the satan in the Chronicler's later account of the census serves a similar function to that of

11. Kelly, *Satan*, 72.

the Angel of the Lord in the Hagar narrative, mediating the presence of God so as to keep humans at a degree of remove, and distancing YHWH from the morally dubious act of entrapment that would lead to nothing less than genocide.[12] Walter Brueggemann invokes the concept of plausible deniability so as to suggest that the invocation of a satan is intended to spare the Deity direct involvement and obvious knowledge of the sting operation.[13] As sinister as the satans of the Hebrew Bible may be, there is little indication that these tempters, testers, and obstructionists constitute enemies of God rather than a manifestation of YHWH's tiger-parenting.

The ominous side of the Deity imagined by the ancient authors is evident in its permissive will, as it allows a satan to inflict unspeakable cruelty upon Job, saying "Very well, he is in your power; only spare his life" (Job 1:6) The narrative introduces the satan as a "son of God, a divinely authorized tempter and tester that extends its remit into the gospels. Such a model of Satan is evident in the gospel accounts of the temptation of Jesus in the desert wherein the distinct agency of God and of Satan may not be as distinguishable as modern Christians might like to believe. Matthew portrays Jesus as being drawn by divine power into an encounter with Satan. He is "led by the Spirit" to be tempted by Satan in the desert (Matt 4:1–11).[14] The motif of Satan as tempter and tester serves as a mythic probe into what might transpire in the relationship between humans and their Maker if a given scenario were to transpire. If, for example, Job were to encounter a sequence of calamities, how might he then regard God? And if Jesus were to succumb to the human desire for comfort and for power, what would this mean for humanity's relationship with God?

A further example of the *ha-satan* role is evident in the Balaam narrative of Numbers 22 when an angel acts as a satan to Balaam and blocks his path. Even when serving as a blocker of paths, the satan role probes possibilities in the God-human relationship. To obstruct one path is to divert the would-be traveler towards other possibilities. When, in Matthew 16:23, Jesus famously snaps at St. Peter "Get behind me Satan!," this may not be quite as harsh a rebuff as it sounds to modern ears, as though Jesus was equating his friend with the most evil being in the universe. Jesus was steeped in the traditions of the Hebrew Bible in which satan denotes an obstruction and arguably an unwelcome intervention by God in the affairs

---

12. McGill, "Evolution of the Christian Motif of Satan."
13. Brueggemann, *Reverberations of Faith*, 188.
14. Alison, "Deliver Us from Evil."

of humanity.¹⁵ In this instance, Peter endeavors to obstruct a path that will foreseeably lead to his friend's slaughter.

SATAN AND THE DUALISTIC WORLDVIEW

In 539 BC, King Cyrus of Persia conquered Babylon, repatriated the Israelites who had been exiled there, and bankrolled the construction of the Second Temple. Jews exiled in Babylon encountered Zoroastrianism, the religion of ancient Persia that viewed the universe as gripped in tension between a principle of goodness and a principle of evil.¹⁶ Although Zoroastrianism is, in modernity, usually classified as a monotheistic religion, its worldview is deeply dualistic, envisaging the existence of a benign deity, Ahura-mazda, and a rival, malevolent spirit, Ahrimam. The fact that the liberated Jews regarded Cyrus as a messianic figure underscores the benign view of Persia adopted by Second Temple Judaism.

While neither Judaism nor Christianity fully embraced the cosmic dualism of Zoroastrianism so as to teach that the devil is God's equal opposite, the Judeo-Christian tradition nonetheless inherited some of its dualistic assumptions. The influence of Zoroastrian dualism is clearly evident in the writings of the Qumran community that view reality as gripped by a cosmic struggle between a spirit of light and a spirit of darkness also referred to as the spirit of perversion or Belial.¹⁷ Its long-term influence, however, is more insidious and usually evades critical scrutiny.

SATAN FALLS FROM GOD'S GOOD GRACES

The complications entailed in tracing any coherent evolution of the motif of Satan are greatly compounded by linguistics as Hebrew, Greek, Latin, and English terms are insidiously blended to form the composite motif of Satan as presented in the Catechism. While the Hebrew books of the Old Testament present functionary satans as faithfully serving the will of God, it is an Old Testament text authored in Greek that first ascribes a personal motive to a biblical satan. Wisdom 2:21–22 asserts that "through the devil's envy, death entered the world." Henry Ansgar Kelly exegetes the text, concluding that the author is rendering in Greek an equivalent of the common noun,

---

15. Alison, "Deliver Us from Evil," 39–40.

16. Isbell, "Zoroastrianism and Biblical Religion"; Kronen and Menssen, "Defensibility of Zoroastrian Dualism," 185–205.

17. Brown, "Qumran Scrolls," 10–11.

ha-satan, rather than referring to the devil as a distinct being.[18] Nonetheless, this reference to diabolical envy suggests that the devil's motives are not entirely in line with the dictates of its divine overlord.

The Catechism invokes this passage to support its assertion that Satan facilitates the intrusion of death into human history.[19] Henry Ansgar Kelly, however, argues compellingly that the "devil" or "accuser" referenced by the Book of Wisdom may be a human satan—the mythical character Cain who committed the first murder related in the canon, an act that the Wisdom authors may have regarded as more grievous than the theft of fruit.[20]

The Book of Wisdom invokes the indefinite article so as to assert that it was through the envy of "a devil," in Greek, *diabolos* that death entered the world.[21] While the term "Satan" derived from Hebrew suggests an "enemy" and "obstructionist," the term *diabolos* suggests a "slanderer" or "accuser." Thus, the Hebrew and Greek terminology associated with the devil or Satan have somewhat different connotations. Nonetheless, the terms "*diabolos*" and "*Satanas*" are used interchangeably in the Greek texts of the synoptic gospels so that "the devil" and "Satan" have to all intents and purposes become synonyms in Christian thought.[22]

To modern ears, the term "devil" may signify a specific being rather than a role or category in the sense that the term "demon" does. However, this has not always been the case in English wherein reference to a plurality of "devils" was once more common as instantiated in Shakespeare's remark in Othello, "When devils will the blackest sins put on / They do suggest at first with heavenly shows."[23] Again, in *The Tempest*, the bard exclaims, "Hell is empty. And the devils are here."[24] Biblical references to the term "devil" are no more certain to refer to the role or name of a specific being than are references to Satan.

It is in the New Testament, specifically Luke 10:181–89 and Revelation 12:10, that the biblical authors envisage Satan as a celestial being expelled from heaven so as to be "thrown down."[25] The motif of beings being thrown out of heaven finds precedence in intertestamental literature and appears to

18. Kelly, *Satan*, 72.
19. CDF, *Catechism of the Catholic Church* 398.
20. Kelly, *Satan*, 77–78.
21. Kelly, *Satan in the Bible*, 29.
22. Green et al., *Dictionary of Jesus and the Gospels*, 164; Kittel et al., *Theological Dictionary of the New Testament*, 151–52.
23. Shakespeare, *Othello* II.iii.62–63.
24. Shakespeare, *Tempest* I.ii.216.
25. Kelly, *Satan*, 155.

be an allegorical expression of conflict and treachery on earth.[26] Conflicts with Jewish and Roman authorities prompted the New Testament authors to envisage God meting out justice to enemies in high places. However, the separation of Satan from God seemed inevitable on philosophical grounds alone as ethical monotheism emerged from monism. A God whose very will constitutes goodness cannot actively or tacitly encourage evil. If the capricious will of a morally ambiguous God can no longer be blamed for the evil that befalls us, a vacancy ensues. Satan, relieved of its office in the heavenly cabinet, is gradually conscripted by the Christian imagination to serve as a new explanation for evil, exonerating the morally purified model of God.[27]

The fallen Satan is hence a byproduct of the development of ethical monotheism. If God is the one and only God, and hence is God for all people, it is less plausible that God would unleash angels of destruction upon Egyptian first-borns, Canaanites, or *goyim* in general. From a monotheistic perspective, it is difficult to imagine that evil, cruel, or destructive spirits could enjoy a divine mandate.[28] If objective goodness is not defined in terms of God's will, it might be asked, what standard distinguishes good from evil? This is the basis of a divine-command ethic wherein God is the source of goodness and not accountable to some extraneous moral standard. From such a perspective, God cannot, by definition, will evil, and the satan or Satan is released from its celestial contract so as to operate on a free-lance basis.

THE MOTIF OF SATAN REFLECTS EARTHLY ADVERSARIES

While Henry Ansgar Kelly traces the emergence of Christian models of Satan largely in relation to a gradual disassociation of God from evil, Elaine Pagels emphasizes another, though not at all contradictory, strand of development. Pagels highlights the influence of Israelite nationalism, treachery, and intra-Jewish rivalry in the evolution of the concept of Satan as a trope signifying the demonization of earthy adversaries.[29]

Pagels points to the extracanonical *Book of the Watchers* and its depiction of the fall of mythic personas, Semihazah, Azazel, Mastema, Belial, and Satanail.[30] The fall of these entities, on Pagel's reading, symbolizes the

26. Pagels, *Origin of Satan*, 48.
27. Kelly, *Satan*, 17–30.
28. Cook, "Can God Take Responsibility?"
29. Pagels, *Origin of Satan*, 49; McGill, "Evolution of the Christian Motif of Satan."
30. Pagels, *Origin of Satan*, 55; Almond, *Devil*, 8.

treachery of those Israelites who sided with Greek invaders and opposed the Maccabean revolt.[31] Pagels regards the litany of fallen beings in *Watchers* as signifying an ancient belief that tumult on earth implies a cosmic upheaval. The emphasis is thus on a universal conflict rather than the ontological reality of the fallen ones. So when Philip Almond comments in relation to the litany of fallen beings in the intertestamental literature that "The Prince of Demons went by many different names," it is important to note that only in retrospect have these celestial rejects been blended into the composite motif of Satan, yet alone taken to denote a particular ontological reality.[32]

Later, as Pagels notes, Essene separatists would specifically invoke the name of Satan to demonize Jews who embraced Hellenistic culture.[33] "More radical than their predecessors," Pagels observes, "these dissidents began increasingly to invoke the *satan* to characterize their Jewish opponents; in the process they turned this rather unpleasant angel into a far grander—and far more malevolent figure."[34] Our exploration of the motif of Satan in the canonical gospels will suggest further instances of demonization as the Jesus movement vied with other Jewish sects for the hearts and minds of diaspora Jews.[35] A particularly explicit trope reflecting bitter conflict between the Jesus movement and other Jewish groups is evident in the Book of Revelation, in its explicit reference to the "synagogue of Satan" (2:9; 3:9). This libelous outburst follows the expulsion of the Jewish Christians from the synagogues by 80 AD, a decade or more before the authorship of Revelation.

The term "satan" means enemy and had long been invoked to denote human or inhuman adversaries who functioned on behalf of God. In time, however, the dualist influence of Zoroastrianism, the bitterness of the Maccabean revolt, intra-Jewish sectarianism, and the exoneration of God from complicity with evil contributed towards the evolving perception of a Satan that was something other than a role subservient to the Deity, morphing into a more sinister entity with a mind of its own. As the enemy of humanity became the enemy of God, that which had been thought of as a role, a guise, and at most a shadowy functionary insidiously acquired, in popular perception, the trappings of personhood.[36]

---

31. Pagels, *Origin of Satan*, 48.
32. Almond, *Devil*, 22.
33. Pagels, *Origin of Satan*, 47.
34. Pagels, *Origin of Satan*. 47.
35. Pagels, *Origin of Satan*, 38–39, 46–47.
36. Pagels, *Origin of Satan*, 49.

THE CHURCH COUNTERACTS EXAGGERATED NOTIONS OF SATAN

Impelled by the teachings of Jesus, Christianity exorcized any trace of moral complexity, yet alone the demonic, from the Godhead, as epitomized by the assertion of 1 John 4:16 that "God is love." On the fringes of second-century Christianity, however, Gnostic movements speculated the existence of other, less benign gods, demigods, or demiurges who, independent of God, created the physical realm. If references to the satan in the Hebrew Bible denoted an obstructionist, adversarial role as opposed to a being, it is Gnosticism that aggrandized Satan as a formidable opponent of God that did not owe its existence to the Deity.

The apologetic Patristics including Justin Martyr, Tatian, Athenagorus, Irenaeus, and Origen sought to refute Gnostic models of Satan as the creator of the physical world, or, alternatively, as a creature of the demiurge, rather than a creature of God.[37] Rejecting such views, Justin Martyr, in the mid-second century, associated Satan with the snake of the Adamic myth, hence identifying Satan as a creature of God, rather than existing as an evil deity.[38] Justin's disciple, Tatian, pioneered the classification of the fallen angels as demons, an association that had not hitherto been widely assumed. Tatian also advanced the view that Satan is a fallen angel and hence a demon.[39] Athenagorus and Tertullian built on Tatian's position so as to emphasize that Satan, as a fallen angel, was a creature of God, with an originally good nature, and a character corrupted through its exercise of free will.

The implications of these Patristic speculations are still deeply embedded in Christian assumptions regarding the spiritual realm. The position that demons are fallen angels has contributed to the stark moral dualism envisaged by Christian doctrine, whereby inhuman spirits are either angelic or demonic—celestial or damned. Such dualism may also reflect the Zoroastrian influence upon Second Temple Judaism. Why it, might be asked, could shades of moral complexity not exist among inhuman spirits? Terms such as "elemental" or "nature spirit" as associated with Pagan worldviews and some of the literature on paranormal investigation, on the other hand, suggest that not all inhuman spirits, should they exist, are entirely heavenly or hellish. To imagine stark dualism as existing in the spiritual realm, it might be argued, leads to a somewhat apocalyptic view of creation in which the battle lines between good and evil are clearly drawn.

---

37. Russell, *Satan*, 27, 47, 227.
38. Russell, *Satan*, 65.
39. Russell, *Satan*, 73–74.

Consistent with the Patristic endeavor to identify Satan as a creature rather than an evil deity, Clement of Alexandria distinguished between the being of the Satan creature versus pure evil in and of itself. This distinction served to refute the position that God created evil. Clement advanced the model of evil as a privation, a "nothingness," void, or lack, and hence distinct from the being of Satan.[40] If all being is created by God and is hence inherently good, evil can be thought of as no-thing. Origen, for his part, suggested the possibility ultimately rejected by the bulk of Christian thought, that Satan's inherently good being might be redeemed since it is separable from the privation of evil.[41] Origen's distinction between the privation of evil and the inherently good being of Satan, assumed and reinforced the position that Satan exists as a being. Origen identified Satan with the motif of the morning star of Isaiah 14, addressed as having fallen from the heavens, and invoked the term "Lucifer," that is, "light-bearer," an association popularized in St. Jerome's Vulgate in 382 AD, and further reinforced by Milton's *Paradise Lost* in 1608.[42]

While refuting the Gnostic idea of a co-eternal evil principle, God's "opposite number" who is the cosmic source of evil, the Patristics also sought to exonerate God of having directly created evil.[43] In rejecting depictions of Satan as a creator-demiurge, or as a creation of the demiurge, the Patristics emphasized that Satan was a creature of the one true God, and used its free will to opt for the privation of evil.[44] On the face of it, only a free-willed sentient being, a person, that is, could make this choice. Still, the driving motivation of the Patristics seems to have been "negative," that is, to correct the exaggerated notion of a quasi-divine Satan that arose in Gnosticism rather than to proactively engender certainty in Satan's existence as a fallen creature of God.

Long after the Gnostic heresies regarding Satan have faded into historical curiosity, the counterargument of the Patristics remains ensconced as orthodox Christian thinking, that is, Satan was regarded as a corrupted creature of God, and hence a being. While the initial motivation of the Patristics was to reject overblown versions of Satan and to defend monotheism, in the process they perpetuated misplaced certainty about the existence of Satan as a free-willed creature, an angel, and hence, a person. Jeffrey Burton Russell comments that Patristic ruminations on Satan became excessively

---

40. Russell, *Satan*, 188.
41. Russell, *Satan*, 147.
42. Almond, *Devil*, 46.
43. Russell, *Satan*, 27–28.
44. Russell, *Satan*, 27–28.

speculative. Russell's own assessment is that we are incapable of knowing whether the devil exists "objectively" or "transcendentally"—an agnostic position with which the present work concurs.[45]

When Church Councils taught on the subject of the devil, as is the case for doctrine in general, they did so to counteract the heresies at large in their milieu. Thus, the First Council of Braga in 561 AD, confronted with Manichean versions of the devil, reiterated the broad thrust of Patristic thought that Satan is a fallen angel and hence a creature of God. Still, Gnostic versions of Satan proved resilient through the centuries and the Fourth Lateran Council of 1215 AD confronted the model of Satan espoused by the Albigensian movement, also known as Cathars, that regarded the physical creation as evil and as the handiwork of Satan, again elevating Satan to the status of a creator.[46] The councils of Braga I and Lateran IV effectively ensured that Christianity did not adopt a cosmic dualism along the lines of that evident in ancient Zoroastrianism that envisaged the existence of a self-created principle of evil.

On an anecdotal note, students of theology routinely object to the position that there are no compelling philosophical arguments for the ontological reality of a personal Satan, countering that "if there is a God, then surely there must also be a devil since everything has an opposite." Revealing an impoverished understanding of the mystery of God as though God exists in the form of a thing that can be contrasted with other things, this response may suggest that cosmic dualism exercises a certain seductiveness, implying that the devil is an evil version of God and somehow a logical corollary to the existence of the Deity. Whereas God, from a monotheistic perspective, is the cause of all causes, the reason why there is something instead of nothing, the figure of the devil holds no such existential significance.

Despite the massive differences in their respective versions of Satan, the Catholic Church and the Albigensians both agreed that Satan existed as a being of some kind.[47] It could, however, be asked whether the Council assumed rather than formally defined the existence of Satan and other demons.[48] Paul Quay proposes that, given the exaggerated role that the Cathars afforded Satan as the creator of matter and of the demons, it would have been expedient if the Council Fathers could have avoided attracting any attention whatsoever to the doctrine, and that the fact they did so indicates that they

---

45. Russell, *Satan*, 220, 225

46. Russell, *Satan*, 220, 225; *Lucifer*, 95n9; Denzinger, *Enchiridion Symbolorum* 237–38, 242–43; Lateran IV, "Canons" 1.

47. Quay, "Angels and Demons," 42.

48. Quay, "Angels and Demons," 42.

are consciously making a theological assertion.[49] This argument invokes the "criterion of embarrassment" as utilized by biblical scholars, suggesting that it would have been more convenient for the Council to have said nothing that might encourage speculation concerning Satan. What is certain is that the Council sought to challenge anything approaching a deification of the devil. When, as we shall later see, modern theologians challenge the existence of Satan as a particular being, they continue this endeavor to deflate exaggerated notions of the devil—from demigod to mere creature, and, in contemporary thought, to something less than a creature.

SET: A CASE OF RETROSPECTIVE SATANIZATION

Another strand of mythology that has arguably contributed to the evolution of Christian motifs of Satan is that associated with the Egyptian god Set. While Joshua Mark posits that "Set was incorporated into the early mythology of Christianity *as the devil*," this development is only thinly evidenced beyond the more general demonization by Christians of all the gods and supernatural entities of paganism.[50]

Still it must be admitted, given his identikit, Set does seem to have been an obvious candidate for demonization and conflation with Satan.

> Set's relationship to darkness and wickedness, as well as the color red and the popular image of him as a red-haired beast, all leant themselves to the iconography of the Christian Satan. Like Satan, he brought about the end of paradise and was cast out of the land of the gods for rebelling against harmonious rule. His association with deceit, cunning, war, destruction and close connection with the serpent also worked well in fashioning the Christian concept of the great supernatural deceiver of human beings, who swore eternal enmity with God.[51]

It would however lose sight of other elements of the Set tradition to simply write off this mythical being as an ancient Egyptian forerunner of the Christian Satan. Set was not universally feared or hated, being viewed as a hero-god and worshipped in the city of Ombos. Further, it reflects the dualistic assumptions of ethical monotheism to cast Set as the enemy of "God" designated with an upper-case G, whereas Set was imagined as a god among gods in a polytheistic worldview within which mutual combat

---

49. Quay, "Angels and Demons," 42.
50. Mark, *Set*; Russell, *Satan*, 74–75
51. Mark, *Set*.

between the gods was rampant. So when commentators steeped in Western culture and informed by the iconography of Christianity, refer to Set as a demon, as does Paul Carus when he describes Set as "the nefarious demon of death and evil in Egyptian mythology," this is a retrospective imposition of Christian categories where these would have made little sense to the original audiences of the myth.[52] While Carus regards Set as a demon, to go beyond that and identify Set as an Egyptian model of Satan would amount to retrospective satanization—a fate to which a range of biblical and extra-canonical motifs have fallen prey. An association with Satan has much the same effect on the reputation of a mythical persona as a comparison with Adolf Hitler has for the reputation of a politician, while the designation of a mythical persona as a "demon" has all the endearing connotations of the politician being deemed a Nazi. Unbiased analysis of the character becomes very difficult beyond that point, suspicion lingering that there is no smoke without hellfire.

Long before its demonization in the Christian imagination, however, Set's popularity does seem to have plummeted in ancient Egypt so as to be, as Joshua Mark notes, "transformed from a god of love, protector, and hero into the villain who stood for everything the Egyptians feared and hated: disorder, chaos, waste, drought, famine, destruction, hunger, and foreign invasion/influence."[53] Still, Mark acknowledges that, even after Set's ratings slipped, Rameses II remained a loyal devotee in a reminder that one man's demon is another's God.

The identification of Set with Satan evokes the difficulties entailed in trying to distinguish whether the motif is an influential forerunner of Christian models of Satan or a mythical persona retrospectively demonized in light of Christian doctrine. This is, to a large extent, the same problem that arises when students of World Religions insist upon classifying the non-Christian religions in terms of Christian doctrine so that, for example, Ramadan is described as the "Muslim Lent."

Granted, when Christian authors regard mythical characters as depictions of Satan, they are not necessarily assuming that the ancients envisaged a Satan in the manner that the Christian imagination would in time. Neither are they necessarily claiming to know better than the ancient audiences of the myth by detecting something that the pre-Christian audience could not. Sometimes their position is a form of reader-response interpretation, arguing that, regardless of the intentions of the pre-Christian authors, the

---

52. Carus, *History of the Devil*.
53. Mark, *Set*.

Christian reader should interpret all of reality through the lens of the Christ event and Christ's conquest of evil.

In a case in point, Rivka Nir advocates a distinctively Christian reading of the first-century Jewish text, *The Greek Life of Adam and Eve*. Nir argues that a struggle between Adam's son, Seth, and a beast should be understood as a struggle between the image of God and Satan.[54] This suggestion that Seth was attacked by Satan is a good case in point from which to illustrate the complications entailed by transposing mythical characters from one myth and culture to another. Set the Egyptian god or demon is sometimes dubbed "Seth," a named shared with Adam's son.[55] Joshua Mark notes depictions of the Egyptian Set or "Seth" as a "red-haired beast" so that if one were to accept that Set or Seth is an Egyptian depiction of Satan, one might say that Seth was attacked by Seth. Such a crosspollination of nomenclature may seem ridiculous, but it is no more outrageous than much of the transplantation of Satan nomenclature that has transpired in the Christian tradition. Motifs as disparate as the Joban "son of God," the fallen star of Isaiah 14, the fallen angels of the extracanonical *Book of the Watchers,* the talking snake of Genesis 3, the gods of the gentiles, the dragon, serpent, and beast of Revelation, the chaos monsters of the psalms, Belial, Baal'zebul, and the antichrist of the first letter of John have all contributed towards the discovery of the "Christian" Satan popularly imagined in Western culture, its pedigree very much that of a mongrel.[56]

CONCLUSION

This chapter offers an account of the evolution of Christian motifs of Satan through the cross-pollination of mythical narratives and tropes. It detects a common characteristic shared by the various strands of Satan tradition. Models of Satan have evolved in relation to their corresponding models of God and the gods—henotheistic, monist, and eventually ethical monotheistic. Contemporary presentations of the doctrine of Satan, however, are not always attentive to these formative influences. The theodicist challenges associated with the emergence of ethical monotheism, the influence of Zoroastrian dualism on Second Temple Judaism, the bitter epithets vented against adversaries in intra-Jewish conflicts, the demonization of pagan gods, and Patristic polemics against the Gnostic deification of Satan tend

---

54. Nir, "Struggle between the 'Image of God.'"
55. Mark, *Set*.
56. D'Aragon, "Apocalypse," 482.

to be forgotten as a mishmash of motifs and traditions are blended and assumed to correspond to a particular supernatural being.

Historically, models of Satan have evolved in keeping with developing insights into the mystery of God, and as thinking about God continues to evolve, so must thinking about Satan. Surely, the controlling image must be the image of God and any theological construct that is no longer compatible with the guiding image of God has lost its theological credibility.

3

Can the Existence of Satan Be Demonstrated without Recourse to Myth?

So far, our argument has been that the Catholic Church's presentation of the doctrine of Satan's existence as an ontological being hinges upon a historicized misinterpretation of myth coupled with a Patristic endeavor to deflate the Gnostic glorification of Satan as a God or demiurge. So as to counteract Gnostic attempts through the centuries to deify Satan, the Councils of Braga I and Lateran IV asserted a deflated account of the devil as a creature of the one and only God. While largely successful in suppressing the model of Satan as a God or demiurge, these councils effectively canonized Satan's perceived existence as an ontological being. The language of myth became the language of doctrine.

Let us now consider an objection to this argument, asking whether the magisterium's exposition on the personal Satan, rather than an erroneous literalization of myth, might be founded upon philosophical arguments that are expressed with recourse to mythical language. If natural theology can construct arguments from creation, design, and contingency, suggesting the existence of a divine Creator of some kind, then natural Satanology might reflect an argument from violence and destruction, indicating the existence of Satan as the instigator behind evil, the one who facilitated creation's deviation from the plan of a loving God. Since there is a creation, there must be a Creator or creators, it might be argued, and by the same token, since there is destruction, there must have been a first component of creation to utilize free will so as to break with the Creator's plan and set in motion a cycle of evil and suffering.

From the outset, it is clear that many aspects of the doctrine of Satan cannot be justified by rational argument alone since they relate to the interpretation of specific scriptural passages. It does not seem possible, for example, to demonstrate solely by recourse to philosophical argument that Satan tempted Jesus in the desert. Other aspects of the tradition, for example, that of a horned devil, reflect the imaginative interpretation of mythical motifs and are also beyond the scope of rational argument alone.

This thought experiment in natural Satanology will focus therefore on three dimensions of the Satan tradition as endorsed by the Catechism. First, we will test the argument that humanity's initial abuse of its freedom indicates the influence of a non-human tempter.[1] Second, we will test the position that humanity's ongoing propensity to sin is influenced by the agency of a non-human being.[2] Finally, we will test the position that it is possible to individuate a particular fallen being that constitutes a nemesis to God.[3]

IS SATAN NECESSARY TO EXPLAIN THE FALL OF HUMANITY TO SIN?

We have already discussed at some length the Catechism's historicized account of Satan's temptation of Adam and Eve. If God is the Creator of all that is, and if all that God creates is good, it then stands to reason that evil must have arisen in creation due to an aberration that is at odds with God's plan. Within the Christian worldview, this aberration is due to the exercise of creaturely free will. In this vein of thought, the Catechism invokes the mythical motif of the Fall of the Angels in order to illustrate the first emergence of evil in creation. "The Church teaches that Satan was at first a good angel, made by God: 'The devil and the other demons were indeed created naturally good by God, but they became evil by their own doing.'"[4]

By presenting the Fall of the Angels as part of the same overarching narrative as the Fall of humanity, the Catechism can appear to imply that one chronologically preceded the other. Satan, however, understood as a

---

1. CDF, *Catechism of the Catholic Church* 391.
2. CDF, *Catechism of the Catholic Church* 395.
3. CDF, *Catechism of the Catholic Church* 395.
4. CDF, *Catechism of the Catholic Church* 391.

disembodied being in heaven, might be considered to have existed outside of time. So as to avoid the impression of a chronological timeline, it might therefore be argued that Satan fell from grace in and through its role in the temptation of Adam and Eve. In any case, the Catechism is constrained by spatiotemporal language and, in its defense, need not be interpreted as presenting a chronological account of the Fall of the angels that preceded the Fall of humanity.

The text continues to grapple with temporal language, asserting that "The devil 'has sinned from the beginning'; he is 'a liar and the father of lies.'"[5] The reference to sinning "from the beginning" stands in some tension with the assertion of having been created good by God. It may be understood as a distinction between the inherent goodness of the creature's being by virtue of its creation by God and, on the other hand, the corruption of its character by means of its own choices. Such an interpretation may be more helpful than to imagine that the devil existed in a state of Original Innocence for some period of "time" before its exercise of free will in a catastrophic choice against God (which would be the devil's one and only choice in relation to God, based upon the scholastic speculation that angels cannot change their minds, an argument we will examine in due course.)

In contrast with the vaunted position that John Milton would in his seventeenth-century epic poem *Paradise Lost*, attribute to Satan, the Catechism does not explicitly recognize Satan as the instigator and leader of an angelic mutiny, but refers to the Fall of "the devil and the other demons," locating Satan's rejection of God in the context of a rebellion that included multiple demons.[6] Hence, the Catechism does not individuate Satan as the "first" being, as it were, to fall from grace, or assert that Satan's Fall is in itself any different from that of the other demons.

It is in its indictment of Satan for facilitating the Fall of humanity that the Catechism first individuates Satan from its demonic brethren. "Behind the disobedient choice of our first parents lurks a seductive voice, opposed to God, which makes them fall into death out of envy. Scripture and the Church's Tradition see in this being a fallen angel, called 'Satan' or the 'devil.'"[7] What we are left with then is the claim that Satan tempted the first humans to sin, ending a period of original innocence, whatever its duration. Could, therefore, the emergence of human sin point compellingly to the existence of a non-human tempter?

---

5. CDF, *Catechism of the Catholic Church* 391.
6. Milton, *Paradise Lost*, 206–469.
7. CDF, *Catechism of the Catholic Church* 391.

So as to constitute a credible natural theology, an account of the emergence of human sin must take into consideration the scientific theory of evolution. Acceptance of the theory of evolution is essentially compatible with Catholic doctrine as clarified by Pope John Paul II in his 1996 "Message to the Pontifical Academy for the Sciences: On Evolution."[8] From an evolutionary standpoint, long before a mammal could make a moral choice, natural systems inflicted suffering on a massive scale in the animal world. Nature was "red in tooth and claw" as reflected in the food chain and the struggle for dominance in the animal world.[9] Within an evolutionary framework, moral consciousness emerges gradually among primates so that there may be no crystal-clear line to demarcate animal brutality from the emergence of moral evil as perpetrated by primitive humans.

The discussion as to how evil emerged in creation must contend with the question of natural evil. For our purposes, natural evil denotes the situation whereby the non-human environment, including weather, diseases, and non-human creatures cause suffering that it is difficult to reconcile with the plan of a loving God, such as we can imagine it to be. Either God sanctions the destructive effects of these natural forces or else they function in a manner contrary to the divine plan and are hence in terms of a divine command ethic, evil. Granted, such a view is predicated upon ethical monotheism and a presupposition that the lives of humans and of other creatures matter, and are not simply collateral damage that is incidental to the emergence of a greater good. In deciding whether one recognizes a category of natural evil, one might ask oneself whether the suffering and death inflicted by cancers, earthquakes, and tsunamis seem to reflect God's will as we might glimpse it through the life and teachings of Jesus.

While the forces of nature are not conscious in the way that human persons are, neither are they micromanaged by God—at least not in terms of the models of God embraced by many contemporary Christians. Within such a worldview, God does not decide that it will rain heavily in London while there will be a drought in Melbourne, and a light drizzle in Dublin, or that one person's grandmother will live to a hundred and three years of age while another's will die of cancer in her late sixties. Not to recognize some form of natural evil would seem to indict God for each and every tragedy inflicted by natural causes.

Granted, it might be argued that Satan or other demons may manipulate natural systems and hence facilitate natural evil. However, in

---

8. John Paul II, "Message to the Pontifical Academy of Sciences." See also Chardin, *Phenomenon of Man*, 218, 220, 223, 227, 228, 277.

9. Tennyson, "In Memoriam LVI."

the endeavor to build a natural Satanology, the question is whether such diabolical instigation is not only possible but necessary in order to explain the phenomena in question.[10] The argument that demons tinker with natural forces seems tinged with a degree of arbitrariness. Unless one were to imagine that demons cause every rain shower and breeze, at what point on the Beaufort Wind Scale, the Richter Scale, or the barometer, do natural conditions become sufficiently severe as to offer evidence of demonic manipulation?

An account of the gradual evolution of moral consciousness stands in stark contrast with a scenario in which an evil genius, that is, Satan, tempted two humans who were equipped with full knowledge and conscious choice—for such must be the case in a literalized account of the sin of Adam and Eve, or else the Fall of humanity was occasioned by a merely venial sin committed by cognitively low-functioning brutes. It is implausible that the first humans, moreover, could have had any inkling of the catastrophic consequences entailed by their foraging for fruit. The narrative simply does not make sense as an account of cause and effect in the world beyond the myth. Why one might ask, would the humans need a snake or a Satan to suggest that they eat the forbidden fruit? If they were so dull-witted not to have considered the possibility themselves, they would seem too oblivious to be culpable for mortal sin, being akin to simpletons tricked by a devious fraudster.

Granted, the argument for a continuum between natural evil and moral evil does not rule out the possible role of a devil or demons, operating behind the scenes, but such intervention is not necessary. The misguided use of human freedom, emerging from the general freedom of the cosmos, provides ample explanation for personal sin, without necessary recourse to the role of Satan as a tempter. Thus fails our first possible basis for a natural Satanology.

DOES THE ONGOING REALITY OF PERSONAL SIN POINT CONVINCINGLY TO SATAN?

Moving from Original Sin to the ubiquitous reality of sin in every time and place, a Christian worldview need not envisage that a being identified as Satan directly influences every human person in every sinful choice. Rather, the human propensity to sin can be explained in terms of personal freedom and with reference to the doctrine of the Fall, regarded as a mythical means of speaking about how humans in all times and places fall short of the vision

10. Plantinga, *Analytic Theist*, 16–48.

of a loving God. An existential account of the Fall, rejecting biblical literalism, requires no reference to diabolical influence.

St. Augustine of Hippo's fifth-century account of vice represents a strand of Catholic moral theology that requires no reference to Satan's involvement in each instance of temptation and sin. Augustine explains vice in terms of disordered desires for things that are good in and of themselves.[11] The desires are disordered to the extent that they lose sight of priority and proportionality so as to, for example, commit an armed robbery so as to provide a more comfortable lifestyle for one's family. The stolen resources in themselves, as part of the grace-infused creation, are good. So too is the desire to provide for one's family a good thing—but not at the expense of depriving, threatening, injuring, or killing an innocent person in the process. This overwhelming desire for things that are in themselves good can, without any reference to Satan, serve to explain sinful choices. Even crimes that might be, in a colloquial sense, termed "diabolical" may be interpreted as involving a perverted desire for justice that in actuality extracts revenge, a desire for sexual intimacy that has become distorted, or a sadistic act that feeds some dark psychological need. In each instance the moral agent seeks something that is, in itself, good, but loses all sense of proportionality in relation to the hierarchy of goods and the rights of others.

Augustine's account of vice in no way underestimates its evil or mitigates personal responsibility. Indeed, an account of Satan as the agent provocateur behind each instance of temptation is far more suggestive of entrapment and the mitigation of human responsibility. Rather, St. Augustine's theory accounts for the emergence of vice in the creation of a good God. St. Augustine as a man of his time does seem to have believed in the ontological reality of the devil, but the point of relevance is that his account of vice is not dependent upon the direct involvement of Satan as a tempter who incites each human sin.[12]

An objection might be suggested that some evil acts do not seem to be driven by a disordered desire for the good since there is nothing good to be gained. These acts seem entirely destructive and evocative of a diabolical mayhem such as when a father dismembers his family with a hacksaw and then rides his bicycle to the local train tracks and cycles under a train. In such cases there is no "loot" or personal gain—and apparently no pursuit of the good, however disordered. Without completely discounting the influence of the devil or demons, which may be ultimately unfalsifiable, the involvement of supernatural beings does not seem to be a necessary condition for

---

11. Augustine, *City of God*, 10.
12. Finney, "Empty Evil," 3.

such senseless evil which may be caused by mental illness. Evil acts brought about because of mental illness may be regarded as natural evil or could represent the collusion of natural and moral evil. The point of relevance is that even the most horrific instances of violence do not point ineluctably to the influence of an inhuman Satan. Indeed, given the unspeakably evil acts that humans have committed, why should the tradition posit that the most notoriously evil being in creation is inhuman?

SATAN AS A PSYCHOLOGICAL ARCHETYPE

Having argued that humans are quite capable of exercising their free will for evil without the complicity of a disembodied being, we now turn to an argument from psychology to see if Satan can be located as a reality that exists within the human person. Richard Stromer posits that "satan—or the devil as he is alternatively known—has remained among the most popular of archetypal figures of Western Civilization for more than two millennia."[13] Carl Jung regards archetypes as a priori and universal, the psychic equivalent of instincts. They are pictures or patterns of behavior embedded in the subconscious. Jung asserts, "All the most powerful ideas in history go back to archetypes."[14] Jung holds this to be especially true in relation to religious constructs, but it applies also to scientific, ethical, cultural, and philosophical ideas. "The archetype concept derives from the often-repeated observation that myths and universal literature stories contain well-defined themes which appear every time and everywhere. We often meet these themes in the fantasies, dreams, delirious ideas and illusions of persons living nowadays."[15]

Jung suggests that the archetype of Satan exists within the psyche, representing the internal conflict of binary forces.[16] Jung's evocation of the archetype of Satan refers to the shadow-side of the person, usually subdued by the conscious ego.[17] In Jung's view, there are forces within each person that can impede their journey toward self-actualization and these forces cannot be obliterated, only integrated.

Jung's reference to a Satan within raises the question as to how a "external" Satan harassing or possessing a human could be distinguished from a force that resides in the person's subconscious. After all, the designations

13. Stromer, "On Satan, Demons and Daimons."
14. Storr, *Essential Jung*, 16.
15. Jung, *Archetypes and the Collective Unconscious*, 153–54.
16. Oglesby, *C. G. Jung and Hans Urs von Balthasar*, 63.
17. Post, *Jung and the Story of Our Time*, 205–29.

of "inner" and "external" are but spatial metaphors—and highly ambiguous ones since something "within" a person is not necessarily something of which they are conscious or in control. Does, we might ask, religious discourse about Satan tend to objectify a dimension of the subconscious? Sallie Nichols suggests that, as Christianity essentially rejected the morally complex image of God with the *ha-shatan* operating on its behalf, it cast Satan as an enemy of God.[18] Perhaps, in exorcising any trace of Satan or darkness from its dominant image of the Godhead, Christianity also exorcised Satan from the *imago Dei*, that is, the human person, instead objectifying Satan as Other, even as another person.

While Stromer and Jung before him refer to Satan as an archetype, that is, a universal image, no version of Satan, whether drawn from sacred texts or the wider culture, has been recognized universally. Each motif of Satan is, after all, influenced by historical and cultural factors, so the authors of the Book of Job, for example, could not have been privy to the construct of Satan as later conceived by St. Augustine, or by the 1992 Catechism. Clearly, no particular model of Satan appears every time and everywhere. This poses a compelling argument against overstating the degree to which any particular mythic image of Satan, as depicted in a given tradition, can be identified with the Jungian archetype.

Voicing cynicism regarding the correspondence of the archetype of Satan with any ontological reality, Jean Knox is unconvinced that the collective subconscious reveals a glimpse of anything beyond itself, being nothing more than "a mere product of psychic functions."[19] The collective subconscious is, after all, a form of representation and is not things-in-themselves. Archetypes are not in and of themselves proof of the existence of any corresponding noumenal reality. That is to say, the fact that children from medieval Munich to twenty-first-century Manhattan have feared the nightmarish archetype of the hag does not prove the ontological existence of some corresponding noumenal hag. In this vein of thought, Stephanie de Voogd rejects a model of the archetype as representation and argues that the archetype is "contentless," and should be distinguished from images and representations.[20] Hence our second possible basis for a natural Satanology is also doomed to failure, unable to show that humanity's ongoing propensity to sin is influenced by the agency of a non-human being, that is, Satan. Indeed, Satan may be a projection of the human.

---

18. Nichols, *Jung and Tarot*, 269–70.
19. Knox, *Archetype, Attachment, Analysis*, 32.
20. Voogd, "C. G. Jung," 175–82.

Can the Existence of Satan Be Demonstrated without Recourse to Myth? 53

INDIVIDUATING A MOST EVIL BEING IN CREATION

We now turn to our third and final proposed basis for a natural Satanology, testing the prospect that it is possible to individuate a particular fallen being that constitutes a singular nemesis to God. The greatest evil in creation, it might be argued, must be rooted in mortal sin, that is, the most serious category of sin, rather than the relatively minor category of venial sin. Traditional criteria for the classification of a mortal sin include the agent's full knowledge of the grave matter at hand, and freedom to choose how to act.[21] The possession of free will and full knowledge carries with it a proportionate culpability for the perpetration of an evil act.

If a sane and cunning person skillfully executes a plan to push a man underneath a moving train so as to usurp his wealth, his wife, or some other benefit, this entails a greater degree of moral culpability than if a mentally ill person, while hallucinating, and imagining himself to be fighting off extraterrestrial monsters, commits the same act. On the other hand, if someone who had neither a premeditated plan to commit murder, nor suffered from delusions caused by mental illness, were, in a fit of temper or under the influence of illegal drugs, to commit the lethal offence, their culpability would seem to fall somewhere between the extreme culpability of the cold-blooded, calculated killer, and the diminished culpability of the deranged person who had no idea what he was doing. As such, degrees of culpability reflect degrees of knowledge, and of freedom to act. Hence, we might argue, the worst evil is likely to be committed by an agent or agents with superior intelligence, knowledge, and freedom to act. There is, however, no necessary correlation between superior intelligence and the greatest evil. It is conceivably possible that more intelligent beings live virtuous lives so that the misdeeds of some relatively low-functioning miscreant constitute the greatest evil—though history's pantheon of evil geniuses suggests otherwise.

It might be argued that if, hypothetically, there existed some species of inhuman extraterrestrials with greater intelligence and knowledge than that available to humans, such beings would be better equipped to commit the worst evil so that the most evil being in creation may well arise from their ranks.[22] Within a Christian framework, such as that envisaged by St. Thomas Aquinas, there exists a classification of persons with supra-human intelligence that is better equipped than humanity to perpetrate the worst evil. While the existence of supra-human angels would not in itself prove that angels are responsible for the worst evil, it would cast some degree of

---

21. CDF, *Catechism of the Catholic Church* 1857.
22. O'Meara, "Vast Universe and Extraterrestrials," 1–7.

suspicion upon these beings. Since Christian claims for the ontological reality of angels are rooted in myth—as is the case for Satan, the fallen angel, this diversion into myth derails the attempt to, within a broadly Christian worldview, construct a natural Satanology.

FROM NATURAL SATANOLOGY TO ANGELOLOGY AND MYTH

Catholic doctrine affirms the existence of angels, and teaches that these spirits are endowed with free will, and with superior capacities to those possessed by humans.[23] "As purely *spiritual* creatures angels have intelligence and will: they are personal and immortal creatures, surpassing in perfection all visible creatures, as the splendor of their glory bears witness."[24] As such, the Catechism suggests that the abilities of the angels surpass those of visible creatures such as human beings.

Aquinas holds that there are ranks of angels and that their degrees of knowledge vary.[25] The saint speculates that an angel possesses the "full knowledge" allotted to it by God.[26] According to Aquinas, angels do not learn or gradually grow in knowledge. They are, however, upon Aquinas's account, free-willed.[27]

The Catechism suggests that angels exceed human beings in their knowledge of God. With reference to Luke 2:81–4 and Mark 16:57, the Catechism asserts that the angels perpetually enjoy the Beatific Vision.[28] If this is the case, angels possess a knowledge of God that is not usually, if ever, directly accessible to humans, at least this side of the grave. This immediate access to the face of God, and the knowledge of God this would yield, would entail a heightened moral obligation for angels.

When human beings say that they are rejecting God, they are usually rejecting particular images of God, some of which may deserve to be rejected. Michael Paul Gallagher remarks that many atheists reject a "solitary and unrelating" God, a "Christian Zeus" that has little in common with the Triune Godhead professed by Christians.[29] Granted, Karl Rahner argues that the ultimate decision for or against God is played out implicitly in

---

23. CDF, *Catechism of the Catholic Church* 328.
24. CDF, *Catechism of the Catholic Church* 330.
25. Aquinas, *Summa Theologiae* I-I, q55, a3.
26. Aquinas, *Summa Theologiae* I-I, q58, a1.
27. Aquinas, *Summa Theologiae* I-I, q59, a1.
28. CDF, *Catechism of the Catholic Church* 339.
29. Gallagher, "Reflection on Rublev's Icon of the Trinity," 104.

Can the Existence of Satan Be Demonstrated without Recourse to Myth?

decisions about the creation in which God is mysteriously present, so that one could incrementally reject God without having access to the Beatific Vision.[30] Still, humans, at least in the earthly realm, are not in an epistemic position to reject God in Godself.

What is true for Spiderman, would be true for Satan: "With great power comes great responsibility."[31] A foray into angelology affirms this argument, implying that beings who gaze upon the Beatific Vision are in a position to reject God in Godself in a way that humans are not epistemically equipped to do. While supra-human beings, should they exist, may possess this capacity, this does not mean that any one of them has necessarily rejected God. Further, there is no logical reason to propose the existence of a particular angel who facilitated the fall of humankind, and who holds singular significance in the obstruction of God's saving designs so as to correspond to the Satan described in the Catechism. To envisage such a singular villain is to imagine an Olympics of evil in which a clear and unbeatable winner has emerged.

SATAN AS THE SPIRIT OF SYSTEMIC EVIL

The problem of individuating a particular Satan from other fallen beings is accentuated by an increased awareness of the role of social structures, systems, and institutions in perpetuating evil that cannot be fully attributed to the choices of any individual person. Whereas the tradition once defined sin almost exclusively in terms of Original and personal sin, Catholic harmatologies now recognize that sin may gather a momentum impelled by structures, systems, and social mores.[32] This would call into question whether the entrance of sin into the world can be attributed to the choice of some villainous individual as opposed to more insidious, social, and psychological processes that build upon biological factors more ancient yet.

Liberation and other self-consciously contextual theologians have been especially vocal in exposing sin that exists in social structures. Gustavo Gutiérrez acknowledges

> In the liberation approach, sin is not considered as an individual, private, or merely interior reality—asserted just enough to necessitate a "spiritual" redemption which does not challenge the order in which we live. Sin is regarded as a social, historical fact,

---

30. Rahner, "Dignity and Freedom of Man," 246.
31. Lee, *Amazing Spiderman Collection*, 1:13.
32. Schoonenberg, *Man and Sin*, 203–8; Gutiérrez, *Theology of Liberation*.

> the absence of brotherhood and love in relationships among men. . . . Sin is evident in oppressive structures, in the exploitation of man by man, in the domination and slavery of peoples, races and social classes."[33]

Similarly, Marjorie Suchocki acknowledges the personal and systemic dimensions of sin, arguing that "Sin is both individual and systemic: individually, the human condition is radical alienation from one's true relationship to self, nature, and God; systemically, this translates into structures of domination and subordination that are enforced by the group in power."[34]

Catholic Social Teaching has also recognized the reality of social sin.[35] Pope St. John Paul II proposed that in order to gain insight into the evil that afflicts the world, it is necessary to acknowledge the existence of structures of sin. "Sin and structures of sin are categories which are seldom applied to the situation of the contemporary world. However, one cannot easily gain a profound understanding of the reality that confronts us unless we give a name to the root of the evils which afflict us."[36] Elsewhere, the pontiff remarks, "The mystery of sin is composed of this twofold wound which the sinner opens in himself and in his relationship with his neighbor. Therefore one can speak of personal and social sin."[37] Even if the agency of a particular being could be ascribed responsibility for the first sin in the cosmos, who is to say, in light of centuries of genocide and starvation, that the first sin was the worst sin and that the worst evil has not been perpetrated and perpetuated by social structures?

Walter Wink advances a model of Satan as the energy that drives systemic evil, but his account of Satan is not that of a supernatural person. Wink describes Satan as the "world-encompassing spirit of the domination system."[38] By "spirit," Wink means the ethos or inner life of an institution.[39] The author interprets the references to the "angels" of churches in the Book of Revelation as an allusion to their "spirit" in this sense.[40] As such, Wink offers a fresh perspective on the position that Satan is a "spirit" and a fallen "angel."

---

33. Gutiérrez, *Theology of Liberation*, 75–176.
34. Suchocki, "Original Sin Revisited," 233.
35. USCCB, *Economic Justice* 77.
36. John Paul II, "*Sollicitudo Rei Socialis*" 36.
37. John Paul II, "Reconciliation and Penance" 15.
38. Wink, *Powers That Be*, 27; Eph 6:12.
39. Wink, *Powers That Be*, 24–25.
40. Wink, *Powers That Be*, 3.

Wink argues that St. Paul's references to the "powers and principalities" against which the Church struggles are allusions to the "spirit" of human authorities and structures. Wink believes that the powers exist only within human structures, not as "angelic or demonic beings fluttering about in the sky."[41] Consistent with his view of the powers, Satan, for Wink, is neither a being nor pure evil in and of itself, but rather, the momentum of corrupt human structures that dominate persons and render violence to all who resist.[42]

On Wink's reading, "The myth of Satan's rebellion and expulsion from heaven symbolically depicts the fate of any creature that lusts after ultimate power and authority."[43] Interpreting the myth as referring to *any* creature, Wink does not regard it as a reference to one particular being. Indeed, the thrust of Wink's argument suggests that the myth of Satan's fall expresses the fate of structures (that is, powers) as well as that of creatures who seek to oppress creation.

These ruminations on social, institutional, or systemic evil challenge the supposition that the worst evil must take the form of personal sin. It might, on the other hand, be objected that social, systemic, or institutional sin must be set in motion by the sinful choices of a particular being. This objection, however, takes too narrow a view of social sin. While the example of genocide may conjure up a scenario whereby an evil tyrant, by his personal choices, mobilizes the state-sponsored machinery of death, social sin also includes far more ubiquitous and pervasive forms of evil that lay the foundation for genocide. The evils of racism, sexism, homophobia, and other sinful "isms," and the primal drive towards brutal competition, cannot be attributed to the choice of any particular evil being. Such cannot be definitively traced to the agency of an inhuman Satan any more than to the agency of a particular human villain. The escalation of negative emotion fed by the frenzied mob, the uncritical blindness of groupthink, and the callously self-serving momentum of bureaucracies spawn evil that is social, institutional, and systemic in nature. Social structures are brimming with natural talent in this endeavor and require no coaching from an invisible being.

CONCLUSION

Our attempt to construct a natural Satanology cannot provide a compelling basis to affirm the specific characteristics or agency of the supernatural

---

41. Wink, *Powers That Be*, 3; Wink, *Naming the Powers*, 105.
42. Wink, *Naming the Powers*, 105.
43. Wink, *Naming the Powers*, 68.

Satan as described in the Catechism. It cannot, with any degree of certitude, affirm the existence of the inhuman tempter of a prototypal human couple, a singular facilitator of human sin more generally, or a particular being responsible for the worst evils in creation so as to stand out as God's most fervent enemy.

The emergence of evil in creation can be adequately explained in terms of natural forces exercising a non-personal form of freedom to deviate from the vision of a loving God. Further, if one accepts the scientific theory of evolution, the emergence of human persons from the animal world included the emergence of moral consciousness from animal instinct so that personal sin insidiously emerged from animal brutality, in no way requiring the influence of a Satan.

Neither does the ongoing phenomenon of temptation point ineluctably to the existence of an inhuman tempter, being explicable in terms of a disordered desire for things that are in and of themselves good. While the literature of Jungian psychology speaks of Satan as an archetype etched in the human psyche, symbolizing a destructive dimension of the human person, the archetype cannot be directly identified with the Christian doctrine with which it shares a name, much less with a supernatural being.

Our third and final proposed point of departure for a natural Satanology identified Satan as the most evil being in creation, the being responsible for the worst evil and, as such, a nemesis of God, distinguishable from all other sinners for the scale and depravity of its misdeeds. While a theology of mortal sin casts suspicion upon beings with superior knowledge, intelligence, and freedom to act, it can only deal in likelihood. At this point, our line of argument segues into a discussion of fallen angels as supra-human beings, a construct conveyed through mythology and revealed religion. We are hence no longer dealing in natural Satanology.

The recognition of systemic, social, or institutional evil deals a further blow to the attempt to construct a natural Satanology, frustrating any attempt to identify a single most evil being in creation. The moral evil that wreaks the most devastating consequences is often that perpetuated by institutions and systems. The chapter notes a sense in which institutional evil could be considered evidence of a Satan insofar as Walter Wink interprets the motif to denote the ethos of corrupt institutions and systems that unjustly exert their dominance. However, Wink is adamant that Satan is not a person and hence his argument does not demonstrate the existence of the Satan described in the Catechism.

Thus, the thought experiment attempted in this chapter suggests that it is not possible to construct a compelling case for the existence of the personal Satan without recourse to scripture and tradition and, in particular, the mythical motif of angels. Our attempt to do so has reaffirmed that the basis for the Christian doctrine of Satan lies in an interpretation of mythical narratives and motifs. This is hardly in itself a problem if the interpretation of myth continues to evolve in keeping with our theology of God and of the world—and so we turn to the question of the development of doctrine in light of the insights of modernity.

4

The "Modernist Crisis": A Refusal to Benefit from the Insights of Modernity

We have seen that the motif of Satan is the product of development and the crosspollination of diverse mythical motifs derived from diverse traditions. The account of Satan in the Catechism of the Catholic Church, however, freeze-frames a myth in motion. To resist continued development of the motif of Satan is arbitrary and stunts the growth of an ancient endeavor to express humanity's ongoing grappling with the mystery known as God.

So as to situate this doctrinal intransigence in historical context, this chapter offers an account of the Modernist Crisis—the years during the mid-nineteenth to mid-twentieth century during which the teaching office of the Church vehemently resisted learning from the emerging insights of modernity, condemning as heretical virtually anything that challenged the doctrinal status quo. Having assigned a chronological timeframe to the Modernist Crisis, it might however be argued that the crisis lingers, or at least its residue does, in some areas of Catholic doctrine—including the Catechism's teachings on Satan.

EARLY ATTEMPTS TO SET CATHOLICISM IN DIALOGUE WITH MODERNITY

Nineteenth-century German Catholic thinkers such as Johann Mohler, Fredrich Von Schegel, and Ignaz Von Doellinger sought to set the Church's doctrine in dialogue with Enlightenment thought. In England, John Henry Newman and John Acton numbered among their counterparts, as did Maurice D'Hulst and Anton Gunther in France. Such thinkers represented an emerging impetus to marshal the benefits of Enlightenment thought for the continued progress of Catholic doctrine.

In 1863, Doellinger called a conference in Munich and presented a keynote paper entitled "The Past and Future of Theology."[1] Doellinger's paper argued that doctrine needed to develop in light of the insights of modern scholarship (with a heavy emphasis on German thinkers).[2] The paper suggested that scholarly analysis and debate, rather than an appeal to magisterial authority, should drive the ongoing development of doctrine. Doellinger also argued for academic freedom for Catholic scholars, unrestrained by magisterial control.

Richard Schaefer notes that exponents of the Catholic enlightenment did not assert the self-sufficiency of reason.[3] Rather, thinkers such as Doellinger viewed intellectual rigor as holding potential to aid and abet a faith perspective. As Richard Schaefer observes, "For Döllinger, theology had authority because it joined religious devotion with ideas in the disciplined pursuit of truth (*Wissenschaft*)."[4] Modern Catholic thinkers from Doellinger to Loisy viewed reason, and the methodologies to which it gives rise, as a means through which divine revelation is mediated, and through which its representation in doctrinal formulae can continue to develop.

On hearing of Doellinger's presentation, Pope Pius IX wrote to the Archbishop of Munich, insisting that Catholic scholars needed to be subjugated to the authority of the magisterium.[5] Indeed, Doellinger's paper was to prove an immediate impetus for Pope Pius IX's publication of the *Syllabus of Errors*.

The fourth article of the *Syllabus* rejects a model of reason as an *innate* strength, rather than a gift implanted by God. It characterizes the position to which it objects as holding that "All the truths of religion proceed from

---

1. Bokenkotter, *Concise History of the Catholic Church*, 124.
2. Bokenkotter, *Concise History of the Catholic Church*, 313.
3. Schaefer, "True and False Enlightenment," 24–45.
4. Schaefer, "True and False Enlightenment," 24–45.
5. Schaefer, "True and False Enlightenment," 24–45.

the innate strength of human reason; hence reason is the ultimate standard by which man can and ought to arrive at the knowledge of all truths of every kind."[6] It is not at all clear as to who exactly the *Syllabus* is seeking to paraphrase and critique in this regard, so the stated position is something of a straw man argument. Its characterization of reason as an innate human faculty without reference to God is contrary to Immanuel Kant's understanding of reason as a gift implanted by God in the human person.[7] By suggesting that modern scholars regarded the truths of religion as proceeding from reason, this article of the *Syllabus* necessitates a distinction that proves crucial to our entire argument, that is, the difference between truth and the way it is presented, between revelation and doctrinal formulae.

Cautioning against the equation of doctrinal formulations with revelation itself, Avery Dulles argues that a model of "revelation as doctrine" could give rise to the misunderstanding that doctrinal formulae come directly from God.[8] Also, Dulles notes that, if taken in isolation, a model of revelation as doctrine "forgets God's presence in one's own life and experience" and excludes "a faith that probes and questions."[9]

Doctrinal formulations and creeds are distinct from revelation itself since they are a human endeavor to express revealed truth amidst the limitations of human language. While the eternal truths themselves are not the product of reason, the formulae that seek to express them hopefully are. This is not problematic in the Catholic tradition wherein Aquinas regarded reason as a divine gift that operates in harmony with divine revelation.[10] However, for those who are unwilling to concede this distinction between the truth and its representation in doctrinal formulae, an argument for the development of doctrine in light of modern insights may appear to be an arrogant assertion of human reasoning as the ultimate standard to which revelation itself should be subjugated, in effect, denying its divine origin and authority.

Despite an arguable underestimation of the role of reason in the formulation of doctrine, it would be simplistic to regard the *Syllabus* and the later anti-Modernist writings as going quite so far as to equate doctrine with revelation itself. Rather, these writings seem to reflect the position that as grace builds on nature, revelation builds upon reason, and transcends it. Lawrence Cunningham regards the dictum, "Grace builds on nature," as a

6. Pius IX, "Syllabus of Errors" 4.
7. Kant, *Religion within the Boundaries of Mere Reason*, 80.
8. Dulles, *Models of Revelation*, 45–46.
9. Dulles, *Models of Revelation*, 45–46.
10. Aquinas, *Summa Theologiae* I-I, q3, a7.

paraphrasing of Aquinas's statement in *Summa Theologiae*, Part 1, 1:8 that "Grace does not abolish nature but perfects it."[11]

The notion of grace building upon nature suggests a two-tier structure whereby grace in some purified form, unmediated by reason, takes over when reason reaches its limits. Doctrine, from a scholastic viewpoint, is informed by both reason and by grace, that is, by revelation.[12] Hence, a scholastic perspective may view it as problematic to submit doctrine to rational analysis that cannot account for the revealed dimension of doctrine that transcends reason's grasp. Such an account of the relationship between grace and reason can then be invoked to justify the downright unreasonable in presentations of doctrine. That which is downright unreasonable can, within such a mindset, be fideistically explained away as attributable to grace that exceeds reason—a matter of faith. So much then for the Catholic vision of the universe wherein God is present in all of creation, including the faculty of reason. The First Vatican Council perpetuated this dichotomy between faith and reason and between faith and revelation, condemning the position of those who viewed revelation as working in and through human processes for "utterly confusing nature and grace, human science and Divine faith."[13]

REJECTING BIBLICAL INTERPRETATION ROOTED IN SECULARIZED REASON

Resenting the application of rational interpretative systems to truths informed by supra-rational revelation, the *Syllabus of Errors* casts its aspersions upon the historical-critical method in scripture scholarship. In its reference to literary genres, it particularly targeted the method of form criticism. Article seven denounces the exegetical position that "prophecies and miracles set forth and recorded in the Sacred Scriptures are the fiction of poets."[14] This reference to fiction carries dismissive undertones, suggestive of that which is invented and untrue.

The present work, benefiting from the insights of modern biblical scholarship as eventually endorsed by the Catholic Church, will argue that some truths can only be told through fiction of a kind. The truth conveyed by poetry and myth relates to that which is universally possible rather that which is particular and actual. Indeed, if the Catholic faith is concerned with

11. Cunningham, "Four American Catholics and their Chronicler," 113–17.
12. Oliver, "Parallel Journey of Faith," 113–130; Anselm, *Proslogium*, 8; Kent, "Review," 123–24; McDonald, "Theories of Revelation," 384.
13. Vatican I, "*Dei Filius*."
14. Pius IX, "Syllabus of Errors" 7.

"eternal" truth, that is, the supra-historical rather than the particular and empirical, fiction and poetry may be especially well-poised to express such truth. Pope Pius IX, however, writing some sixty years before the Church's official endorsement of modern biblical scholarship, did not recognize the capacity of myth, narrative, and poetry to convey eternal truth in a way that doctrinal propositions cannot do—at least not without borrowing from the language of these literary genres.[15]

REJECTING SCHOLARSHIP THAT COULD FACILITATE THE DEVELOPMENT OF DOCTRINE

In a curious sense, if Enlightenment thought enforced a dichotomy between faith and reason, ousting faith from the public square to the ghetto of personal piety, it might be argued that Scholasticism furthered the marginalization of faith by envisaging it as too rigidly segregated from reason.[16] By contrast, scholars such as Alfred Loisy, regarded by the magisterium as Modernists, advanced a much more integrated model of reason, faith, and revelation.[17] The Modernist position seemed conducive to maintaining a place for faith-based perspectives in interdisciplinary discourse and the effects of its suppression may still be felt.

Loisy was influenced by John Henry Newman's account of the development of doctrine which saw the process of development as entirely compatible with a belief in the inspirational role of the Holy Spirit.[18] Loisy, writing under the pseudonym, "A. Firmin," posited that the biblical tradition too had developed in and through human processes.[19] For Loisy, the process of development was a means through which divine revelation was mediated.[20] Therefore, Loisy believed that it was entirely appropriate to draw upon a historical-critical method in the interpretation of both scripture and of doctrine.[21]

Loisy was critical of Adolf von Harnack's arguable assumption that the essence of a pure, unadulterated Christianity had been lost as the Church

---

15. Pius XII, "*Divino Afflante Spiritu*" 37.
16. Loisy, *Gospel and the Church*, 211.
17. Turvasi, *Condemnation of Alfred Loisy*, 148, 167.
18. Turvasi, *Condemnation of Alfred Loisy*, 148, 167.
19. Morrow, "Alfred Loisy's Developmental Approach," 326; Newman, "On the Inspiration of Scripture," 185–99; *Essay on the Development of Christian Doctrine*.
20. Morrow, "Alfred Loisy's Developmental Approach," 329; Turvasi, *Condemnation of Alfred Loisy*, 148, 167.
21. Turvasi, *Condemnation of Alfred Loisy*, 148, 167.

reflected upon Revelation and developed its doctrine.[22] Harnack's position seemed to play into the hands of a magisterium that equated development with corruption—if such development was influenced by contemporary scholarly insight. Loisy, on the other hand, argued that the tradition had always been in flux and there had never been a static, pristine Christianity.[23]

Loisy contended that those who denied the possibility of a legitimate development of doctrine, in fact, corrupted the tradition.[24] The author defended his insistence upon the possibility and necessity of a legitimate development of doctrinal formulae by offering myriad examples as to how doctrines ranging from Trinitarian to Eucharistic had evolved.[25] Christianity was already, in Loisy's view, a product of development, and this merely needed to be recognized more explicitly. He wrote, "Christianity is in a very true sense a development from post-exilic Judaism, which is a development of the religion of the prophets which is a development from primitive Mosaic Yahwism."[26] Given that Christianity was already the product of development, Loisy suggested that "It is just the idea of development which is now needed, not to be created all at once, but established for a better knowledge of the past."[27]

Loisy's position that revelation is mediated in and through processes of interpretation and development might be regarded as a defense of "tradition" in its most dynamic sense, and quintessentially Catholic. His view exemplifies the sacramental vision of Catholicism whereby grace, and we might say, God's very presence, is mediated in and through creation, not depending upon sporadic interventions from beyond. Sacramental theologian, Michael Himes captures this dimension of Catholicism when he suggests that "at its best, Catholicism is shaped by the conviction that grace lies at the root of all reality. And if that conviction is true, all the humanities, as well as the sciences, become religious enterprises."[28] For Loisy, the interpretation and development of revealed truth was a religious enterprise, not a secular process imposed upon religion. However, what Himes purports of Catholicism "at its best" has not always characterized the attitudes of Catholics. Flannery O'Connor, a Catholic author writing in the preconciliar twentieth-century era, opined that "the average Catholic reader . . . [is] more of a Manichean

---

22. Harnack, *What Is Christianity?*, 234.
23. Loisy, "Le Développement Chrétien"; Pius X, *Lamentabili Sane Exitu* 1.
24. Morrow, "Alfred Loisy's Developmental Approach," 328.
25. Loisy, "Le Développement Chrétien," 16–18.
26. Loisy, *L'Evangile et L'Eglise*, 161–62; Talar, *Prelude to the Modernist Crisis*, 94.
27. Loisy, *L'Evangile et L'Eglise*, 161–162.
28. Himes, "Finding God in All Things," 102.

than the Church permits. By separating nature and grace as much as possible, he has reduced his conception of the supernatural to the pious cliché."[29]

Loisy's sense that the developmental processes can mediate the divine concurs with the thought of his contemporary, Teilhard de Chardin, who saw no contradiction between the scientific theory of evolution and a belief in God as Creator—a position that the Catholic Church has come to accept.[30] If God created humanity through what science describes as the process of evolution, God reveals to humankind through processes of development, processes that are historical, literary, cultural, and equally well sacred in nature. Just as Teilhard did not think of God's creation of humankind as a process separable from that of evolution, so Loisy did not think of divine revelation as a process separable from the communication, interpretation and development of the Word of God. For Loisy, it was less the case that grace builds on nature than that grace saturates nature. If grace saturates nature, then it can infuse human nature and its rational processes, flawed and fallen though they may be.

C. J. T. Talar acknowledges that, since Loisy sought zealously to redress what he perceived as an imbalance whereby the role of development in Christian doctrine has been understated or largely ignored, the mistaken impression might be given that he denied the transcendent dimension of revelation altogether. "Loisy's preoccupation with the role of experience in revelation would lead many of his eventual critics to overlook his effort to maintain a transcendent dimension."[31] Loisy did not deny the transcendent but saw it as capable of working in and through the agency of rational human beings inspired by God. For Loisy, as for the Catholic sacramental tradition, God's transcendence is radical immanence, transcending particularity so as to permeate everything.

Loisy jettisoned the notion of literal inspiration. "There is nothing to indicate, nor has the Church ever taught, that in those who are the inspired organs of revelation, the movement of thought takes a totally irregular course."[32] Here lies the heart of the dispute between Loisy and the magisterium. Loisy saw the "movement of thought" governed by its regular course, that is, by reason, as a means through which divine inspiration is mediated.

---

29. O'Connor, *Mystery and Manner*, 146.

30. Chardin, *Phenomenon of Man*, 218, 220, 223, 227–28, 277; John Paul II, "Message to the Pontifical Academy of Sciences."

31. Talar, *Prelude to the Modernist Crisis*, xxi.

32. Talar, *Prelude to the Modernist Crisis*, 57.

In July 1907, Pope Pius X issued a decree, *Lamentabili Sane Exitu*, condemning sixty-five Modernist positions in relation to the interpretation of the scriptures and of doctrine.[33] The introduction to the decree decried what it regarded as the regrettable results of the allegedly immoderate application of modern interpretative methods to the scriptures and tradition of the Church, implying a lack of prudence and an irresponsible sensationalism. "With truly lamentable results, our age, casting aside all restraint in its search for the ultimate causes of things, frequently pursues novelties so ardently that it rejects the legacy of the human race."[34]

Lamentabili proceeds to regard the modern age, and its pursuit of novel insights, as posing a threat to the authority of the magisterium. "Thus it falls into very serious errors, which are even more serious when they concern sacred authority, the interpretation of Sacred Scripture, and the principal mysteries of Faith."[35] The decree condemns the attempts of exegetes and theologians to contribute to the development of doctrine as transgressing non-negotiable boundaries and nothing short of destructive. "The fact that many Catholic writers also go beyond the limits determined by the Fathers and the Church herself is extremely regrettable. In the name of higher knowledge and historical research (they say), they are looking for that progress of dogmas which is, in reality, nothing but the corruption of dogmas."[36] Granted, this statement does not preclude all possibility of doctrinal development. Such a position would be untenable in view of the manner in which ecumenical councils had defined dogma and developed the Church's understanding on subjects such as the Virgin Mother, the person of Christ, and the Trinity. Rather, *Lamentabili* specifically condemns the prospect of the development of doctrine impelled by modern scholarship.

THE DIFFICULTY IN DEFINING MODERNISM

As Michael Morton observes, "Modernism itself is really very hard to define. Even the name was conjured up to embrace a whole array of what were considered unacceptable ideas and subjects of study."[37] Morton's reference to 'conjuring" up the name is appropriately suggestive of the manner in which the magisterium, to some extent, constructed the Modernist enemy. That is, Modernism is not a specific heresy such as Arianism. It is not a corrupted or

33. Pius X, "*Lamentabili.*"
34. Pius X, "*Lamentabili*" 1.
35. Pius X, "*Lamentabili.*"
36. Pius X, "*Lamentabili.*"
37. Morton, "Catholic Modernism."

deficient account of some specific doctrine of the Church and could not be counteracted in relation to a specific question or issue. Rather, it is a worldview which Morton describes in terms of three characteristics.[38] First, Modernism espoused a historical consciousness that views developments in Christianity, including doctrine, in the context of their evolution, under the guidance of the Holy Spirit. Second, and related to this, is Modernism's endorsement of a historical-critical approach to the scriptures, attentive to questions of authorial context and genre. Third, Modernism offered an unwelcome critique of the excesses of Scholasticism that had all but eclipsed other approaches to Catholic theology. Modernism may be understood as the endeavor to interpret scripture and tradition in light of reason, placing Christian doctrine in dialogue with the sciences, both social and hard. Pope Pius X referred to the Modernists as a hidden danger lurking in the midst of the Church. "They lie hid, a thing to be deeply deplored and feared, in her very bosom and heart, and are the more mischievous, the less conspicuously they appear."[39]

CONCLUSION

Far from a concession to secular modernity, the case for the development of doctrine in light of the insights of modernity is entirely consistent with the sacramental worldview of Catholicism. The sacramental perspective is open to the possibility that grace may be mediated through any part of creation. If the divine can be mediated through bread, wine, oil, and religious artifacts, "fruit of the earth and work of human hands," so then why not also through other forms of human ingenuity such as processes of expression, interpretation, and development? Grace not only builds on nature as a distinct and separate layer, as supposed by some forms of Scholasticism. Rather, grace infuses all of creation, including human nature, literature, and hermeneutics. Indeed, as we shall later note with reference to St. Augustine of Hippo, even the being of Satan, should such a creature exist, is infused with grace insofar as it is a component of God's sacred creation.[40]

---

38. Pius X, "*Pascendi Dominici Gregis*" 2.
39. Pius X, "*Pascendi Dominici Gregis*" 2.
40. Augustine of Hippo, *Confessions*, 160.

5

Vatican II and the Case for the Ongoing Development of Doctrine

While this book would, no doubt, have been condemned by the anti-Modernist magisterium of Popes Pius IX and X, it finds a clear mandate in the teachings of the Second Vatican Council which encouraged ongoing candid dialogue between the Catholic tradition and the modern world. In order for such dialogue to be genuine, it must be open to the possibility of the development of doctrine, and in 1973, the Congregation for the Doctrine of the Faith (CDF) published the declaration, *Mysterium Ecclesiae*, arguing that the human words and constructs used to express a doctrinal truth in any given time are distinct from the eternal truth itself, and must be open to the possibility of a new formulation that expresses the eternal truth more completely, and more clearly, so as to be better understood in a given age. As such, this chapter shows that it is entirely consistent with the Church's understanding of the nature of doctrine to develop its exposition on Satan in light of the exegetical and theological insights of modernity.

THE COUNCIL THAT WOULD NOT CONDEMN

Church councils have, historically, served a corrective function, defining doctrine so as to counteract erroneous understandings—as Braga I and

Lateran IV did in relation to the doctrine of Satan.[1] Early councils of the Church had responded to heresies by formulating orthodox stances in relation to the identity of Jesus Christ and the Trinity. In more recent centuries, the Council of Trent had condemned the Protestant Reformation, and the First Vatican Council had condemned the position that doctrine can develop significantly in view of modern scholarly insights, declaring "If anyone says: it may happen that to doctrines put forward by the Church, sometimes, as knowledge advances, a meaning should be given different from what the Church has understood and understands, let him be anathema."[2]

In calling a council in 1959, Pope St. John XXIII was not, however, proposing another assault on the Modernists. Yet, as John W. O'Malley, insightfully observes, there was, in a sense, a crisis to be confronted.[3] The Church appeared to be thriving in terms of its bulging congregations, overflowing seminaries, and smorgasbord of pious devotions, but it was in danger of spiritual and intellectual stultification. And so, Pope John proposed a pastoral council, not characterized by a reaction to heresy but, in a sense, a reaction to orthodoxy, that is, a reaction to the inertia, triumphalism, and complacency, that can typify those hierarchs who become overinvested in the status-quo.

JOHN XXIII'S HERMENEUTIC OF CONTINUOUS DEVELOPMENT

In his inaugural speech at the opening of the Second Vatican Council on October 11, 1962, Pope John XXIII exhibits a commitment to both conservation and progress in relation to doctrine. The pontiff speaks of the importance of treasuring the deposit of faith as mediated in scripture and tradition, not by simply preserving it, but by developing it so that it may speak effectively to the modern era.

> Our duty is not only to guard this precious treasure, as if we were concerned only with antiquity, but to dedicate ourselves with an earnest will and without fear to that work which our era demands of us, pursuing thus the path which the Church has followed for twenty centuries.[4]

---

1. Congar, *Meaning of Tradition*, 16, 55.
2. Vatican I, "*Dei Filius*" 4.3.
3. O'Malley, *What Happened at Vatican II?*, 1–30.
4. John XXIII, "*Gaudet Mater Ecclesia.*"

Vatican II and the Case for the Ongoing Development of Doctrine 71

Pope John bestowed a mandate to go beyond antiquarianism so as to continue the development that had characterized the dynamic tradition at its best—though not consistently—for twenty centuries. The pontiff, in his exhortation to work fearlessly, appears to anticipate resistance to the development of doctrine. Yet John XXIII also sensed a widespread readiness for such development.

> The whole world expects a step forward toward a doctrinal penetration and a formation of consciousness in faithful and perfect conformity to the authentic doctrine, which, however, should be studied and expounded through the methods of research and through the literary forms of modern thought.[5]

Pope John clearly envisages modern approaches to research, analysis, and communication being utilized in service of the tradition. The "doctrinal penetration" envisaged by John XXIII is essentially a development of doctrine, penetrating the doctrinal formulae by subjecting them to scrutiny, while also more deeply penetrating the eternal truth to which the formulae refer. Hence, this "penetration" can take the form of both hermeneutics and constructive theology.

John XXIII cut a distinction between the eternal truths in themselves, and the doctrinal formulations that seek to express these truths through a given language for a given epoch. "The substance of the ancient doctrine of the deposit of faith is one thing, and the way in which it is presented is another."[6] Giuseppe Alberigo suggests that John was referring to adaptations necessary for the presentation of doctrine to those whose worldviews were formed by Marxism, and the liberal institutions of modernity in general.[7] In any case, Pope John's distinction between eternal truths and the Church's attempts to articulate them, acknowledges that improvement is conceivably possible in the formulation of doctrine so as to more effectively mediate divine revelation.

John XXIII's reference to the importance of adherence to the "entirety" of Church teaching may be interpreted as a comment upon the selective manner in which the tradition had, for the most part, been presented in the centuries since the Council of Trent.[8] That is, the Tridentine Church had been selective as to which aspects of the ancient tradition it emphasized.

---

5. John XXIII, "*Gaudet Mater Ecclesia.*"
6. John XXIII, "*Gaudet Mater Ecclesia.*"
7. Alberigo and Komonchak, *Formation of the Council's Identity*, 17.
8. John XXIII, "*Gaudet Mater Ecclesia.*"

George Lindbeck, a Lutheran observer at the Council, believes that the Council Fathers fulfilled Pope John's vision, recognizing the riches of a two thousand year-old tradition.[9] The Council moved beyond those strands of the tradition that were a reaction to the Reformation and to the Modernist crisis. Lindbeck recalls, "The renewers argued circles around the traditionalists. They unmasked their opponents as mistaking the post-Tridentine developments, not least the Marian and papal advances of the nineteenth century, for the total Catholic heritage."[10] Lindbeck's reference to the nineteenth century appears to evoke Pope Pius IX's definition in 1854 of the doctrine of the Immaculate Conception, and the First Vatican Council's declaration of papal infallibility.[11] These two pronouncements could be considered instances of the development of doctrine, underscoring the point that the anti-Modernist magisterium was not opposed to doctrinal development per se so much as developments of doctrine influenced by insights arising from modern intellectual inquiry, science that is, in the broadest sense.

John XXIII's references to the entirety of Church teaching, beyond the emphases of Trent and Vatican I, may be read as an endorsement of *ressourcement*. The return to early sources would pose a significant challenge to the Neo-Scholasticism that had all but eclipsed other perspectives within the tradition. The Council, however, welcomed among its *periti*, theologians who advocated a return to the scriptural and patristic sources of theology that had been all but obscured by Scholasticism.

During the decade before the Council, *ressourcement* theologians, including John Courtney Murray, Edward Schillebeeckx, Henri de Lubac, and Karl Rahner had been held in suspicion by the magisterium while endeavoring to recover the riches of Christian antiquity. Now, in the environs of St. Peter's Basilica, they brushed shoulders with their former detractors. As James Carroll remarks, "Formally censored and censured scholars were all at once the darlings of Catholic thought."[12]

The Council would revive ancient practices and ways of thinking as much, if not more, than it inaugurated new ones. Daniel Donovan observes, "Although Vatican Two has seemed to many people to represent something new, in many ways what it said . . . was quite traditional. It represented a return to values and insights that in many cases had been widely held in the early Church."[13] The Council was more friend than foe to ancient Christianity.

---

9. Lindbeck, "How a Lutheran Saw It," 16.
10. Lindbeck, "How a Lutheran Saw It," 16.
11. Pius IX, "*Ineffabilis Deus*"; Vatican I, "*Dei Filius*" 4.9.
12. Carroll, *Practicing Catholic*, 163.
13. Donovan, *Distinctly Catholic*, 25.

Donovan notes that ancient practices and formulations were not revived on the grounds that their antiquity in itself made them somehow pure and authentic. Rather, the author notes a similarity between the situation of the Church in patristic times and in late modernity. "It was almost as if the bishops, recognizing that the kind of intertwining of church and society that had marked medieval Christendom had come to an end, decided to turn to early Christian experience for insight into how they might renew the life of the church in a pluralistic and increasingly secular world."[14] This suggests a pastoral pragmatism, reinstituting practices of the Patristic era in response to a pastoral context, rather than for the sake of primitivism.

Lindbeck regards the Council's historical consciousness as distinguishing it from previous councils. The author argues that the Council adopted a new view of the world, seeing the Church and the broader world as works in progress, evolving towards their fulfillment in the Kingdom of God.[15] Lindbeck describes this perspective as "realized futuristic eschatology."[16] By this term, the author refers to an evolutionary view of the Church and the world, in which the Kingdom of God is a reality experienced as "already" and as "not yet," a tension to which Walter Kasper, Teilhard de Chardin, Karl Rahner, and J. B. Metz have been attentive.[17] Lindbeck argues that this perspective is closer to the Hebraic worldview held by many of the biblical authors, than to more static views of the world held by Hellenistic perspectives.[18] Insofar as it reflects the "already," a realized futuristic eschatology is conducive to an understanding of doctrine as authoritative. Insofar as it reflects the "not yet," a realized futuristic eschatology is conducive to an understanding of doctrine as provisional, reflecting the "not yet" status of a pilgrim Church. Hence, realized eschatology suggests an understanding of doctrinal formulae as provisionally authoritative.

MYSTERIUM ECCLESIAE: AFFIRMING JOHN XXIII'S VIEW ON THE DEVELOPMENT OF DOCTRINE

In 1973, the CDF issued a declaration "In Defense of the Catholic Doctrines of the Church against Certain Errors of the Present Day," *Mysterium*

---

14. Donovan, *Distinctly Catholic*, 25.

15. Lindbeck, "Vision of a World Renewed," 4; Kasper, *Dogma unter dem Wort Gottes*, 36; Sullivan, *Creative Fidelity*, 37.

16. Lindbeck, "Vision of a World Renewed," 9.

17. Lindbeck, "Vision of a World Renewed," 4; Kasper, *Dogma unter dem Wort Gottes*, 36; Sullivan, *Creative Fidelity*, 37.

18. Lindbeck, "Vision of a World Renewed," 9.

Ecclesiae.[19] The declaration endeavors to address erroneous and ambiguous accounts of the nature of doctrine that had arisen since the Council. Pope Paul VI was, at this time, deeply troubled by an atmosphere of dialogue and of innovation in the postconciliar Church and in academia.[20] However, despite the defensive title of the declaration, it is infused with an intellectual humility largely unknown in previous defenses of the Church's infallibility. The declaration candidly admits "during her earthly pilgrimage the Church, embracing sinners in her bosom, is at the same time holy and always in need of being purified."[21] A Church that is always in need of being purified is a Church that had better be open to the possibility of change.

Mysterium Ecclesiae is deeply reminiscent of the distinction made by Pope John XXIII between the deposit of faith and the way it is expressed. The declaration affirms his mandate that the best of modernity's insights and methodologies be marshaled so as to accomplish "a step forward toward a doctrinal penetration and a formation of consciousness in faithful and perfect conformity to the authentic doctrine, which, however, should be studied and expounded through the methods of research and through the literary forms of modern thought."[22] True to the influence of John XXIII, *Mysterium Ecclesiae* recognizes that the effectiveness of any doctrinal formulation is relative to its context.

> The dogmatic *formulas* of the Church's Magisterium were from the beginning suitable for communicating revealed truth, and that as they are they remain forever suitable for communicating this truth to those who interpret them correctly. It does not however follow that every one of these formulas has always been or will always be so to the same extent.[23]

The declaration proceeds to approve a role for theologians in the exegesis and formulation of doctrinal formulae at the service of the teaching office. "For this reason theologians seek to define exactly the intention of teaching proper to the various formulas, and in carrying out this work they are of considerable assistance to the living Magisterium of the Church, to which they remain subordinated."[24] *Mysterium Ecclesiae* notes that while some ancient doctrinal formulae remain effective, others need to be

---

19. CDF, *Mysterium Ecclesiae*.
20. McClarey, "Pope Paul VI and the Smoke of Satan."
21. CDF, *Mysterium Ecclesiae* 6.
22. John XXIII, "*Gaudet Mater Ecclesia*."
23. CDF, *Mysterium Ecclesiae* 5.
24. CDF, *Mysterium Ecclesiae* 5.

replaced by new ones that present the same meaning more completely or more effectively.

> For this reason also it often happens that ancient dogmatic formulas and others closely connected with them remain living and fruitful in the habitual usage of the Church, but with suitable expository and explanatory additions that maintain and clarify their original meaning. In addition, it has sometimes happened that in this habitual usage of the Church, certain of these formulas gave way to new expressions which, proposed and approved by the Sacred Magisterium, presented more clearly or more completely the same meaning.[25]

Thus, the formulae can develop so as to communicate more clearly in the idiom of the age, and more completely so as to take account of new insights into the original deposit of faith.[26] Hence, in *Mysterium Ecclesiae*, the case for the development of doctrinal formulations is vindicated. As Francis Sullivan observes, "This statement of the CDF provides official clarification of the sense in which dogmatic statements can be said to be 'irreformable.' Irreformability is predicated of their meaning. . . . On the other hand, the fact that this meaning can be expressed with greater clarity or more developed shows that irreformability is not predicated of dogmatic formulas as such."[27] Sullivan's interpretation of *Mysterium Ecclesiae* signifies the Church's acknowledgment of the possibility of the legitimate development of doctrine based on both the need for an articulation of the ancient deposit that will be better understood in a new epoch, and also on new insights regarding the truth to which the doctrine refers.

THE EPIDEICTIC TONE OF THE COUNCIL

Cardinal Godfried Daneels recalls that the majority of the Council Fathers were quickly won over to John XXIII's dialogical disposition toward the modern world. Noting that most of the Fathers were initially suspicious of the "world," Daneels remarks that, within a few weeks, they displayed a more open and optimistic attitude."[28] As Oliver Putz notes, "Regardless of the ideas with which they came to Rome, virtually all of the participants

---

25. CDF, *Mysterium Ecclesiae* 5.
26. CDF, *Mysterium Ecclesiae* 5.
27. Sullivan, *Creative Fidelity*, 35.
28. Daneels, "Vatican II."

transformed their views."²⁹ Putz regards the Council as having facilitated a conversion experience for its participants.³⁰

O'Malley argues that the manner in which the Second Vatican Council spoke to the world, its style that is, held massive implications for the way in which Church teaching would henceforth be understood.³¹ Unlike previous councils, the Second Vatican Council did not teach by way of canons. Canons, as exemplified in the anti-Modernist writings, are essentially prohibitions declaring that anyone who holds some stated position should be regarded as "anathema." In a sense, they are a series of condemnations. However, as Ladislas Orsy notes, "The fathers of the Council wanted no threats or punishments in their documents; they trusted that faith will persuade by its own beauty and persuasive power."³² Thus, Orsy implies, the persuasive style of the Council's documents reflects an infectious quality that is integral to the faith, rather than a marketing ploy, extraneous to the faith itself.

In contrast with the canonical style, the Second Vatican Council teaches, as O'Malley observes, in the epideictic style, that is, by presenting a vision of the ideal so as to invite, exhort, and persuade.³³ When John XXIII referred at the opening of the Council to "making use of the medicine of mercy rather than severity," such language heralded the style that would be embraced by the Council Fathers.³⁴ In the years preceding the publication of the conciliar documents, John's own encyclicals, *Mater et Magistra* (1961) and *Pacem in Terris* (1963) had epitomized the epideictic style.³⁵ Garry Wills notes the misgivings of the curia, commenting that "Those letters' openness towards the world, their call for cooperation with it, were considered naïve by the pope's own staff, as well as his calling of the Council."³⁶

In relation to the question of style, Marshall McLuhan's axiom that "The medium is the message" is pertinent.³⁷ That is, the manner in which Church teaching is expressed cannot be neatly separated from the teaching itself.³⁸ The epideictic style is not merely a question of ancient teachings in

29. Putz, "I Did Not Change, They Did!," 23.
30. Putz, "I Did Not Change, They Did!"
31. O'Malley, "Vatican II," 12.
32. Orsy, *Receiving the Council*, 117.
33. O'Malley, "Vatican II," 3–33.
34. John XXIII, "*Gaudet Mater Ecclesia.*"
35. John XXIII, "*Mater et Magistra*"; "*Pacem in Terris.*"
36. Wills, *Papal Sin*, 82.
37. McLuhan, "Medium Is the Message," 23–35, 63–67.
38. Daly, *Transcendence and Immanence*, 218.

new wrapping, a more diplomatic rendition of the party-line. Rather, in a case in point, *Gaudium et Spes* invites the entire human family to conversation, signaling openness to genuine discussion.[39] This does not imply a concession to relativism, an acquiescence to the secular status quo, or a denial of the Church's authority, rather, it suggests the possibility of a spirited, constructive dialogue.

INVITING THE MODERN WORLD TO DIALOGUE

If the medium had changed, so had the message. O'Malley observes that "The Council took as axiomatic that Catholicism was adaptive even to the modern world."[40] The author notes that "This was a shift from the integralism that marked most Catholic thinking from the early nineteenth century and well into the twentieth."[41] *Gaudium et Spes*, Vatican II's *Pastoral Constitution on the Church in the Modern World* expresses the Council's desire for dialogue with the contemporary world, including those who are not explicitly followers of Christ. "This Council can provide no more eloquent proof of its solidarity with, as well as its respect and love for the entire human family with which it is bound up, than by engaging with it in conversation," and again, specifically with regard to non-Catholics, "We want frank conversation to compel us all to receive the impulses of the Spirit faithfully and to act on them energetically." Significantly, Pope John XXIII in his 1963 encyclical *Pacem in Terris* set a precedent for addressing "all men of good will," as opposed to Catholics only. This signaled an impetus to persuasively engage contemporary people in dialogue, appealing to their best motives. In a sense, therefore, Pope John XXIII envisaged the modern world as a conversation partner, not merely the incidental background against which the Church taught unilaterally.

It may be fair to suggest that the "modern world" within the Council's terms of reference is primarily suggestive of its contemporary global population—first and foremost persons of flesh and blood rather than a paradigm or worldview. This focus on the world's people is apparent when *Gaudium et Spes* opens with the words, "The joys and the hopes, the griefs and the anxieties of the men of this age, especially those who are poor or in any way afflicted, these are the joys and hopes, the griefs and anxieties of the followers of Christ."[42] That is, the Fathers were primarily interested in

39. Paul VI, "*Gaudium et Spes*."
40. O'Malley, "Vatican II."
41. O'Malley, "Vatican II," 113; Paul VI, "*Gaudium et Spes*" 92.
42. Paul VI, "*Gaudium et Spes*" 1.

the concerns of living people, especially the poor and oppressed. *Gaudium et Spes*, by its reference to the Council's solidarity with the poor, reinforces the sense that the Council's outreach to the modern world is primarily in relation to its people rather than to ideologies per se.

Many of the poor, inhabiting the developing world, did not in the 1960s, live in the context of the modern paradigm. Many lived in cultures that suffered the effects of colonialism or its aftermath, enjoying few of the benefits of modernity, practical or intellectual. Such contexts may not have been characterized by Western Christianity or the ideals of the enlightenment. Therefore, to some extent, the Council's references to the "modern world" could have been considered synonymous with the term, "contemporary," rather than modern in the sense of Modernity.

While the Council sought solidarity and dialogue primarily with all contemporary people, its invitation also extended to those invested in the modern paradigm. For example, *Gaudium et Spes* extols the benefits of modernity in separating religion from superstition, and hence militating for a more mature, critical, intentional faith.[43] Similarly, the *Decree on the Media of Social Communications* recognizes, though not uncritically, the benefits to be derived from this aspect of modernity.[44] The Council envisaged the Church learning from the world, from culture, and from the sciences. "The experience of past ages, the progress of the sciences, and the treasures hidden in the various forms of human culture, by all of which the nature of man himself is more clearly revealed and new roads to truth are opened, these profit the Church, too."[45] This statement recognizes the store of wisdom offered by "past ages" and also the "progress of the sciences" that may in some instances serve to illuminate ancient truths that have been obfuscated.

Leo O'Donovan detects in *Gaudium et Spes* an affirmation that modernity's efforts for human development are in continuity with the divine plan. O'Donovan notes that the constitution suggests that modern humans can, in this regard, "justly consider that by their own efforts they are unfolding the creator's work."[46] O'Donovan remarks that several theologians have detected in *Gaudium et Spes* an optimistic, evolutionary perspective such as that advanced by Teilhard de Chardin.[47] Henri de Lubac considers that Teilhard's evolutionary theology exerted "a certain influence, at least

---

43. Paul VI, "*Gaudium et Spes*" 7.
44. Paul VI, "*Inter Mirifica*."
45. Paul VI, "*Gaudium et Spes*" 44.
46. O'Donovan, "Was Vatican II Evolutionary?," 497.
47. O'Donovan, "Was Vatican II Evolutionary?," 495.

indirect and diffuse on some orientations of the Council."[48] Otto Spülbeck recalls four occasions on which the Council Fathers, while deliberating on *Gaudium et Spes*, discussed de Chardin's theology, and regards chapter 3 of that pastoral constitution as particularly informed by Teilhard's optimistic view of development as progress towards unity with the divine.[49]

Vatican II's mandate for dialogue with the modern world is powerfully affirmed by the Council's inclusive model of Church as the "People of God."[50] This broad and inclusive ecclesiology means that the modern voices originating new insights need not be regarded as operating outside the Church. The Church's dialogue with the modern world need not, therefore, be understood as a conversation between the magisterium and extra-ecclesial perspectives, so much as an exchange of views within the bounds of Church, the People of God. The designation of the Church as the "Pilgrim" People of God in *Lumen Gentium*, with overtones of the realized futuristic eschatology detected by Lindbeck, suggests a Church that is still making its way, and open to progress.[51]

While inviting the modern world to partake in dialogue, however, the Council Fathers were not in naïve denial regarding the fallen state of humankind. On the contrary, *Gaudium et Spes* states that humanity was influenced by the "evil one" at the very start of history.[52] But *Gaudium et Spes* makes no explicit argument for a personal Satan. In its ruminations upon the topic of evil, the document acknowledges the role of human experience in confirming that which is made known through revelation. "What divine revelation makes known to us agrees with experience."[53] This affirmation of the life experience of modern people reflects a theology of correlation that underlies the document.

---

48. Lubac, *Athéisme et sens de l'homme*, 130; O'Donovan, "Was Vatican II Evolutionary?," 495.

49. Spülbeck, "Teilhard de Chardin und die Pastoralkonstitution"; Hampe, *Die Autorität der Freiheit*, 86–87; Spülbecke, "Fortschrittsglaube und Evolution," 85–107; O'Donovan, "Was Vatican II Evolutionary?," 494.

50. See chapter 2 in Paul VI, "*Lumen Gentium*."

51. See chapter 7 in Paul VI, "*Lumen Gentium*"; Lindbeck,"Vision of a World Renewed," 4.

52. Paul VI, "*Lumen Gentium*" 13.

53. Brown, "Pater Noster as an Eschatological Prayer," 208.

VATICAN II AND THEOLOGY OF CORRELATION

Gaudium et Spes, in its mandate for the Church to engage in conversation with the contemporary world, exemplifies the concerns of a correlational theology. A theology of correlation, as understood by Paul Tillich, is one that seeks to mediate between the Christian tradition and contemporary culture.[54] Widely regarded as the father of an explicitly correlational approach to theology, Tillich was Lutheran by denomination. However, Francis Schüssler Fiorenza notes that the Catholic pioneers of the *nouvelle théologie* could also be regarded as exponents of a theology of correlation.[55] David Tracy concurs, suggesting the fact "that several of these theologies do not call themselves 'correlational' is less important than the methodological-as-correlational character of the theologies themselves."[56]

The *nouvelle théologie* pioneered by authors such as Rahner, Congar, and Schillebeeckx had helped blaze an intellectual trail for Vatican II, challenging the position that all Catholic theology must be done within the framework of Scholasticism. These thinkers observed a correlational method by recognizing the revelatory potential of life experience in the modern world, and by harnessing insights derived from modern philosophies.

Karl Rahner's method, for example, is informed by a correlation between the search for meaning in, on the one hand, German Idealist philosophy, and on the other, the Roman Catholic tradition.[57] Rahner's recourse to Idealist philosophy signified his position that Neo-Scholasticism is not the only philosophical system that can profitably inform Catholic theological methodology. Thematically, Rahner's theology is characterized by a correlation between nature and grace.

While Tillich's use of the term "correlation" suggests the manner in which theologians and the Church envisage their relationship with the broader culture, and strive to proclaim the kerygma, the author also views divine revelation as inherently correlational. George Kendall posits that "Paul Tillich's theology of revelation and, by extension, of salvation, has as its center his principle of correlation. This principle affirms that God's revelation to His creatures must, in its form, be correlated to the conditions under which creatures have their being, that is, the conditions of existence."[58]

---

54. Clayton, *Concept of Correlation*, 8.
55. Rahner, *Spirit in the World*, 41.
56. Tracy, "Uneasy Alliance," 553.
57. Fiorenza and Galvin, *Systematic Theology*, 40.
58. Kendall, "Existence and Revelation."

Dei Verbum, Vatican II's *Dogmatic Constitution on Divine Revelation*, affirms the inherently correlational nature of revelation when it states that the interpreter of scripture in order to discern what God sought to reveal "must investigate what meaning the sacred writer intended to express and actually expressed in particular circumstances by using contemporary literary forms in accordance with the situation of his own time and culture."[59] Hence, *Dei Verbum* affirms Tillich's view that divine revelation is the Word of God in human words, and, more broadly, that revelation transpires when the Word of God engages with a particular culture and way of life. The recognition that God reveals in a human fashion, working through human authors, their cultures, their historical contexts, and the literary forms associated with these contexts, legitimizes the use of the historical-critical method of biblical exegesis. A theology of correlation, in Tillich's use of the term, views revelation as occurring in and through culture.

Rigby, Hengel, and O'Grady regard the method of correlation as central to liberal thought. "Rational progress and truth are at the heart of the liberal enterprise. Its method is one of mutually critical correlations."[60] The authors imply that the degree to which a method of correlation constructively engages our current reality may depend upon the accuracy or veracity with which it characterizes the present situation.

> Certain correlations can be shown to be . . . more rationally progressive, and therefore, to disclose more truth for the theological enterprise. . . . Some social science theories and some interpretations of doctrine offer us more authentic possibilities of life than others because they present us with a more accurate redescription of our present reality.[61]

The reference to a "more accurate redescription of our present reality" implies an inductive methodology, beginning with a candid examination of life experience, rather than a deductive approach. Some degree of correlation, whether acknowledged or not, is inherent to the theological enterprise. As soon as the theologian utilizes language with its mores and assumptions, culture is then related to the kerygma. In this sense, perhaps no theology, however apophatic or radically orthodox, simply by virtue of its use of human language, is correlation-free.

---

59. Paul VI, "*Dei Verbum*" 12.
60. Rigby et al., "Nature of Doctrine and Scientific Progress," 688.
61. Rigby et al., "Nature of Doctrine and Scientific Progress," 688.

CONTRASTING ATTITUDES AT THE COUNCIL TOWARDS DIALOGUE WITH MODERNITY

Neither the Council Fathers nor the worldwide Church since the Council unanimously endorsed a dialogical, correlational stance in relation to the modern world. Even before an agenda was made known for the Council, opposition was mounting. As Greg Tobin remarks, "While the direction the Council might take was unclear . . . it was clear that anything could happen. And the Curia, as well as other cardinals of the Church, did not like it at all."[62] Cardinal Spellman of New York opined, "I do not believe that the pope wanted to convoke a Council, but that he was pushed into it."[63] This remark of the New York prelate reveals a suspicion, even before the Council, that some ominous agenda was at work behind the scenes. Tobin notes that Giovanni Montini, the future Pope Paul VI, newly incardinated by John, and well-disposed towards him, confided, "This holy old boy doesn't seem to realize what a hornets' nest he's stirring up."[64] Thirteen years later, as we shall later see, Montini in his role as Pope Paul VI would use terminology far more damning than his allusion to a hornets' nest to describe the situation stirred up by the Council. John XXIII, in the most constructive sense, did indeed stir up the episcopacy, writing to 2,598 bishops and ordinaries of religious orders, soliciting agenda items for discussion at the Council and receiving a 77 percent response rate representing some 1,800 cardinals, bishops and superiors of religious orders.

Having remarked upon the manner in which the majority of Council Fathers were won over to St. John XXIII's dialogical disposition toward modernity, Cardinal Daneels adds, "There remained a minority—privileged by the bishops and the cardinals of the curia—who suspected the majority of disloyalty and betrayal of the tradition."[65] Daneels hence asserts that this conservative minority of Council Fathers was favored by the Curia.

This brings us to the role of Cardinal Alfredo Ottaviani, Prefect of the Holy Office, tasked with chairing the Theological Commission and preparing an agenda of theological topics for discussion at the Council. Ottaviani's motto read *Semper Idem*, "always the same," and the cardinal was faithful to it, resisting the prospect of progress within the Church. Such intransigence, it could be argued, characterized the ethos of the Roman Curia more broadly. James Carroll recounts

---

62. Tobin, *Good Pope*, 112–13.
63. Tobin, *Good Pope*, 112–13.
64. Tobin, *Good Pope*, 112–13.
65. Tobin, *Good Pope*, 112–13.

> Ahead of the Council, numerous schemata or outlines, were prepared by members of the Roman Curia, the conservative Vatican Bureaucracy that was determined to thwart change. These documents reiterated the traditional propositions on revelation, morality, family life, chastity, the liturgy, and the exalted place of Mary.[66]

Thus, Carroll characterizes the body of clerics charged by John XXIII with preparing the schemata as intransigent, with overtones of integralism. Hindsight suggests that John XXIII was not entrusting the direction of the Council to the curia, but rather, in a pragmatically effective move, using an existing infrastructure to do the preparatory work required. Furthermore, whether by the pope's design or not, the paternalistic behavior of the curia would jolt the Council Fathers into action, impelling them to find their voices. Essentially, the curia provoked the Council Fathers, each one the leader of a diocese or religious institute and accustomed to being heeded, to take ownership of the Council and revise its agenda, albeit within parameters. It might not be too great a stretch to say that Pope St. John XXIII allowed a paternalistic curia to do what it did best, in hope that it would ignite the ire of some two thousand prelates who would not allow themselves to be controlled like "schoolboys" as one hierarch put it.[67] However, for one who knew the intransigent nature of the "prophets of doom," and who was aware that some 1,800 prelates had felt strongly enough about the Council to submit agenda items, a clash could not have been completely unforeseen.[68]

If Cardinal Ottaviani and the curia can be characterized as resistant to change, Cardinal Augustine Bea, and the Secretariat for Promoting Christian Unity could be broadly characterized as open to development. Tobin suggests that John XXIII instituted this secretariat and appointed Bea its leader, so as to counterbalance the culture of the curia.[69] With sad irony, it might be argued that the establishment of the Secretariat for Christian Unity demarcated clear battle-lines in the Church. This endorsement of ecumenism must have occasioned concern, or even disdain, on the part of those who feared for the preservation of the status quo, and accentuated existing tensions between conflicting ecclesiologies.

An early indication that the majority of Council Fathers was prepared to challenge the curia became evident on October 13, 1962, when the curia presented the Council with a slate of possible candidates to chair

---

66. Carroll, *Practicing Catholic*, 110.
67. Tobin, *Good Pope*, 175.
68. John XXIII, "*Gaudet Mater Ecclesia*."
69. Tobin, *Good Pope*, 146.

the Council's various commissions, and Cardinal Lienart, Bishop of Lille, argued that the Fathers needed three days to consider the matter.[70] Upon discovering that the slate prepared by the curia stacked the decks in favor of ultra-conservatives, the bishops compiled their own list of candidates, in a move dubbed "The Revolt of the Bishops."[71]

The theological differences that existed between, on the one hand, Ottaviani's curia and, on the other, Bea and the majority of Council Fathers, bubbled to the surface once more in relation to the reform of the liturgy. O'Malley notes that this was the first substantive issue facing the Council, whereby the Fathers would show whether they were prepared to challenge the status quo. Carroll recounts that "The Ottaviani-inspired decree on the liturgy was immediately put before the bishops, as a final draft, ready to be voted on."[72] O'Malley notes that the Fathers upturned the status quo by permitting the use of the vernacular as an alternative to Latin in the celebration of the liturgy. Still, the most dramatic liturgical developments associated with Vatican II, it might be argued, are not micro-prescribed by the texts themselves, so much as the spirit of innovation inspired by the Council. This dynamic may be illustrated with reference to the 1973 *General Instruction on the Roman Missal* which advanced the trajectory of the Council's *Constitution on the Sacred Liturgy* so as to mandate as a goal of all Catholic worship, the "full, active, conscious participation of all the faithful, motivated by faith, hope and charity."[73] The epideictic style of the documents seems to have suggested that they were more a beginning than an end, a springboard for progress, rather than a ceiling to constrain it.

The divide between the curia and the Council majority became evident once more when, on November 14, 1962, the Fathers rejected *De Fontibus*, the draft schema on the sources of revelation as presented by Cardinal Ottaviani. The dispute was in large part concerned with the relationship between magisterial authority and the freedom of exegetes to utilize the best interpretive methods at their disposal in open, intellectual inquiry. Adrian Graffy recalls that

> during the morning no fewer than twelve of the fifteen Council Fathers who spoke were against the draft. While Cardinal Ruffini of Palermo and Cardinal Siri of Genoa approved it and emphasised the need to draw up rules for Catholic biblical scholars, such opinions were not shared by Cardinals Frings of Cologne,

---

70. Tobin, *Good Pope*, 175.
71. Tobin, *Good Pope*, 175.
72. Carroll, *Practicing Catholic*, 111.
73. Tobin, *Good Pope*, 177; Paul VI, "*Sacrosanctum Concilium*" 14.

Alfrink of Utrecht, Suenens of Malines-Brussels, and Cardinal Bea, head of the newly formed Secretariat for Christian Unity.[74]

The proposal that rules should be drawn up for scripture scholars must have rattled Cardinal Bea, himself a scripture scholar, who had served as rector of the Pontifical Biblical Institute for nineteen years and had assisted in the preparation of the 1943 encyclical, *Divino Afflante Spiritu* which sought to emancipate exegetes to use the best available methods.[75]

Ottaviani insisted on the primacy of tradition over scripture, a position deplored by the *peritus*, Joseph Ratzinger, and that, if adopted by the Council, would have placed a stranglehold on scripture scholarship.[76] Tradition, notoriously difficult to pry apart from the magisterial pronouncements that mediate it, could then have been invoked to veto any new insight or clarification with regard to the significance of the biblical text.

Cardinal Joseph Ritter urged the Council Fathers to reject the draft. Cardinal Bea suggested that the draft represented a particular theological agenda, and one not associated with good theology, contending that "the schema represents the work of a theological school, and not what the better theologians think."[77] Bea called for a more inviting alternative. "What our times demand is a more pastoral approach, demonstrating the love and kindness that flow from religion."[78] Tobin notes that Cardinals Maximus IV Saingh and Joseph De Smelt of the Secretariat of Christian Unity, and Cardinal Lineart of France called for a more pastoral and less dogmatic tone.[79]

The Council Fathers sought a new style that would characterize the Church's interaction with the world, in effect, the epideictic style.[80] Edward Hannenberg comments, "Those who criticized the text wanted a new start. They wanted to free the Council from the anti-modern mentality that had hung over the Church in recent decades."[81] Hannenberg identifies not only the impetus on the part of the majority of Council Fathers to reject the mentality that had impelled the Modernist crisis, but also their desire to recover aspects of the ancient tradition that had been suppressed in Tridentine Catholicism. "They saw, paradoxically, that the key to moving forward was to

---

74. Graffy, "Story of *Dei Verbum*."
75. Graffy, "Story of *Dei Verbum*"; Pius XII, "*Divino Afflante Spiritu*" 37.
76. See Wicks, "Six Texts by Prof. Joseph Ratzinger," 269–79.
77. Graffy, "Story of *Dei Verbum*."
78. Graffy, "Story of *Dei Verbum*."
79. Tobin, *Good Pope*, 191.
80. Tobin, *Good Pope*, 191.
81. Hannenberg, "*Dei Verbum*," 81.

recover the deeper wisdom of the past."[82] Tobin posits that the Council's rejection of *De Fontibus* was so pivotal as to change the course of the Council from the rubber-stamping that it might have been.[83] Similarly, O'Malley views the affair as effectively removing power from the doctrinal commission. The bitter disappointment of the curia, and a minority of Council Fathers with regard to the Council's teaching on revelation and scripture, would continue to haunt the Church, perpetuating the disconnect between the insights of biblical scholarship and the presentation of doctrine.

CONCLUSION

The Second Vatican Council, especially its *Pastoral Constitution on the Church in the Modern World*, signaled a dialogical stance on the part of the Church in relation to modernity. The Council invited the entire human family to engage in candid conversation and recognized that the modern paradigm could help to distinguish mature faith from superstition. However, the Council was polarized, and an ultra-conservative minority among the Fathers resented what it saw as unwarranted accommodation to the modern zeitgeist. This polarization and resentment would hold great implications for the question of the postconciliar development of doctrine—or the lack thereof. Openness to dialogue with modernity is ultimately openness to the possible—and to grace. On the other hand, if one believes that one's current understanding and articulation of the truth are complete in every regard, then genuine, open dialogue is pointless.

---

82. Hannenberg, "*Dei Verbum*," 81.
83. Hannenberg, "*Dei Verbum*," 81.

6

Why Doctrinal Formulations Should Respect the Genre of Biblical Texts

Having made the case that the Catholic tradition has always been a dynamic, evolving one, and that the Second Vatican Council envisaged the Church as benefiting from a prudent, critically conscious openness to the insights of the modern world, this chapter narrows our focus so as to document the Church's stated receptivity to developments in one specific form of contemporary inquiry, that is, modern biblical scholarship.

Holding enormous implications for the presentation of doctrine, Catholic teaching on the interpretation of scripture not only allows, but mandates, the use of the historical-critical method as "indispensable" for the interpretation of scripture. This indispensable method of biblical interpretation as described by the Pontifical Biblical Commission includes as an integral consideration, the literary characteristics of the biblical text, including that of genre. The Church cannot then, with any credibility, interpret scripture without regard for the implications of genre, for example, treating myth as history.

The chapter contributes to the evolution of our central argument by providing a basis from which to insist, that according to the Church's own teachings, myth must be interpreted as myth and not as history, etiology, biography, or any other literary form.

TRACING THE CHURCH'S ACCEPTANCE OF THE HISTORICAL-CRITICAL METHOD

Robert Murray notes that for most of the Church's historical existence, indeed until the closing years of the nineteenth century, the judgments of scripture scholars in the catechetical schools, monasteries, and universities were generally trusted by the popes and bishops, including those at the Council of Trent.[1] However, Murray observes that around the time of the Modernist crisis, use of the term "magisterium" seemed to narrow so as to exclude theologians and exegetes, and refer more exclusively to the Holy Office.[2] The author supports his observation by pointing to the fact that six sevenths of the ecclesial documents regarding scripture, as contained in the *Enchirdion Biblicum,* originate in the period 1893–1953 with less than a seventh originating before, and little since.[3]

The Pontifical Biblical Commission (PBC), founded in 1902 in the midst of the Modernist crisis, rigorously enforced the magisterium's oversight of Catholic exegesis, issuing decrees on the interpretation of virtually every passage of scripture. In 1943, however, an emancipatory development transpired with the publication of Pope Pius XII's *Divino Afflante Spiritu.* The encyclical, which Raymond Brown considered a *magna carta* for Catholic biblical scholarship, openly acknowledged that responsible interpretation of the Bible required attention to historical and literary factors.[4]

> No one who has a correct idea of biblical inspiration will be surprised to find, even in the Sacred Writers, as in other ancient authors, certain fixed ways of expounding and narrating, certain definite idioms, especially of a kind peculiar to the Semitic tongues, so-called approximations, and certain hyperbolical modes of expression, nay, at times, even paradoxical, which even help to impress the ideas more deeply on the mind.[5]

The encyclical openly recognizes that divinely inspired writing is subject to the particularities of its authorial context with its linguistic and stylistic mores—a position that would in time be affirmed by Vatican II's *Dogmatic Constitution on Divine Revelation* and in the 1992 Catechism of the Catholic Church. Given this acknowledgment that the inspired Word of

---

1. Murray, "Further Reflection on Magisterium," 34–35; McGill, "Reading the Bible through Stained Glass," 31–42.
2. Murray, "Further Reflection on Magisterium," 34–35.
3. Murray, "Further Reflection on Magisterium," 34–35.
4. Brown, *New Testament Essays,* 49.
5. Pius XII, *"Divino Afflante Spiritu"* 37.

Why Doctrinal Formulations Should Respect the Genre of Biblical Texts 89

God is mediated by human words, languages, genres, and mores, the encyclical mandates exegetes to consider "to what extent the manner of expression or the literary mode adopted by the sacred writer may lead to a correct and genuine interpretation," adding with a note of urgency, "and let him be convinced that this part of his office cannot be neglected without serious detriment to Catholic exegesis."[6] The encyclical goes so far as to censure as neglect any failure on the part of scripture scholars to use the most effective methods available while promoting the broad approach that constitutes the historical-critical method. Of particular importance for our present purposes, *Divino Afflante Spiritu* emphasizes the importance of interpreting scripture in light of the "literary mode adopted by the sacred writer."[7]

A further watershed in the magisterium's gradual acceptance of the historical-critical method was a 1950 statement by the PBC in the *Enchiridion Biblicum*, in which the commission undertook to allow exegetes full freedom to reach their own scholarly conclusions.[8] Again, in 1964, the PBC's *Sancta Mater Ecclesiae* urged exegetes to freely exercise the best methods at their disposal:

> There are still many things, and of the greatest importance, in the discussion and explanation of which the Catholic exegete can and must freely exercise his skill and genius, so that each may contribute his part to the advantage of all, to the continued progress of sacred doctrine.[9]

While mandating exegetes to freely pursue their craft and influence the development of doctrine, the instruction also exhorts the exegete to "always be disposed to obey the magisterium of the Church" and "never to depart in the slightest degree from the common doctrine and tradition of the Church."[10] On one reading, it seems as though a mixed message was conveyed to exegetes who were encouraged to use the best methods at their disposal, provided these methods did not yield results that challenged the status quo. If, however, doctrine is understood as the truth to which the formulations point, and tradition is understood as an evolving engagement with the faith, the injunction makes more sense. In terms of the first reading, the encouragement for exegetes to "freely pursue their craft and influence the development of doctrine" would be completely contradicted.

---

6. Pius XII, "*Divino Afflante Spiritu*" 38.
7. Pius XII, "*Divino Afflante Spiritu*" 38.
8. PBC, *Enchiridion Biblicum*.
9. PBC, "*Sancta Mater Ecclesiae*."
10. PBC, "*Sancta Mater Ecclesiae*."

Lending support to our second interpretation of the PBC's reference to doctrine and tradition, *Dei Verbum* reinforces the mandate for exegetes to work "toward a better understanding and explanation of the meaning of Sacred Scripture, so that through preparatory study the judgment of the Church may mature."[11] Again though, there is some suggestion of a mixed message. While signaling openness to the possibility of maturation in the Church's understanding of scripture, this statement also issues a reminder that the magisterium possesses ultimate interpretative authority: "For, of course, all that has been said about the manner of interpreting scripture is ultimately subject to the judgment of the Church which exercises the divinely conferred commission of watching over and interpreting the Word of God."[12] While fully appreciating that the canon of scripture is a work of the Church to be interpreted by the Church, it would seem that those members of the Church best equipped to interpret it are those skilled in the science of exegesis.

Dei Verbum envisages exegetes working with theologians, in a comment recognizing the implications for new exegetical insights for theology—which would then hold implications for doctrine too. Still, this recognition is immediately followed by a remark that the magisterium would closely monitor the specialized work of exegetes and theologians.

> Catholic exegetes and other workers in the field of sacred theology should zealously combine their efforts. Under the watchful eye of the sacred magisterium, and using appropriate techniques, they should set about examining the sacred texts in such a way that as many as possible of those who are ministers of the divine word should be able to distribute fruitfully the nourishment of the scriptures to the People of God.[13]

The reference to exegetes as a body that stands apart from the magisterium and should be subjugated to it, seems to reflect Murray's observation concerning a widening chasm since the late nineteenth century between Catholic scholars and the official teaching office of the Church.[14] Extending hermeneutical charity, however, the "watchful eye" might suggest magisterial attentiveness and interest rather than oppressive supervision. Such an interpretation might be supported with reference to *Dei Verbum*'s subsequent remarks on the pastoral applicability of the work of the exegete who performs "an ecclesial task, for it consists in the study and explanation of

---

11. Paul VI, "*Dei Verbum*" 13.
12. Paul VI, "*Dei Verbum*" 21.
13. Paul VI, "*Dei Verbum*" 23.
14. Murray, "Further Reflection on Magisterium," 34–35.

Why Doctrinal Formulations Should Respect the Genre of Biblical Texts

holy Scripture in a way that makes all its riches available to pastors and the faithful."[15] If the work of exegetes is to be pastorally enriching for Catholic communities, it stands to reason that the magisterium must watch with interest as exegetes propose interpretations with theological and pastoral implications.

The same 1992 Catechism that presents a historicized account of the Fall and a literalized account of the motif of Satan affirms the importance of historical-critical criteria as conveyed in *Divino Afflante Spiritu* and in *Dei Verbum*, admittedly without identifying the historical-critical method by name. "In Sacred Scripture, God speaks to man in a human way. To interpret Scripture correctly, the reader must be attentive to what the human authors truly wanted to affirm, and to what God wanted to reveal to us by their words."[16] The Catechism outlines the considerations that must be taken into account in order for the reader to uncover what the human authors endeavored to communicate. Attention must be paid to the historical factors that influenced the authorial context. Also, the literary form in question must be taken into consideration: "In order to discover the sacred authors' intention, the reader must take into account the conditions of their time and culture, the literary genres in use at that time, and the modes of feeling, speaking and narrating then current."[17] This statement, although it does not explicitly name the historical-critical method, clearly describes it. This is the understanding of the historical-critical method as advocated throughout this book, a necessary step in the interpretation of that which "God speaks to man in a human way."[18]

The Catechism proceeds to acknowledge the manifold ways in which truth can be conveyed. Truth need not be expressed in a historical or empirical manner. "For the fact is that truth is differently presented and expressed in the various types of historical writing, in prophetical and poetical texts, and in other forms of literary expression."[19] Essentially the Catechism in this section recounts Pius XII's 1943 encyclical *Divino Afflante Spiritu* 38 which mandates Catholic exegetes to utilize the most effective methods at their disposal, and *Dei Verbum* 12 that exhorts the interpreter of scripture to take into account historical context and literary forms so as to discover what the sacred authors sought to convey and what God seeks to reveal through their words, and hence contribute "to the continued progress of

15. PBC, "Interpretation of the Bible in the Church."
16. CDF, *Catechism of the Catholic Church* 109.
17. CDF, *Catechism of the Catholic Church* 110.
18. CDF, *Catechism of the Catholic Church* 110.
19. CDF, *Catechism of the Catholic Church* 110.

sacred doctrine."[20] Granted, the magisterium cannot uncritically endorse each novel, revisionist, and possibly conflicting theory by each and every exegete and theologian. However, in order for exegetes to contribute "to the continued progress of sacred doctrine," the magisterium must be open to the possibility of development, embracing a dialogical rather than entirely supervisory disposition in relation to the guild of biblical scholars as a whole.[21]

In 1993, the PBC published a report entitled *The Interpretation of the Bible in the Church*, explicitly mandating recourse to the historical-critical method.[22] This report affirms that the historical-critical method is "the indispensable method for the scientific study of the meaning of ancient texts."[23] It posits that the approach is a historical method, both because it studies the significance of ancient texts "from a historical point of view," and also because "it seeks to shed light upon the historical processes which gave rise to biblical texts."[24] The PBC asserts that it is a critical method, because "it operates with the help of scientific criteria that seek to be as objective as possible."[25] Hence, the historical-critical method may for our present purposes be defined as an approach to discovering the meaning intended by inspired authors, informed by historical research, literary criticism, and other applicable sciences including anthropology, philosophy, and archeology.

When the PBC mandates the historical-critical method as indispensable for the "scientific study" of scripture, a question might be raised as to what counts as "scientific study" and whether this applies to the Church's interpretation of scripture. Its applicability becomes clear with reference to the preceding fifty years of Church teaching that exhorted the Church and its theologians to be attentive to exegetes as they interpret the sacred texts in light of what clearly amount to historical-critical considerations. Readings of scripture that do not count as "scientific study" would include its use in personal prayer, such as Lectio Divina—though this too can be enriched by historical-critical exegesis. In any case, subjective readings of scripture, however pious, are not a basis for the formulation of doctrine—as made clear in the Church's teachings since *Divino Afflante Spiritu*.

---

20. Pius XII, "*Divino Afflante Spiritu*" 38; Paul VI, "*Dei Verbum*" 12; PBC, "*Sancta Mater Ecclesiae.*"
   21. McGill, "Reading the Bible through Stained Glass."
   22. PBC, "Interpretation of the Bible in the Church" 1, 34.
   23. PBC, "Interpretation of the Bible in the Church" 1, 34.
   24. PBC, "Interpretation of the Bible in the Church" 1, 34.
   25. PBC, "Interpretation of the Bible in the Church" 37.

Why Doctrinal Formulations Should Respect the Genre of Biblical Texts

THE CONSIDERATION OF GENRE IN THE HISTORICAL-CRITICAL METHOD AS MANDATED BY THE PBC

The PBC in *The Interpretation of the Bible in the Church* views the historical-critical method as concerned with both historical and literary analysis.[26] In the view of the PBC, the method approaches the biblical text in the same manner as it would approach any ancient text. "As an analytical method, it studies the biblical text in the same fashion as it would study any other ancient text and comments upon it as an expression of human discourse."[27] When the PBC regards the biblical text as "an expression of human discourse," this effectively acknowledges that it is a work of literature. The commission proceeds to describe the role of literary criticism in biblical interpretation.

> The text is then submitted to a linguistic (morphology and syntax) and semantic analysis, using the knowledge derived from historical philology. It is the role of literary criticism to determine the beginning and end of textual units, large and small, and to establish the internal coherence of the text. The existence of doublets, of irreconcilable differences and of other indicators is a clue to the composite character of certain texts. These can then be divided into small units, the next step being to see whether these in turn can be assigned to different sources.[28]

This statement shows that the PBC regards literary criticism, with close attention to genre, linguistics and semiotics, as constituting an integral part of the historical-critical method. The commission encourages exegetes, especially those with a penchant for effectively popularizing insights otherwise confined to the academy, to clearly distinguish the language of myth from that of history.

> This requires that exegetes take into consideration the reasonable demands of educated and cultured persons of our time, clearly distinguishing for their benefit what in the Bible is to be regarded as secondary detail conditioned by a particular age, what must be interpreted as the language of myth and what is to be regarded as the true historical and inspired meaning.[29]

---

26. McGill, "Reading the Bible through Stained Glass," 37.
27. PBC, "Interpretation of the Bible in the Church."
28. PBC, "Interpretation of the Bible in the Church."
29. PBC, "Interpretation of the Bible in the Church," 34.

Granted, there is some ambiguity here regarding the implied relationship between "the true historical" and "inspired meaning" with the possible implication that the inspired meaning is necessarily historical in nature. Further ambiguity may also exist in relation to a possible equation of the language of myth with secondary, cultural assumptions. There is also an arguably elitist undertone in the reference to "educated and cultured persons of our time," raising a question as to how education and culture are to be defined for these purposes. Someone with a stellar education in the hard sciences or business may have ceased all religious education as a child and have a juvenile level of religious understanding. There is even an implied connotation that those less cultured and educated, however this is to be measured, can be left to languish with a less informed interpretation of scripture. Such a situation might not bode well for the Church in the developing world and in other contexts that lack access to formal education. These criticisms and ambiguities noted, however, the relevance of the PBC statement for our present purposes is that it mandates that exegetes should distinguish between genres, and between the expression of the various kinds of truth, so as to counteract both literalism, and a dismissal of the scriptures as fallacious.

Joseph Fitzmyer, with an evident regard for the importance of acknowledging genre, asserts of the biblical author, "since the truth he has enshrined in his text is analogous to the form used, historical criticism teaches us that we cannot read an ancient text without the sophistication that the form calls for."[30] This same regard for the theological implications of the literary genres is evident in the application of the method by exegetes such as Fitzmyer, Brown, Schneiders, and Murphy.[31] These exegetes, far from assuming that the biblical text always seeks to record historical truth, explore the historical origins of the text and its literary character so as to ascertain what kind of truth the sacred authors sought to convey and what God sought to reveal through their words.

DISAGREEMENT REGARDING THE DEFINITION AND SCOPE OF THE HISTORICAL-CRITICAL METHOD

As Luke Timothy Johnson observes, the term, "historical-critical method" can carry a degree of ambiguity.[32] In particular, the prominence of the term

---

30. PBC, "Interpretation of the Bible in the Church" 2; Fitzmyer, *In Defense of the Historical-Critical Method*, 66.

31. Brown et al., *New Jerome Biblical Commentary*.

32. Johnson, *Real Jesus*, 81–82; CDF, *Catechism of the Catholic Church* 390.

Why Doctrinal Formulations Should Respect the Genre of Biblical Texts 95

"historical" in the name of the method may overshadow the "critical" dimension in the sense of literary criticism. Indeed, there is significant divergence of opinion as to what extent the method takes literary considerations into account. "In biblical scholarship," Johnson laments, "critical has come to be associated with historical."[33] Johnson suggests that the method has been implemented so as to be excessively critical of tradition and rather uncritical of its own assumptions.[34] What Johnson identifies, however, seems to be an incomplete and skewed application of the method, rather than a flaw in the method itself. When Johnson calls for a "more inclusive sense of 'criticism,'" this could be regarded as a plea for a more rigorous application of the method, attentive to literary concerns.

Further, Johnson's concern that an over-emphasis on the "historical" dimension of the historical-critical method leads to a neglect of critical considerations might also be explored in terms of the same authors observation that "*history* cannot be used simply for 'the past,' or 'what happened in the past' any more than *historical* can be used simply as a synonym for 'what was real about the past.' History is, rather the product of human intelligence and imagination."[35] Johnson's concern regarding reductionist applications of the historical-critical method seems to warn of a tendency on the part of some interpreters to work from too narrow an understanding of history so that the truth of the biblical text is reduced to questions of facticity.

Walter Wink has also associated the historical-critical method with historicism. Wink segues from a discussion of the ambiguity entailed by the term "the historical Jesus" into a critique of the historical-critical method without any clear differentiation between the former and the latter. Wink remarks with regard to the term "historical Jesus," "It would help immeasurably if we would make clear which meaning we intend when we use the expression."[36] Immediately following this appeal for terminological clarity, Wink makes an unacknowledged leap from a discussion of the term "historical Jesus" to an expression of agreement with Luke Timothy Johnson's assessment of the historical-critical method, announcing, "I agree with Johnson that the historical-critical approach, despite its undeniable contributions, is inadequate as the central or sole means of interpreting scripture."[37] Notably, the PBC regards the historical-critical method as an

---

33. Johnson, *Real Jesus*, 81–82.
34. Johnson, *Real Jesus*, 81–82.
35. Johnson, *Real Jesus*, 81–82.
36. Wink, "Response to Luke Timothy Johnson," 239.
37. Wink, "Response to Luke Timothy Johnson," 239.

indispensable, but not the *sole* means of interpreting scripture.[38] Rather, the method establishes the literal sense as a basis for subsequent canonical exegesis which seeks out the *sensus plenior*, and other forms of interpretation, all of which must begin with a solid grasp of the literal sense. However, the more pertinent point for the issue at stake is that use of the historical-critical method in no way implies sympathy for any particular school of historical-Jesus scholarship which is itself a heterogeneous amalgamation of specialisms and perspectives.

Wink decries a form of historicism that he believes to be dominant in modern biblical scholarship, lamenting that "only those events that can be described as 'historical,' as having 'really happened,' are true. Only facts have verity."[39] However, the historicist mindset described by Wink is not inherently related to the adoption of the historical-critical method. Indeed, it might be argued, insights derived from the application of the historical-critical method have helped emancipate believers from a historicist interpretation of the myths of Genesis, proposing richer theological and existential interpretations.

In a case in point, Eugene Maly, a contributor to the *Jerome Biblical Commentary*, and practitioner of the historical-critical method, asserts, "No scholar today would hold that Gn [sic] presents history in the modern sense of that term."[40] We have already noted that John McKenzie, Pauline Viviano, and Daniel Harlow number among the historical-critical exegetes who explicitly reject historicist assumptions and urge readers to interpret the text in light of its literary form.[41] Proponents of the historical-critical method cannot be fairly attributed a position that "only those events that can be described as 'historical,' as having 'really happened,' are true. Only facts have verity."[42] While the PBC and Joseph Fitzmyer regard literary considerations as integral to the historical-critical method, Luke Timothy Johnson, Walter Wink, and, indeed, George Lindbeck, believe that the method as practiced places a high premium on historical reconstruction but neglects literary considerations.

This divergence of opinion indicates the potential for talking at cross-purposes concerning the historical-critical method. For our working purposes, however, references to the historical-critical method reflect the

38. Fitzmyer, *In Defense of the Historical-Critical Method*, 81.
39. Wink, "Response to Luke Timothy Johnson," 239.
40. Maly, "Genesis," 40.
41. McKenzie, "Aspects of Old Testament Thought," 740–41; Viviano, "Genesis," 43; Maly, "Genesis," 40; Harlow, "After Adam," 179–95.
42. Wink, "Response to Luke Timothy Johnson," 240.

model endorsed by the PBC in *The Interpretation of Scripture in the Church* and reflected in *The Jerome Biblical Commentary, The New Jerome Biblical Commentary,* and the *Collegeville Bible Commentary*.[43] The present work thus understands the method to denote an approach to discovering the intention of the inspired author, informed by historical research, literary criticism, and other applicable sciences. Of great importance to the discussion about Satan, the issue of literary genre falls within the remit of the historical-critical method, demanding that myth be read as myth.

CONCLUSION

This chapter documents the Catholic Church's endorsement of the historical-critical method, noting that the 1993 PBC report *The Interpretation of the Bible in the Church* regards the method as indispensable for the informed interpretation of scripture. In addition to the consideration of the historical context in which a text was authored, the method includes a plethora of components such as form, source, and redaction criticism that explore the biblical text as literature.

While some voices including Luke Timothy Johnson and Walter Wink criticize the method for an overemphasis on attempts at historical reconstruction, and lack of attention to literary considerations, this criticism reflects a skewed application of the method that does not reflect the best practices mandated by the PBC or endorsed in this book. This divergence of opinion concerns the definition of what counts as the historical-critical method, Johnson and Wink agreeing that the scriptures should be interpreted in light of their literary genres.

Further, there is nothing inherent to the historical-critical method that views the approach as the only level of analysis appropriate for the interpretation of scripture. The historical-critical method interprets a text on its own terms so as to uncover the literal sense which can then be considered at the level of canonical exegesis, interpreting the text in light of the canon of scripture.

Notably, the PBC defines the method as including a concern for the implications of literary genre and notes the responsibility of exegetes to help the faithful to distinguish myth from history. It is not therefore tenable for the Church to present doctrine without regard for the genres that characterize its scriptural underpinnings.

---

43. Fitzmyer, *In Defense of the Historical-Critical Method*, 66.

7

What Is Myth and What Kind of Truth Does It Express within the Bible?

Having documented the Church's acceptance of the historical-critical method in biblical interpretation with its integral concern for the implications of the literary genres, we now focus upon the genre of myth. The Catechism's references to Satan are saturated in mythical motifs transposed into the language of doctrine and historicized as though they reflect specific events and the agency of a particular being.

We have noted the possibility of talking at cross-purposes about the historical-critical method, and there may exist an even greater risk of such terminological confusion in relation to myth. Even the writings of the PBC have in at least one instance implied a distinction between that which is mythical and that which is true, as though momentarily lapsing into a colloquial understanding of myth as fallacy.[1]

Whereas some approaches to the interpretation of myth regard the genre as a primitive precursor to history, science, or philosophy, the perspective on myth associated with Paul Ricoeur, and broadly adopted by Catholic scripture scholars, recognizes the capacity of the genre to express deep truths that are otherwise largely inaccessible to conscious thought and vexingly ineffable in terms of propositional discourse. Ricoeur understands

---

1. PBC, "Interpretation of the Bible in the Church" 34.

What Is Myth and What Kind of Truth Does It Express within the Bible? 99

myth as expressing universal actualities and possibilities, as opposed to historical or etiological truth. This view of myth is highly conducive to a development of doctrine which points to universal truths rather than historical and etiological assertions.

MODELS OF MYTH

Robert Segal identifies four distinct ways of understanding myth. While Segal categorizes these in relation to science, what is true of their relation to science, is also, I suggest, true of their relation to history.[2]

First, a model of myth as "true science/true history" is literalistic and regards mythical texts as accurately conveying scientific or historical truth.[3] Exponents of this approach are likely to reject the term "myth" in relation to the narratives that they believe to recount history. They may concede that the narrative utilizes figurative language as exemplified by James Orr's approach to the myths of Genesis in the *Fundamentals* series of tracts that gave its name to fundamentalism, but insist that even the figurative language recounts historical or empirical truth.[4]

Second, a model of myth as "modern science/modern history" seeks to reconcile mythical texts with the insights of modern science and modern history.[5] Segal cites editorial comments in the *Oxford Annotated Bible* (1977) as typifying this model.[6] The editors of that volume seek to scientifically explain the plague in Exodus 7:14–24, asserting a scientific and historically viable possibility that the Nile can turn red and hence blood-like in the summer due to pigmentation from soil or micro-organisms.[7] This model is characterized by its own brand of literalism, differing from the "true science" model in its appeal to natural causes rather than supernatural intervention so as to justify an interpretation of the narrative as recounting a particular event.[8] This approach is evident when interpreters equate a mythic flood with some particular historical deluge, as though the myth amounts to an embellished account of history.

Third, a model of myth as primitive science/primitive history views myth as a flawed attempt to fill gaps in humanity's understanding of

2. Segal, "Myth and Ritual," 355.
3. Segal, "Myth and Ritual," 355.
4. Orr, "Early Narratives of Genesis."
5. Segal, "Myth and Ritual," 355.
6. See May and Metzger, *Oxford Annotated Bible with the Apocrypha*.
7. Segal, "Myth and Ritual," 355.
8. Segal, "Myth and Ritual," 355.

causation.⁹ However, as the expansion of scientific knowledge plugs the gaps in human understanding of the world, myth becomes less and less relevant. Yesteryear's acts of God have become explicable as scientific phenomena. This model would challenge the monogenism advocated by a literal reading of Genesis 3, regarding the myth as scientifically erroneous. As archeological evidence is uncovered, increasing our knowledge of the Ancient Near East, myth as primitive history becomes increasingly redundant.

Carl Jung challenges the position that myth is a kind of primitive science when he proposes that "No science will ever replace myth, and a myth cannot be made out of any science. For it is not that 'God' is a myth, but that myth is the revelation of a divine life in man. It is not we who invent myth, rather it speaks to us as a Word of God."¹⁰ Jung posits that myth is a medium of divine revelation, rather than a figurative way to describe causal relationships.

On a similar note, Bernard Batto stingingly rejects the view that myth is a primitive forerunner of more sophisticated forms of thinking and writing.¹¹ Batto comments that "mythopoeic thought was commonly assumed to be characteristic of 'primitive' societies where abilities to think had not progressed beyond a certain 'prelogical' stage."¹² Redirecting the charge of primitive thinking, Batto adds, "Fortunately, except in uninformed circles, this line of thought is now recognized for what it was, the product of a biased 'first world' mentality that regarded the rest of humanity as inferior in culture to itself."¹³ In Batto's view, the assumption that *mythos* is primitive in relation to *logos* reflects cultural imperialism, and one might add, the worst excesses of modernity, elevating one narrow model of reason as though any worldview that does not conform to it is culturally inferior.

The fourth approach identified by Segal differs from the others in that it does not view myth as an attempt to express science or history—whether true, false, ancient, or modern. Myth, in this view, is the expression of suprahistorical, universal truth regarding the experience of being human.¹⁴ The non-explanatory model of myth recognizes that myth has co-existed with primitive science and with the historical writings of antiquity, and is hence distinct from both.¹⁵ Myth, upon this understanding, serves to reconcile

9. Segal, "Myth and Ritual," 356.
10. Jung, *Memories, Dreams, and Reflection*, 373.
11. McKenzie, "God of Israel," 741.
12. Batto, *Slaying the Dragon*, 7.
13. Batto, *Slaying the Dragon*, 7.
14. Segal, "Myth and Ritual," 236.
15. Segal, "Myth and Ritual," 239.

humans to realities of life, including death, that are beyond their control. Modern authors who recovered this ancient sense of the mythopoetic included Bronislaw Malinowski, Lucien Levy-Bruhl, Claude Lévi-Strauss, Mircea Eliade, and Paul Ricoeur. These thinkers wrote for the most part in the early twentieth century as the science of modern biblical interpretation was coming into its own and meeting opposition in the form of Protestant fundamentalism and Catholicism's condemnation of Modernism.[16]

One exponent of the non-explanatory approach to myth is Claude Lévi-Strauss who characterizes myth as a dynamic form of language that exceeds the explanation of phenomena or the reconstruction of events. The author posits that, "Myth is language, functioning on an especially high level where meaning succeeds practically at 'taking off' from the linguistic ground on which it keeps rolling."[17] Lévi-Strauss's remarks suggest that myth possesses the capacity to liberate meaning from a limited attachment to particular referents as would be the case in allegory wherein particular terms correspond to realities in the world outside the text. Myth, according to this view, is not a vehicle for the delivery of predetermined meaning that could be equally-well expressed in propositional statements. Rather, it empowers truth to roll where it may. This cannot be the case for historical narrative, in a modern sense, the task of which is to reconstruct and interpret a particular event or chain of events.

David Tracy's concept of the "classic" may help to further explicate the superabundance of meaning to which Levi-Strauss refers. By the term "classic," Tracy means "a text(s), event(s), or person(s) that bear an excess of permanence of meaning, yet always resist definitive interpretation."[18] Because myth is concerned with all of history rather than a particular historical event, its universal significance can give rise to fresh interpretations as new contexts arise and elucidate new dimensions of the myth. Tracy proposes that the "classic" claims authority by virtue of its own persuasive merits, that is, by its innate capacity to captivate the imagination. In Tracy's view, "It claims authority because of the intensification of meaning."[19] Lévi-Strauss's assertion of the dynamic surplus of meaning unleashed by myth and Tracy's assertions regarding the classic find synergy in Jean-Luc Marion's notion of "saturated phenomena," that is, phenomena that exceed the interpretive capacity of reason.[20] Saturated phenomena point infinitely

---

16. Segal, "Myth and Ritual," 357.
17. Lévi-Strauss, *Critical Theory Since 1965*, 808.
18. Tracy, *Analogical Imagination*, 100.
19. Tracy, *Analogical Imagination*, 100.
20. Marion, "Erotic Phenomenon," 164; *God Without Being*, 22.

beyond themselves and their meaning cannot be exhaustively stated. They are pregnant with possibility rather than a means to recount that which has actually transpired.

If myth is saturated with meaning so as to resist definitive interpretation, then we might ask whether any reading of myth can be dismissed as a misinterpretation. The present work, after all, is highly critical of historicized interpretations of mythical narratives and motifs that undergird the Catholic Church's current presentation of the doctrine of Satan. This question underlies the hermeneutical debate concerning the relative roles of, on the one hand, reader-response, and on the other hand, the "Otherness" of the text in determining meaning. Grant Osborne identifies this tension, associating Hans-Georg Gadamer with an emphasis on reader-response, and Jürgen Habermas with an emphasis on the alterity of the text.[21] Hence, modern thinkers in the area of hermeneutics seek to negotiate a balance between the extremes of excessively subjective interpretation versus excessive rigidity that neglects the active role of the reader. In short, it might be argued, valid interpretations of myth are manifold and steeped in perspectives ranging from the psychoanalytical to the feminist, but they all recognize myth as myth. On the other hand, a reading that fails to respect the genre in question is a misinterpretation. Once, however, the interpreter recognizes myth as the expression of ubiquitous actualities and possibilities that confront the experience of being human, a mimetic relationship exists between the narrative and the reader with her life experience and concerns. This creative space between the narrative and the reader is what Ricoeur refers to as "possible worlds."[22]

RICOEUR AND THE SUPRA-HISTORICAL MODEL OF MYTH

Ricoeur views myth as the construction of an inner world within which the reader or audience can identify with existential concerns—a theatre, as it were, within which humans can stage and observe features of their existence that defy satisfactory explanation through philosophy and propositional discourse in general.

> Myth is something else than an explanation of the world, of history, and of destiny. Myth expresses in terms of the world—that

---

21. Osborne, *Hermeneutical Spiral*, 368–69; Robinson, "Paul Ricoeur and the Hermeneutics of Suspicion," 1.
22. Kearney, "Myth as the Bearer of Possible Worlds."

What Is Myth and What Kind of Truth Does It Express within the Bible? 103

is, of the other world, or the second world—the understanding that man has of himself in relation to the foundation and the limit of his experience.[23]

This statement encapsulates the understanding of myth that is advanced in the present work. Myth is not concerned with theories of causation or history. Rather, it expresses existential truths, actualities and possibilities that pertain to the experience of being human. Myth is not even a figurative account of history. Rather, it is supra-historical, expressing universally relevant truths "in terms of the world—that is, of the other world, or the second world." An individual reader's or a community's engagement with myth constructs a narrative world within which to express universal truths. As Ricoeur states, "Myth consists in giving worldly form to that which is beyond known and tangible reality."[24] There are realities, the sheer enormity of which makes them inexpressible in an analysis of ontological existence. Within the bounded, imaginal world constructed between the audience and the myth, these enormities can be approximated and expressed.

DISTINGUISHING MYTH FROM ALLEGORY, ETIOLOGY, AND LEGEND

Distancing the genre of myth from history, Ricoeur argues that time and space within the narrative arc of myth "cannot be coordinated with the time and space of history and geography."[25] Its times, spaces, and characters do not directly correspond to particular times, spaces, and characters in the world outside the myth, precisely because they correspond to the situations of all human beings in all times and spaces. Myth is not allegory whereby an author intends a direct correspondence between specific elements within the narrative and specific elements in the world beyond. This is especially important with regard to the motif of "the beginning of the world." Myth, in terms of Ricoeur's supra-historical model, is not a primitive attempt to explain the origins of the physical universe or humanity as a species. Rather, in myth, the trope of the "beginning" is a temporal metaphor signifying the universal.

Ricoeur's view of myth also distinguishes the genre from etiological stories of the "How the Leopard Got Its Spots" variety or, in a biblical context, stories that seek to explain matters such as the name of a person or a

---

23. Ricoeur, "Preface to Bultmann," 60.
24. Ricoeur, "Preface to Bultmann," 7.
25. Ricoeur, "Preface to Bultmann," 18.

place.²⁶ While etiologies seek to explain why something came to be the way it is, myth expresses rather then explains.

It might be objected that the supra-historical model of myth espoused by Ricoeur represents a modern interpretation of ancient narratives, and it cannot be assumed that the ancient authors shared this understanding. What evidence, after all, is there to show that the ancient writers of mythical narrative did not seek to figuratively represent particular events and personages? Who is to say that Cain is not modeled upon some prehistoric murderer, or that the Noah narrative does not recall some actual deluge? After all, the second-century BC mythologist Euhemerus proposed that myths are inflated, figurative reconstructions of particular events and personages so that even the gods of myth once existed as historical characters.²⁷ This argument calls for a distinction between, on the one hand, the influence of the particular and, on the other hand, the reconstruction of the particular.

Mythical narrative, like narrative of any kind, is unavoidably influenced, and even inspired, by particular experiences enshrined in individual or group memory. In a case in point, flood narratives clearly reflect the phenomenon of actual floods, whether personally experienced by the author or held in communal memory. This does not mean, however, that it is the author's intention to figuratively reconstruct these influential events, experiences, or personages. Experience is always particular, and narrative cannot but be influenced by experience. Myth, however, points to the universal and existential significance of experience and is not concerned with the historical veracity of the particular. So while, for example, the Cain and Abel narrative to some extent reflects ancient experiences of jealousy, violence, and murder, the narrative as we have it in Genesis is not a reflection upon the particularities of a given act of fratricide so much as an expression of universal realities including the inscrutability of good fortune whereby the world, the fates, or the divine appears to favor one person over another, stirring up murderous envy in the hearts of some less fortunate.

In contrast with myth, figurative narrative that reflects a kernel of historicity, greatly amplified and stylized by the narrative form, might be classified as legend. This suggestion reflects Hermann Gunkel's use of the term "legend" in relation to the Book of Genesis. Gunkel, a pioneer of form criticism, recognized that the narratives of Genesis do not constitute history in a modern sense. However, he allowed for the possibility that the legend might reflect specific historical events and personages, immortalized in the oral traditions. "Other legends reflect historic events or situations, and in

---

26. Kipling, "How the Leopard Got His Spots"; Barthush, *Understanding Dan*.
27. Brown, "Euhemerus and the Historians," 259.

What Is Myth and What Kind of Truth Does It Express within the Bible?

such cases it was the duty of the narrator to bring out these references clearly enough to satisfy his well-informed hearer."[28] Gunkel's interpretation of the early part of Genesis as legends that expound upon particular historical events is quite distinct from Ricoeur's model of myth as an expression of the universal.

MYTH AND THE SUBCONSCIOUS

In Ricoeur's view, myth utilizes poetic language so as to open us to consciousness of that which is usually subconscious. Endorsing this poetic view of myth, James Dunn posits that myth enables the "expression of a whole area of human experience and awareness of universal values and truths, that can only be presented in symbolic language."[29] For Dunn, the kind of truth that myth is especially well-suited to relate is truth that lingers on the brink of the subconscious. "Myth is the natural and indispensable intermediate stage between unconscious and conscious cognition."[30] This suggests that myth is not an option so much as a necessity in order to express realities that make their presence felt beneath the threshold of consciousness. Myth, according to this poetic view, can evoke and express what other genres cannot. Ricoeur asserts

> My deepest conviction is that poetic language alone restores to us that participation in or belonging-to an order of things which precedes our capacity to oppose ourselves to things taken as objects opposed to a subject. Hence the function of poetic discourse is to bring about this emergence of a depth-structure of belonging-to amid the ruins of descriptive discourse.[31]

This once more emphasizes Ricoeur's position that myth is not a figurative way to explain causes or recount history. It is, rather, an expression of that in which we are saturated and otherwise unable to objectify in thought or word. It allows us to pounce upon ourselves, so as to fleetingly grasp and express our deep relatedness to the world before the critically-conscious self objectifies the world in opposition to itself. Critical consciousness objectifies the world largely by positing causal relationships. Hence, in order for myth to function as the kind of expression envisaged by Ricoeur, it cannot

---

28. Gunkel, *Legends of Genesis*, 75.
29. Dunn, "Demythologizing," 287.
30. Dunn, "Demythologizing," 287.
31. Ricoeur, "Toward a Hermeneutic of Revelation," 1–37.

be an account of cause and effect. Rather, myth is the trapdoor that allows us to go deep and dark, glimpsing the cellar rats before they scatter.

Ricoeur does not regard recourse to myth as a substitute for rational thought, proposing that "The symbol gives rise to thought."[32] Lewis Mudge, paraphrasing Ricoeur, proposes, "symbolic, metaphorical, mythological language *gives* us the capacity to bring experiences of a certain kind to awareness."[33] Mythical language can dredge up from the depths a sense of "belonging" or interrelatedness in the world. Significantly, Ricoeur states that mythical language does its work amidst the "ruins of descriptive discourse."[34] It functions where descriptive, propositional prose fails. Myth can express that which philosophical propositions cannot. As Mudge remarks, "Myth contains more than philosophy can comprehend."[35] Mythical language and motifs articulate experiences that may be largely inexpressible in other registers of language. That which is beyond the comprehension of philosophy, and which usually evades conscious thought must be something other than the history of particular events and persons.

Once more emphasizing the capacity of myth to dredge up that which is usually unconscious, Richard Bell proposes, "Myth is, so to speak, the vertical going down into the layers of reality."[36] Also suggesting a distinctive role of myth, far from that of historical discourse, Joseph Campbell regards the genre as operating on the very limits of language, at the point beyond which words can no longer function. "Mythology is not a lie, mythology is poetry, it is metaphorical. It has been well said that mythology is the penultimate truth—penultimate because the ultimate cannot be put into words. It is beyond words."[37] Campbell's reference to "penultimate" truth alludes to the sense in which myth may come closer than other genres to expressing ultimate truth, but even myth cannot do so in an exhaustive fashion.

MYTHICAL LANGUAGE ENGAGES THE MYSTERY OF EVIL

One existential reality that towers defiantly over the "ruins of descriptive discourse" is that of evil.[38] Propositional discourse lies in ruins in the sense

32. Ricoeur, *Symbolism of Evil*, 15.
33. Mudge, "Introduction," iv.
34. Mudge, "Introduction," iv.
35. Mudge, "Introduction," iii.
36. Bell, *Deliver Us from Evil*, 172.
37. Campbell, *Power of Myth*, 163.
38. Ricoeur, "Toward a Hermeneutic of Revelation," 37.

that it cannot adequately explain evil. To state the obvious and tragic, there is no equivalent of "How the Leopard got his Spots" that satisfactorily explains why we must experience evil, suffering, sickness, and death. Whereas narrative cannot explain these enormities, it can express them—or perhaps more accurately, it can express our plight as we grapple with the inexplicable.

Richard Kearney characterizes Ricoeur as arguing that the distinctive capacity of myth to express the otherwise inexpressible is particularly pronounced in relation to evil. "From the beginning, Ricoeur recognized evil as an experience which could not be adequately dealt with by the human cogito or intentional consciousness."[39] Rather than suggesting that we cannot think rationally about evil, Ricoeur suggests that the symbolism of myth can allow us access to a level of consciousness from which our critical thinking can then proceed. That is, we may proceed from myth to phenomenological and analytical thinking. "When confronted with evil," Kearney proposes, "we are reminded that there are meanings and experiences that defy the transparency of consciousness and contravene our will."[40] Kearney's reference to meanings and experiences that "defy the transparency of consciousness" suggests an epistemological opaqueness that repels conscious thought. Ominous experiences resist the light that thinking, at the level of our usual consciousness, might otherwise shed upon them. Thus, Kearney characterizes Ricoeur's sense of evil as a liminal experience, on the cusp of language and consciousness.

MYTH AS A SYMBOLIC WORLDVIEW AND "SPECIES OF SYMBOLS"

Ricoeur speaks of myth, not only with reference to particular narratives such as those of Gilgamesh, Enuma Elish, or Adam and Eve, but more broadly with reference to a "species of symbols" derived from such narratives.[41] These mythical symbols color a worldview and infuse texts that would properly be characterized as instantiating genres other than myth. Hence, mythical motifs may be found at work in apocalyptic texts, gospels, poetry, and even in catechisms.

A biblical text of any genre may be influenced, implicitly or explicitly, by a mythic worldview. In a case in point, when in Luke 10:18–19, Jesus is depicted as saying "I saw Satan fall like lightning from Heaven," this invokes a mythical motif. Jesus, it might be said, is portrayed as speaking mythically,

39. Kearney, "On the Hermeneutics of Evil," 197.
40. Kearney, "On the Hermeneutics of Evil," 198.
41. Ricoeur, *Symbolism of Evil*, 15.

possibly appropriating texts such as Isaiah 14, Psalm 89, and the *Book of the Watchers*.[42] This is not however to say that the author of Luke's gospel employed the literary genre of myth as narrative form.

This broad use of the term myth signifies what some authors denote by *mythos*, often contrasting this worldview and symbol-system with *logos*, a paradigm rooted in causal relationships. Karen Armstrong, for example, explores this distinction in her account of the development of images of God.[43] Armstrong suggests that a hallmark of fundamentalism is that it tends to interpret *mythos* as though it were *logos*. Armstrong effectively suggests that fundamentalism confuses the symbolic for the explanatory. Such confusion may be exemplified when the Adamic myth is interpreted as an etiological account of a particular event whereby sin and death entered the world thanks to the misdeeds of particular persons.

One further remark may be appropriate concerning a use of the term "myth" to denote more than a literary genre. Jean-François Lyotard defined the postmodern perspective as one characterized by "incredulity to metanarratives."[44] Lyotard's reference to metanarratives implies totalizing worldviews. The idea of narrative as worldview is implicit in Lindbeck's account of intratextuality whereby the author argues that biblical narrative can serve as a lens through which to interpret the world.[45] This notion of narrative as lens is on a par with the use of the term "mythos" or the "mythopoetic" to describe a worldview. In both cases, a literary form is invoked in an allegorical sense so as to denote a perspective on the world.

MYTH ADAPTED TO HENOTHEISM AND MONOTHEISM

Ricoeur's definition of myth does not confine the genre to stories about a multiplicity of gods and goddesses. As Pauline Viviano notes, myth need not necessary endorse polytheism, and can hence be recognized in the henotheistic and monotheistic contexts of the Hebrew scriptures.[46] Similarly, John Hayward comments that in rejecting polytheism, Israelite religion by no means rejected myth.[47] Rather, according to Hayward, writing from a confessional, Christian perspective, the ancient Jews "advanced it, and from

---

42. Torre and Hernandez, *Quest for the Historical Satan*, 767; Pagels, *Origin of Satan*, 55.

43. Armstrong, *Battle for God*, xvi, xvii, 49, 447.

44. Lyotard, *La Condition Postmoderne*, 67.

45. Lindbeck, *Nature of Doctrine*, 117.

46. Viviano, "Genesis," 37.

47. Hayward, "Uses of Myth in an Age of Science," 67.

What Is Myth and What Kind of Truth Does It Express within the Bible? 109

the point of view of our own worldview, they purified it."[48] In the Judeo-Christian tradition, myth is primarily concerned with the expression of truth that applies to the lives of human beings rather than gods, goddesses, or, for that matter, demons.

THE QUESTION OF MYTH IN THE BIBLE

Resistance to the identification of biblical narrative as mythical in itself or informed by mythical motifs may reflect understandings of myth as signifying either primitive naivete, polytheism, or sheer fallacy. Pope Pius XII in his 1950 encyclical *Humani Generis* concedes that the human authors of Genesis may have drawn upon oral or textual sources but insists that divine inspiration rendered any such use of sources inerrant.

> If, however, the ancient sacred writers have taken anything from popular narrations (and this may be conceded), it must never be forgotten that they did so with the help of divine inspiration, through which they were rendered immune from any error in selecting and evaluating those documents.[49]

The encyclical regards myth as an imaginative indulgence rather than a means of expressing truth:

> Therefore, whatever of the popular narrations have been inserted into the Sacred Scriptures must in no way be considered on a par with myths or other such things, which are more the product of an extravagant imagination than of that striving for truth and simplicity which in the Sacred Books, also of the Old Testament, is so apparent that our ancient sacred writers must be admitted to be clearly superior to the ancient profane writers.[50]

While acknowledging that the biblical authors drew upon earlier texts and traditions, the encyclical is at pains to distinguish between the biblical text and "myths or other such things, which are more the product of an extravagant imagination than of that striving for truth."[51] This distinction implies that once material was incorporated into the scriptures, it ceased to be mythical. This may reflect the position that the narratives of Israelite religion are predominantly historical, standing in contrast with the narratives

---

48. Hayward, "Uses of Myth in an Age of Science," 67.
49. Pius XII, *"Humani Generis"* 38.
50. Pius XII, *"Humani Generis"* 39.
51. Pius XII, *"Humani Generis"* 39.

of other ancient peoples.[52] James Barr, for example, has argued that a hallmark of the Judeo-Christian tradition has been the belief that God acted and spoke in *history*. However, both Barr and Langdon Gilkey have wondered what becomes of the tradition's foundational faith in the deeds of God, acting in history, if modern biblical theology no longer regards the narratives in question as historical by genre.[53] When what were once regarded as the theophanies of the Old Testament are read in a figurative manner, where then are the acts of God in history? One response may be that God acts in all of history, sustaining history itself, rather than intervening sporadically.

J. J. M. Roberts challenges the extent to which the narratives of Israel have been regarded as more historical and less mythical than other Ancient Near Eastern texts, remarking that "the contrast between myth in the extrabiblical ancient near east, and history in Israel has been overstated."[54] The henotheistic and monotheistic worldviews of ancient Israel give rise to narratives in which the agency of human characters is more dominant than that of gods, goddesses and other supernatural beings. Such tropes are by no means entirely absent from the narratives, as is evident in references to angels, though they may be intended as figurative personas or serve literary purposes other than an assertion of their ontological existence.

The relatively anthropocentric nature of Israel's narratives, and an ongoing concern for the political theme of Israel's nationhood, may have contributed to an underestimation of the role of myth in these texts. John McKenzie, however, writing in *The New Jerome Biblical Commentary* acknowledges that "The use of mythical language and imagery in the OT has long been recognized."[55] Bernard Batto concurs, arguing that even the ostensibly historical narratives of the Hebrew Bible are characterized by mythical elements, so that the Exodus narrative, for example, is infused with mythical symbolism.[56] McKenzie views the denial of the existence of myth in the Old Testament as indicative of an association of myth with polytheism. "It has become clear that the denial of mythology in the OT implies a questionable definition of myth as essentially polytheistic and false."[57]

It could be argued that the New Testament itself is, at points, informed by a model of myth as fallacy, and is hence dismissive of myth as an

---

52. Lincoln, *Theorizing Myth*.

53. Barr, "Revelation in the Old Testament," 68; Gilkey, "Cosmology, Ontology," 194–205.

54. Roberts, "Myth versus History," 1–13.

55. McKenzie, "Aspects of Old Testament Thought," 740–41.

56. Batto, *Slaying the Dragon*, 1.

57. McKenzie, "Aspects of Old Testament Thought," 740.

What Is Myth and What Kind of Truth Does It Express within the Bible?

expression of truth. As James Dunn notes, the term myth arises five times in the New Testament (1 Tim 1:4; 4:7; 2 Tim 4:4; Titus 1:14; 2 Peter 1:16). Each time, the biblical authors essentially refer dismissively to myth as though it is unsuited to the mediation of divine revelation. However, as Dunn clarifies, the understanding of myth that is being rejected is that of polytheistic stories associated with non-Christian religion. "For these writers, myths are invented and untrue stories, whether Hellenistic speculations about divine emanations or more Jewish speculative interpretations of OT stories. . . . What is rejected here, however, is only one genre of myth. The question of whether other levels of myth and of mythological thinking are present in the NT is neither posed nor answered."[58] Hence, the sacred authors are not rejecting the presence of myth in the sense envisaged by Ricoeur's suprahistorical model.

Related to this antipathy towards myth as exhibited by New Testament writers, Jeffrey Burton Russell identifies a similar suspicion of the genre on the part of the Patristics. Russell notes the unwillingness of Patristic thinkers to admit the presence of myth within the canon of scripture, or the influence of extracanonical myths upon the biblical text. Justin Martyr, on Russell's reading, regarded myths as "inspired by demons to mock Christ and to make people believe that Christians were merely copying the pagan gods."[59] This association of myth with demonic deception, or at least the residue of this association, may help to explain the magisterium's apparent reluctance to acknowledge the mythical nature of biblical motifs of Satan. More broadly, the position that myths are inspired by demons may have done little to foment the Church's recognition of myth as a medium of divine revelation, awakening in humans a deep engagement with the mystery of God.[60]

MYTH AS A MEDIUM OF REVELATION

Richard Bell goes so far as to propose that myth serves as the primary literary form through which divine revelation is mediated, though its implications clearly prevail beyond the narrative arc of myth.[61] "Now Christian Revelation comes to us primarily *via myth* though it is not contained *in it*."[62] Bell's use of the term "myth," in this regard, denotes a worldview and register of

58. Dunn, "Demythologizing," 288.
59. Russell, *Satan*, 70, 74–75.
60. Russell, *Satan*, 74–75
61. Bell, *Deliver Us from Evil*, 172.
62. Bell, *Deliver Us from Evil*, 172.

language as well as a particular literary form, since it would be difficult to defend the assertion that the majority of texts in the bible and the Christian tradition are mythical by genre. Most notably, the gospels are not generally regarded as mythical by genre, if for no other reason than that "gospel" is itself a genre—a proclamation of good news. Gospels may, however, reflect a mythic worldview, infused with the symbolism of the Hebrew Bible. Supporting our point that myth represents a worldview, symbol-system, and register of language as well as mythical narratives per se, Bernard Batto remarks "Myth permeates virtually every layer of the Biblical tradition from the earliest to the latest."[63]

CATHOLIC BIBLICAL COMMENTARIES AND HERMENEUTICS OF MYTH

The *Jerome Biblical Commentary* and the *New Jerome Biblical Commentary* both carry the *imprimatur*, a statement from a Catholic bishop or the major superior of a religious order, assuring the reader that the contents are not in contradiction with the Church's teaching. The *Jerome Biblical Commentary* published in 1968 was granted the imprimatur by Lawrence Cardinal Sheehan, Archbishop of Baltimore, while the *New Jerome Biblical Commentary* published in 1990 was granted the imprimatur by Reverend William J. Kane, the Vicar General of the Archdiocese of Washington. In both volumes, McKenzie acknowledges the presence of myth in the canon of scripture and offers an understanding of the genre that is consistent with that proposed by Ricoeur.

McKenzie quotes Ernst Cassirer who regards myth as a "symbolic form of expression together with art, language and science."[64] Whereas myths undoubtedly include symbolic objects such as trees, fires, and floods, McKenzie also identifies the symbolism of myth with action. "The symbol easiest to employ and to grasp is the symbol of personal activity."[65] Stories taken as a whole, and the agency of personal characters serve as symbols. Yet, myth is not history and its symbols, including its characters, are not historical.[66] The narrative world of the myth creates an eternal now, not limited to a representation of any particular time and place. McKenzie distinguishes between the symbols employed in myth, and the transcendent

---

63. Batto, *Slaying the Dragon*, 1.

64. Cassirer, *Language and Myth*, 8; McKenzie, "Aspects of Old Testament Thought," 77.

65. McKenzie, "Aspects of Old Testament Thought," 77.

66. McKenzie, "Aspects of Old Testament Thought," 77.

reality to which the symbol points. "It does not pretend that symbol is the reality, but it proposes the symbol as that which affords an insight into a reality beyond understanding."[67] Hence, McKenzie concurs with Ricoeur's understanding of myth as symbolic narrative that seeks to express deep, universally-applicable truths that evade other forms of expression, rather than a figurative means to recount historical particularities.

CONCLUSION

If myth is defined strictly in terms of the narratives of polytheism or equated with the primitive and fallacious, it is then understandable that Christians would resent its application to the biblical text. Thinkers such as Paul Ricoeur, however, regard myth as the use of narratives and motifs to express universal human experiences, including the harsh realities of suffering, evil, and death, creating narrative worlds in which to imaginatively play out possible scenarios. Such a model of myth distinguishes the genre from primitive attempts to document history or science and from etiological stories that offer primitive explanations as to why the world is as it is. Ricoeur's non-explanatory account of myth informs the model of the genre adopted in this book. The genre of myth can express truths in relation to the God-human relationship that cannot be as adequately expressed in other genres. The propositional language of theology, doctrine, catechisms, and philosophy can expound upon the truth of myth but cannot effectively replace it. Posing a challenge for doctrinal appropriations of mythical language, myth is not simply a vehicle to illustrate a given premise but a multivalent narrative, saturated in meaning so as to provoke ever-new and challenging interpretations.

---

67. McKenzie, "Aspects of Old Testament Thought," 77.

8

The Doctrine of Satan Entangled in a Conflict about Magisterial Authority

This book has so far endeavored to build a case that Catholic doctrine should, according to the Church's own teaching, be open to critical engagement with compelling insights of modernity and, in particular, the insights of modern biblical scholarship in relation to the genre of myth. Why, it might be asked, is such an argument even necessary? Why has the inconsistency arisen whereby the religious tradition must be persuaded to hold true to its own teachings on the responsible interpretation of its own sacred texts?

One might argue that a dynamic, evolving tradition with a wide array of formally defined doctrines is bound to give rise to some degree of inconsistency as an inevitable delay ensues between a development in one area of doctrine and the full realization of its implications for related areas. In a case in point, it might be said that the doctrinal implications of the Church's acknowledgment of the compatibility of the theory of evolution and Catholic doctrine have yet to be digested in their entirety, for example, in relation to the doctrine of the Fall.[1] Posing a further challenge, modern biblical scholarship continues to propose new interpretations of particular passages and doctrinal formulae may hence lag behind the latest scholarly insight—no matter how compelling it might be.

---

1. Pius XII, "*Humani Generis*" 36.

The Church's anachronistic presentation of the doctrine of Satan, however, is not an innocent delay in realizing the full implications of hermeneutical developments that have been officially embraced by the Church for some seventy years. Rather, the doctrine of Satan was seized upon by a pope as an opportunity to assert the authority of the magisterium, in the narrowest sense of that term, over and against the insights of modern biblical scholarship, theology, and academic research more broadly.

In 1972, a clearly exasperated Pope Paul VI preached a homily in which he regarded modern insights and influences as satanic insofar as they challenged certainty in the current teachings of the Church. Perhaps not surprisingly, the pontiff's subsequent reflections on the subject of Satan did not embrace modern scholarship on the theological and scriptural underpinnings of the doctrine. In this reactionary mode, Paul VI insisted upon Satan's existence as a supernatural being and rejected an understanding of Satan as a figurative personification. Subsequently, Popes St. John Paul II and Pope Benedict XVI would each in their own distinctive way prove reluctant to embrace open dialogue with the modern world or to recognize that its insights can contribute to a valid development of doctrine. The doctrine of Satan has hence languished, the magisterium being unwilling to walk back Paul VI's reactionary tirade, and theologians, for the most part, giving the doctrine a wide berth.

HUMANAE VITAE AND THE QUESTIONING OF AUTHORITY

Following the death of Pope St. John XXIII in 1963, his successor, Pope Paul VI supported the continuation of the Second Vatican Council, three out of the four sessions taking place during his pontificate. However, in 1964, between the third and fourth sessions of the Council, Pope Paul insisted that four issues were not open for conciliar discussion: priestly celibacy, the reform of the Roman Curia, papal infallibility, and artificial birth control.[2]

James Carroll views Paul VI's exercise of papal authority in relation to birth control, as a "dark line" that appeared on the blue horizon of Vatican II.[3] Carroll notes that when Pope Paul precluded the Council's discussion of artificial birth control, "The conservative minority of the fathers welcomed this abrupt manifestation of papal power, but most bishops were deeply unsettled by it."[4] Carroll proceeds to recount that "episcopal protests were

2. Carroll, *Practicing Catholic*, 163–91.
3. Carroll, *Practicing Catholic*, 163–91.
4. Carroll, *Practicing Catholic*, 164.

openly lodged in the nave of the great basilica. These mitered men knew better than anyone what was at stake, both in the pope's violation of the implicit contract of co-responsibility, and in the now proscribed issue itself."[5]

Cardinal Suenens likened the Pope's decision to a great tragedy in the history of the Church. "I beg you my brother bishops, let us avoid a new 'Galileo affair.' One is enough for the Church."[6] Pope Paul, however, sought to honor a precedent set by the 1930 encyclical, *Casti Connubii* which had pitted the modern phenomenon of the rubber condom against what it considered timeless truth.[7] While the newly available rubber condom may have brought the issue of artificial birth control to a head, *Casti Connubii* had condemned all forms of artificial contraception.[8] As Carroll puts it, "Birth Control became a point of institutional loyalty, like devotion to the Blessed Virgin Mary."[9] Artificial birth control, it might be argued, represented for the magisterium, a clearly identifiable way in which science and the modern world in general posed a threat to its authority.

The birth control controversy exacerbated differences between the ecclesiology of the relatively progressive majority of Council Fathers and that of the ultra-conservative minority. Avery Dulles, writing in 1968, acknowledged the polarization that was occurring, and the potential for long-term damage.

> As every thinking Catholic is aware, the present polarization of opinion regarding the encyclical *Human Life* has created a dangerous situation in the church. Enthusiastic proponents of the papal position, using repressive measures in order to enforce a consensus, might unwittingly detonate a widespread revolt among intellectual Catholics, both clerical and lay. On the other hand, opponents of the encyclical, by speaking in an intemperate way, might undermine the respect that ought to be given to the teaching office in the church. In the long run, both these courses of action would produce harmful effects.[10]

Dulles regards both heavy-handed enforcement, and rash rebellion as destructive in their effects upon the Church.

The dispute concerned process as much as substance. The epideictic tone of the Council seems to have given rise to an expectation of greater

---

5. Carroll, *Practicing Catholic*, 164.
6. Hebblethwaite, *Paul VI*, 394, quoted in Carroll, *Practicing Catholic*, 164.
7. Pius XI, "*Casti Connubii.*"
8. Wills, *Papal Sin*, 77.
9. Carroll, *Practicing Catholic*, 166.
10. Dulles, "Karl Rahner on *Humanae Vitae.*"

collegiality in relation to the exercise of magisterial authority. Germain Grisez, a moral theologian who remains committed to the ban on artificial contraception, believes that false expectations had arisen regarding the advisory role of the largely lay commission on birth control. Grisez opines, "It would help the Church now if people had a more sound notion of what actually did happen—an understanding of Paul VI's actual mentality, wanting to study the question without wanting to hand over his authority."[11] Grisez suggests that Paul's appointment of a commission to study the issue of birth control evolved into something that the pontiff had never intended. Grisez asserts, regarding a leak of the commission's draft recommendations, that, "when the documents were leaked in 1967, Paul VI was extremely upset about it. He sent a letter to all the bishops and cardinals who were on the commission, about the documents. It wasn't what he had in mind at all."[12] What transpired was a clash of expectations. The epideictic style of Vatican II had created a climate in which it would be more difficult to effectively exercise papal authority in an apparently unilateral manner.

Even before the publication of *Humanae vitae*, F. X. Murphy observed the troubled disposition of Paul VI.

> The Pope was a man obviously torn by doubts, tormented by scruples, haunted by thoughts of perfection, and above all dominated by an exaggerated concern—some called it an obsession—about the prestige of his office as Pope. His remarks on this score at times displayed an almost messianic fervor, a note missing in the more sedate utterances of his predecessors. His innumerable statements on the subject were made on almost every occasion, from casual week-day audiences or Sunday sermons from the window of his apartment, to the most solemn gatherings in season and out of season.[13]

Murphy detects a preoccupation, not so much with birth control or the other reproductive issues to be addressed in *Humanae Vitae*, as with the issue of papal authority. The author alludes to a strategy on the part of the minority of ultra-conservative Council Fathers to leverage issues, so as to accuse the more progressive majority of disloyalty towards the pope. "Since it was part of the strategy of the [conciliar] minority to accuse the majority of disloyalty toward the Holy Father, Paul's constant harping inevitably

---

11. Mann, "New Documents."
12. Mann, "New Documents."
13. Murphy, *Vatican Council II*, 94.

caused the majority to think that he perhaps did share these misgivings, at least to a certain extent."[14]

This alleged strategy on the part of those who had been the embittered minority did not lack probable cause. In 1964, Paul VI had appointed Cardinal Ottaviani as prefect of the birth control commission. Ottaviani's ultra-conservative plans for the Council had been consistently rebuffed by the relatively progressive majority of Council Fathers. During the debate on liturgy, the cardinal exceeded his allotted fifteen minutes to speak, and his microphone was turned off. The installation of an electronic sound system in St. Peter's Basilica could be regarded as quite symbolic of the endeavor for the Church to benefit from modernity so that its message could be heard anew. Ottaviani walked out of the Council and did not return for two weeks.[15] As prefect of the commission on birth control, Ottaviani was again in a minority position, greatly outnumbered by those laity, theologians, and bishops who advocated for an end to the ban on artificial contraception.

Kenneth Whitehead reproaches the bishops who, he believes, "tolerated dissent and thus fostered widespread disloyalty within the Church."[16] Many of these bishops had numbered among the Council majority that had resisted attempts by the curia to constrain conciliar discussions. In a similar vein, Vincent Foy condemns the positions of Karl Rahner and Bernard Lonergan who were critical of the encyclical.[17] Cardinal Journet in Switzerland wrote, "It does not make sense for a son of the church to oppose the authority of the church."[18] While it was clearly not the only divisive issue in the postconciliar Church, Andrew Greely regarded the papal ban on artificial birth control as a watershed event.[19] Greeley asserts,

> The encyclical *Humanae Vitae*, issued in the summer of 1968, is the most important event of the last twenty-five years of Catholic history. . . . Unlike the changes of the Vatican Council, which had only marginal impact on the lives of the Catholic laity, the encyclical endeavored to reach into the bedroom of every Catholic married couple in the world.[20]

Greeley suggests that the encyclical made a greater impact on married Catholics, than had the entire proceedings of the Council, observing in a

14. Murphy, *Vatican Council II*, 94.
15. Argan, "Vatican II"; Tobin, *Good Pope*, 190,
16. Whitehead, "How Dissent Became Institutionalized," 18–20.
17. Foy, "*Humanae Vitae* and Canada."
18. Seidler and Meyer, *Conflict and Change in the Catholic Church*, 99.
19. Greely, *American Catholic*, 104.
20. Greeley, *Catholic Myth*, 91.

US context that "Many of the most devout Catholics (especially of Irish and Polish backgrounds) for the first time deliberately disobeyed the pope."[21] Their disobedience and that of priests, bishops, medics, and scientists, to the nostrils of Paul VI, reeked of the smoke of Satan.

PAUL VI'S MODERNIST CRISIS AND THE SMOKE OF SATAN

On June 29, 1972, the Solemnity of the Holy Apostles, Peter and Paul, a beleaguered Pope Paul VI delivered a homily in which he asserted that, "from some fissure, the smoke of Satan has entered the temple of God."[22] The Holy Father characterized the Church of 1972 as plagued with doubt. He argued that trust in the teaching office of the Church seemed to have been replaced with trust in new theories and movements. In a remark poignantly reminiscent of the image of the Council as "opening the windows to the world," Paul VI commented that "Doubt has entered our consciences, and it entered by windows that should have been open to the light."[23] George Weigel approvingly attributes a comment to Michael Novak, appropriating the image of the windows opened to the world. "The blinds were raised and the windows opened just as the train entered a dark tunnel full of toxic gases."[24] It is not quite clear whether the poisonous gases correspond to the modern world, elements within it, or otherworldly, satanic influences as identified by Pope Paul VI.[25]

Weigel polemically dismisses the Council's desire for conversation with the entire human family, implying that there is something sinful about wanting to open the Church to dialogue with modernity. Criticizing what he calls "Catholic Presentitus," that is, a postconciliar concern for relevance in the modern world, Weigel charges that "Its originating image, some might say its original sin—was to imagine Vatican II as the Council that 'opened the Church's windows to the modern world' in order to initiate a dialogue with secular modernity."[26] Granted the analogy of opening the windows to the world, though apocryphally attributed to Pope John XXIII, evades attempts to source it precisely. However, when Weigel implies it is sinful to imagine that the Council opened the Church's proverbial windows to the

21. Greeley, *Catholic Myth*, 91.
22. Paul VI, "Mass on the Ninth Anniversary"; McClarey, "Pope Paul VI."
23. Paul VI, "Mass on the Ninth Anniversary."
24. Weigel, *Evangelical Catholicism*, 11.
25. Paul VI, "Mass on the Ninth Anniversary."
26. Weigel, *Evangelical Catholicism*, 102.

modern world in order to initiate a dialogue with secular modernity, his position is difficult to reconcile with the manner in which *Gaudium et Spes* explicitly mandates conversation with the "entire human family," and seeks to benefit from "the progress of the sciences, and the treasures hidden in the various forms of human culture."[27]

Paul VI's "smoke of Satan" homily proceeded to chide modern science for undermining faith, lamenting that "science exists to give us truths that do not separate from God, but make us seek him all the more and celebrate him with greater intensity; instead, science gives us criticism and doubt."[28] The pope's choice of words implies that scientists should actively seek to present findings that bolster religious faith and even implying that more challenging findings should be avoided. In counterpoint, it might be argued that truth cannot, by definition, separate humanity from God who is Truth. Paul VI's injunction might have been more deservedly aimed at the manner in which discoveries by the empirical sciences can be mistakenly interpreted as evidence militating against (or for) belief in God, in effect reducing God to some empirical artifact. Such is the folly of scientism, and Paul VI might have been well justified in critiquing this trespass by empirical science into questions of meaning that lie well beyond the scope of empirical inquiry.

Paul's critique of science is too sweepingly vague to address the real challenge of scientism and continues in an intemperate and scathing manner, complaining that scientists have fomented uncertainty. In a tone approaching mimicry, Paul exclaims "I don't know, we don't know, we cannot know."[29] The pontiff's grievance appears to be that science, in a broad and undifferentiated sense, has called into question that which has previously been assumed to be true. His characterization of the situation is ambiguous since there is a world of difference between the two stances he invokes, "we don't know" and "we *cannot* know."

In a remark suggesting deep cynicism towards purported progress, Paul VI laments that "Progress is celebrated, only so that it can then be demolished with revolutions that are more radical and more strange, so as to negate everything that has been achieved, and to come away as primitives after having so exalted the advances of the modern world."[30] The reference to primitives suggests pessimism, as though the progress in question is illusory and leads to degeneration rather than advancement.

27. Paul VI, "*Gaudium et Spes*" 3, 44.
28. McClarey, "Pope Paul VI."
29. McClarey, "Pope Paul VI."
30. McClarey, "Pope Paul VI."

The pontiff does not appear to be speaking of the form of destruction that is ultimately constructive, that is, Joseph Schumpeter's notion of "creative destruction" whereby new insights and developments render older ones obsolete.[31] Neither does Pope Paul's rhetoric seem to reflect Thomas Kuhn's argument in his 1962 work, *The Structure of Scientific Revolutions*, with regard to the manner in which a new paradigm can supplant the assumptions of a previous one.[32] Rather, Paul's words suggest the fear of the integralist—that if any thread of the tradition is picked at, the entire tapestry might come undone.[33]

Wistfully, Pope Paul lamented, "There was the belief that after the Council there would be a day of sunshine for the history of the Church. Instead, it is the arrival of a day of clouds, of tempest, of darkness, of research, of uncertainty."[34] The statement carries apocalyptic undertones in its imagery of light, darkness, and clouds and, notably, the pontiff associates research with darkness and turbulence.

The "smoke of Satan" homily expresses a yearning for the consoling effects of a faith whereby the interpretation of scripture is harmonized with the exercise of reason. "Faith gives us certainty and security, when it is based on the word of God accepted and found consenting with our very own reason and with our own human soul."[35] This harmonization of our reading of scripture with our reasoning could amount to either a well-reasoned approach to scripture, or else, a restricted exercise of reason that never challenges prevailing interpretations of scripture. In this context, Paul VI is extoling the "certainty and security" offered by faith, rather than its searching, questioning dimension, so it may be a restricted use of reason that the Pope longingly endorses.

Paul VI identifies what he believes to be the underlying cause of the wave of postconciliar doubt that he detects, stating that "there has been an intervention of an adverse power. Its name is the devil."[36] Pope Paul expounds upon this assertion, stating, "We believe in something that is preternatural that has come into the world precisely to disturb, to suffocate the fruits of the Ecumenical Council, and to impede the Church from breaking into the hymn of joy at having renewed in fullness its awareness of itself."[37]

31. Schumpeter, *Capitalism, Socialism and Democracy*, 82–85.
32. Kuhn, *Structure of Scientific Revolutions*.
33. Daly, *Transcendence and Immanence*, 141.
34. Paul VI, "Mass on the Ninth Anniversary."
35. Paul VI, "Mass on the Ninth Anniversary."
36. Paul VI, "Mass on the Ninth Anniversary."
37. Paul VI, "Mass on the Ninth Anniversary."

The pontiff suggests that the implementation of Vatican II, as he would like to have seen it unfold, had been sabotaged by the devil.

Pope Paul VI's "smoke of Satan" homily does not imply that the Second Vatican Council itself was in any sense a satanic ploy. When Paul VI laments that darkness entered the Church through windows that should have admitted light, the pontiff regards the smoke of Satan as something that counteracts the benefits offered by the Council. The pontiff views the smoke of Satan as distinct from and opposed to the true fruits of the Council, implying that certain postconciliar trends were not so much a valid implementation of the teachings of the Council as diabolical sabotage. Pope Paul's vitriol reflects a long tradition of evoking the motif of Satan in response to perceived treachery, polarization, and apostasy.[38] Polarization in this life, to some religious sensibilities, reflects a cosmic conflict.

On November 15, 1972, some fourteen weeks after his "smoke of Satan" homily associating modern scholarly research and debate with Satanic influences, Pope Paul VI asserted with regard to the doctrine of Satan that "evil is not simply a force in the background but rather truly present, a living being who is spiritual, perverse and who renders perverse."[39] Having described Satan as a "living being," the pontiff situates this assertion in the context of a biblical and Christian worldview.

> It is a departure from the picture provided by biblical and Church teaching to refuse to acknowledge the Devil's existence; to regard him as a self-sustaining principle who, unlike other creatures, does not owe his origin to God; or to explain the Devil as a pseudo-reality, a conceptual and fanciful personification of the unknown causes of our misfortunes.[40]

The question arises as to whether Paul VI sought to make a first-order truth claim or rather to exhort faithfulness to the aesthetics of a particular tradition. Such a distinction is reminiscent of the one forged by Pope St. John XXIII between the eternal truths that constitute doctrine, and the way in which these truths are formulated so as to speak to a given age. "The substance of the ancient doctrine of the deposit of faith is one thing, and the way in which it is presented is another."[41] In this instance, the argument might proceed, Pope Paul is lamenting a departure from a traditional presentation of the faith informed by biblical and traditional imagery, rather than directly asserting the ontological existence of Satan as a particular creature.

---

38. Pagels, *Origin of Satan*, 48.
39. Tornielli, "To What Extent?"
40. Paul VI, "Deliver Us from Evil."
41. John XXIII, *Gaudet Mater Ecclesia.*

Indeed, it might be ventured that Paul VI's allusion to the "smoke" of Satan is clearly figurative—at least in its invocation of smoke. However, it does not seem plausible that the Pope's vehemence is intended to make a purely aesthetic point, merely insisting that Catholics continue to invoke traditional imagery and language. The pontiff's November 15 reference to Satan as a "living being" suggests a first order, ontological assertion as opposed to adherence to the aesthetics of a particular tradition. Some months before, in his "smoke of Satan" homily of June 29, he had asserted that something "preternatural" had come into the world to disturb faith. Pope Paul's use of the term "preternatural" suggests something other than evil in its human, social, and systemic forms, being more consistent with the evocation of a spiritual entity. Furthermore, Paul VI's reiteration of the teachings of Braga I and Lateran IV that Satan owes "his" existence to God suggests a creature, and by extension, a being—an implication heightened by the use of the possessive personal pronoun, "his."

On balance, it would seem as though Pope Paul VI, on November 15, 1972, asserted the existence of Satan as a particular being. Heightening the impression that Paul VI is making a first order truth claim, he rejects the prospect of referring to Satan only in a figurative sense. His scathing reference to "fanciful personification" would set the tone for a subsequent study on the devil, published by the CDF, which would condemn figurative interpretations of the doctrine of Satan.

Reinforcing Paul VI's characterization of the devil as a living being and his chiding of contemporary intellectuals who challenged the doctrinal status quo, in 1975 the CDF published an anonymously authored study, *Christian Faith and Demonology*, vehemently rejecting insights gleaned through modern biblical scholarship regarding the devil and demons.[42] The study argued that Jesus, transcending the influence of his culture and its understanding of Satan and demons, made important pronouncements asserting the existence of Satan as a particular supernatural being. It implies that any other interpretation dismisses Satan as a primitive superstition and thus calls into question Jesus' clarity of mind.

POPE ST. JOHN PAUL II REASSESSES THE CHURCH'S RELATIONSHIP WITH THE MODERN WORLD

Following the death of Pope Paul VI in 1978 and the thirty-three-day papacy of Pope John Paul I, Popes St. John Paul II and Benedict XVI each, in their own distinct way, challenged the vision of the Second Vatican Council

42. CDF, "Christian Faith and Demonology."

for dialogue with the modern world. St. John Paul II, having observed a time of debate and turbulence during the postconciliar papacy of Paul VI, recognized that the modern world was dynamic and changing. So too, he would suggest, the Church's disposition towards the world needed to be dynamic, not stuck in the dialogical mode promoted by *Gaudium et Spes*.

John Wilkins suggests that, as Archbishop of Krakow, Karl Wojtyla, the future Pope John Paul II, had witnessed the ambivalent manner in which bishops' conferences around the world had responded to Paul VI's exercise of papal authority in reaffirming the Church's ban on artificial birth control.[43] Wilkins opines of John Paul II, "He lost no time in reminding the bishops where they stood: he was in charge."[44] In his first encyclical, *Redemptor Hominis*, (1979) John Paul praised Paul VI remarking, "I keep thanking God that this great Predecessor of mine, who was also truly my father, knew how to display ad extra, externally, the true countenance of the Church, in spite of the various internal weaknesses that affected her in the postconciliar period."[45] John Paul implies in the encyclical that the Council and its aftermath were characterized by excessive criticism of the ecclesiastical status-quo, and an insufficiently critical stance in relation to modernity.

> The Church that I—through John Paul I—have had entrusted to me almost immediately after him is admittedly not free of internal difficulties and tension. At the same time, however, she is internally more strengthened against the excesses of self-criticism: she can be said to be more critical with regard to the various thoughtless criticisms, more resistant with respect to the various "novelties," more mature in her spirit of discerning, better able to bring out of her everlasting treasure "what is new and what is old."[46]

John Paul's comment regarding that which is old and that which is new implies the restoration of a balance between *ressourcement* and *aggiornamento*. In *Redemptor Hominis*, John Paul II commits to a correlational, adaptive stance towards the contemporary world, attentive to the "signs of the times," though not necessarily the same form of correlation envisaged in 1965 by the Council.

> While keeping alive in our memory the picture that was so perspicaciously and authoritatively traced by the Second Vatican

---

43. Wilkins, "Bishops or Branch Managers," 18.
44. Wilkins, "Bishops or Branch Managers."
45. John Paul II, "*Redemptor Hominis*" 4.
46. John Paul II, "*Redemptor Hominis*" 4.

Council, we shall try once more to adapt it to the "signs of the times" and to the demands of the situation, which is continually changing and evolving in certain directions.[47]

John Paul regards the situation of the modern world as one characterized by flux. He wryly implies that the Council's dialogical stance towards the world needed to be itself updated. In counterpoint to John Paul II's argument that the postconciliar Church should evolve its relationship with the modern world so as to counter a more challenging *zeitgeist*, Daniel Donovan has suggested that the Council had sought to reclaim elements of the early Church and its disposition precisely because it foresaw the decline of the institutionalized, cultural Catholicism of Western Europe, and had had adopted a dialogical disposition towards the world, specifically in response to this challenge.[48]

In a 1996 encyclical, *Redemptoris Missio*, John Paul II identified a pastoral concern that many of the baptized in culturally Catholic regions and more recently established dioceses had ceased to participate in the life of the Christian community.[49] The Pope regarded the situation as "intermediate," fearing that it would in time lead to a new situation whereby the next generation would not be baptized.

> There is an intermediate situation, particularly in countries with ancient Christian roots, and occasionally in the younger Churches as well, where entire groups of the baptized have lost a living sense of the faith, or even no longer consider themselves members of the Church, and live a life far removed from Christ and his Gospel. In this case what is needed is a "new evangelization" or a "re-evangelization."[50]

This statement envisages the new evangelization as a re-evangelization intended to counteract disengagement from the sacramental and communal life of the Church, and offer moral remediation so as to challenge lives "far removed from Christ and his Gospel."[51] Avery Dulles identifies this realignment in the Church's envisaged relationship with the world with reference to an "evangelical turn," observing, "In my judgment, the evangelical turn in the ecclesial vision of Popes Paul VI and John Paul II is one of the most surprising and important developments in the Catholic Church since

---

47. John Paul II, "*Redemptor Hominis*" 15.
48. Donavon, *Distinctly Catholic*, 25.
49. See chapter 2 in John Paul II, "*Redemptoris Missio*."
50. John Paul II, "*Redemptoris Missio*" 33.
51. John Paul II, "*Redemptoris Missio*" 33.

Vatican II."[52] Ralph Martin notes that, since 1983, John Paul "began to refer frequently to a "new evangelization," denoting a mandate to re-evangelize individuals and cultures to whom the gospel had been proclaimed but who have lost a living commitment."[53] This evangelical effort would focus primarily upon traditionally Catholic countries wherein a significant portion of the population was nominally Catholic but not practicing. Evangelization, although by no means inherently opposed to dialogue, suggests a tone that is more assertive than dialogical.

POPE BENEDICT XVI DOWNPLAYS THE TRANSFORMATIVE VISION OF THE COUNCIL

Whereas Pope St. John Paul II called for a change of tone in the postconciliar Church's engagement with a changing world, a shift from the dialogical to the assertively evangelical, his successor, Pope Benedict XVI denied that the texts of the Council had ever in the first place justified a transformation in the Church's disposition towards the world. He viewed the Council as an incremental corrective rather than a revolutionary event in the life of the Church.

On December 22, 2005, as Joseph Ratzinger prepared to celebrate his first Christmas as Pope Benedict XVI, he asked, "What was the outcome of the Council? Has it been implemented in the right way? What, in the implementation of the Council has been good and what has been inadequate or mistaken? What remains to be done?" and "Why has the implementation of the Council, in large parts of the Church, thus far been so difficult?"[54] Benedict regards the difficulties as emerging from the mutual opposition of two starkly contrasting interpretations of the Council: a "hermeneutic of reform" of which he approves, and a "hermeneutic of discontinuity and rupture" which, Benedict warns, "risks ending in a split between the pre-and post-conciliar Church."[55] Benedict associates the hermeneutic of discontinuity or rupture with a misguided view that the "true spirit of the Council" is not fully reflected in the conciliar texts.[56] Those who embrace the hermeneutic of discontinuity, Benedict suggests, argue that the conciliar texts were compromised for the sake of consensus at the Council, believing that "it was found necessary to keep and reconfirm many old things that

52. Dulles, "John Paul II and the New Evangelization," 96–100.
53. Martin, "What Is the New Evangelization?"
54. Benedict XVI, "To the Roman Curia."
55. John Paul II, *Redemptoris Missio* 33.
56. John Paul II, *Redemptoris Missio* 33.

are now pointless."⁵⁷ Adherents of this erroneous hermeneutic, according to Benedict, seek to "go courageously beyond the texts."⁵⁸ Benedict further characterizes the hermeneutic of continuity as suggesting, "In a word, we should not follow the texts of the Council but its spirit."⁵⁹ Such an argument, Benedict remarks, raises "the question as to how this spirit should subsequently be defined."

Benedict XVI fears that reliance on the undefined "spirit" rather than the texts of the Council "gives space for every whim."⁶⁰ Benedict's position hence places great store by ecclesial documents and seems ambivalent towards the "spirit." The Church at its inception, it might however be argued, relied precisely on Spirit from which the earliest Christian texts emerged. The question arises as to whether Benedict's suspicion of the "spirit" might impede openness to the Holy Spirit. If Catholics had always adhered rigidly to the letter of ecclesial texts, how, one wonders, could the tradition ever have developed under the guidance of the Holy Spirit? While Benedict castigates an appeal to the spirit of the Council rather than to its texts, the question remains as to what is to be made of the texts that explicitly mandated dialogue with the modern world and openness to progress in light of the insights of modernity.

POPE BENEDICT XVI'S HERMENEUTIC OF CONTINUITY

Addressing the question as to whether the Council mandated substantive change, Benedict states that a Church Council is not a new constitution that is adopted to replace a previous one. Benedict argues that change of this kind requires a mandate that the Council Fathers did not have. "The Fathers had no such mandate and no one had ever given them; anyone, for that matter, could have done so, because the essential constitution of the Church comes from the Lord and was given to us so that we may attain eternal life, and from this perspective, we are able to illuminate life in time and time itself."⁶¹ Without denying that the Church has inherited its mission from Jesus, the Lord did not leave his Church a written constitution to be followed according to its letter. Rather, he left a spirit, the Holy Spirit, that is, and memories preserved and developed through an oral tradition. Hence,

57. John Paul II, "*Redemptoris Missio*" 33.
58. John Paul II, "*Redemptoris Missio*" 33.
59. John Paul II, "*Redemptoris Missio*" 33.
60. John Paul II, "*Redemptoris Missio*" 33.
61. John Paul II, "*Redemptoris Missio*" 33.

there is no constitution given directly by Christ that the Council Fathers could have changed.

Benedict's position raises the question as to what constitutes legitimate change in doctrine and the life of the Church more generally. St. Vincent of Lerins had, in the fifth century, asked, "Is there to be no progress of religion in the Church?"[62] Vincent answered his own question by drawing a distinction, "There is, certainly, and very great. . . . But it must be a progress and not a change."[63] The question then arises, however, as to how "progress" is to be demarcated from "change" within a Catholic tradition, that Loisy and later, Congar, showed to have been dynamic and evolving from the start.[64] As Carl Trueman observes, continuity is so often "in the eye of the beholder" rather than objectively distinguishable from fundamental change.[65]

Herbert McCabe proposes that Tradition may be defined in terms of a continuous engagement with questions rather than continuity in terms of particular answers. McCabe suggests "we do not just have to know what people said in the past, but we have to be in continuity with their wrestling and with their problems."[66] This suggests that continuity can lie in an ongoing grappling with mystery rather than in imagining that our forebears had achieved a static understanding of the faith that we are obliged to preserve.

In support of this hermeneutic of reform over and against a hermeneutic of discontinuity, Benedict XVI engages the remarks of St. John XXIII at the opening of the Council, the speech that the present work has regarded as offering a mandate for the legitimate development of doctrine. Benedict characterizes St. John XXIII's speech as an endorsement of the hermeneutic of continuity as opposed to that of transformation.

> I would like to here mention only the well-known words of John XXIII, which unequivocally express this hermeneutic when he says that the Council "wants to transmit the doctrine, pure and integral, without any attenuation or distortion," and continues: "Our duty is not only to guard this precious treasure, as if we were concerned only with antiquity, but to dedicate ourselves with an earnest will and without fear to that work which our era demands of us. . . . It is necessary that this certain and

---

62. Hanahoe, "Ecclesiology and Ecumenism," 328.
63. Vincent of Lerins, "Commonitory," 26–28.
64. Congar, *Meaning of Tradition*, 16–55; Loisy, *Birth of the Christian Religion*.
65. Trueman, "Traditional Troubles."
66. McCabe, *God Still Matters*, 206; McCaughey, "Reason, Reality."

unchangeable doctrine, which must be faithfully respected, both in-depth and presented in a way that meets the needs of our time."[67]

A translation of John XXIII's speech as it appears on the website of the Holy See does indeed use the phrase, "unchangeable doctrine," that is, *dottrina certa ed immutabile*.[68] This translation may, at first glance, suggest that John XXIII was, in this instance at least, supportive of a hermeneutic of continuity in the sense proposed by Benedict XVI. However, upon closer inspection, in its given context, Pope John seems to be using the term "doctrine" to refer to the eternal truths themselves rather than the formulae through which they are presented.[69] John XXIII very deliberately distinguished between the deposit of faith which is one thing, and the "way in which it is expressed" which is quite another.[70] Indeed, John XXIII cannot have regarded doctrinal formulae themselves as unchangeable while advocating that they should be "presented in a way that meets the needs of our time," in a world that "expects a step forward toward a doctrinal penetration expounded through the methods of research and through the literary forms of modern thought."[71]

Benedict's address proceeds to confront directly the question of the relationship between the Church and the modern world.[72] The pontiff recounts low-points in the Church's relationship with modernity, asserting that "radical liberalism" had provoked the anti-Modernist writings that the pontiff recognizes to have been a "bitter and radical condemnation of this spirit of the modern age."[73] For all his misgivings about dialogue with modernity, Benedict's characterization of the anti-Modernist writings sounds distinctly unsympathetic as he distances himself from the reactionary, anti-Modernist perspective.

Pope Benedict proposes that the Second Vatican Council faced a question concerning the relationship between the Church and the sciences, suggesting that as the sciences matured so did the Church's reaction to them. "Natural sciences began, more and more clearly, to reflect on their own limitations imposed by their own method which, while achieving great things, was not able to comprehend the totality of reality. Thus, both sides were

---

67. Benedict XVI, "To the Roman Curia."
68. John XXIII, "*Gaudet Mater Ecclesia*."
69. John XXIII, "*Gaudet Mater Ecclesia*."
70. John XXIII, "*Gaudet Mater Ecclesia*."
71. John XXIII, "*Gaudet Mater Ecclesia*."
72. Benedict XVI, "To the Roman Curia."
73. John XXIII, "*Gaudet Mater Ecclesia*."

gradually beginning to open up to each other."[74] Benedict's reference to an acknowledgment of limitations on the part of scientists, may reflect a recognition that theological and philosophical questions lie outside the scope of the natural sciences. However, Benedict diagnoses a more oppositional relationship between the magisterium and the science of biblical interpretation, alleging overreach on the part of practitioners of the historical-critical method.

> First, it was necessary to define in a new way the relationship between faith and modern science; this concern, moreover, is not only the natural sciences but also historical science because, in a certain school, the historical-critical method claimed to have the last word on the interpretation of the Bible and, demanding total exclusivity for its understanding the Holy Scriptures, was opposed to important points in the interpretation that the faith of the Church had developed.[75]

It is not clear as to what representative of the historical-critical method made the totalizing claim that Benedict cites. As we have seen, the PBC has unequivocally mandated the use of the historical-critical method and regarded it as highly compatible with other interpretative approaches, particularly canonical exegesis. The canonical exegete must work from an accurate literal sense of the text as established by means of historical-critical interpretation.[76] That is, it is necessary to ascertain what the ancient author intended to say so as to work out a correct trajectory for canonical exegesis.

Summarizing the Second Vatican Council's vision of the relationship between the Church and the modern world, Benedict asserts, "The Second Vatican Council, with the new definition of the relationship between the faith of the Church and certain essential elements of modern thought, has reviewed or even corrected certain historical decisions, but in this apparent discontinuity it has actually preserved and deepened her inmost nature and his true identity."[77] Hence, Benedict suggests that what may have appeared discontinuous actually affirmed what has always been at the core of the Church's mission. It might indeed be argued that Vatican II and the *nouvelle théologie* that had paved the way for it were characterized by *ressourcement*, the recovery of ancient truths and practices. This does not in itself, however, mean that the Council should be regarded more in terms of continuity than

---

74. John XXIII, "*Gaudet Mater Ecclesia.*"
75. John XXIII, "*Gaudet Mater Ecclesia.*"
76. Pius XII, "*Divino Afflante Spiritu*" 37, 30; PBC, "Interpretation of the Bible in the Church" 34.
77. Benedict XVI, "To the Roman Curia."

transformation. The teachings and practices recovered by the Council had, in many cases, been suppressed for centuries, especially since the Council of Trent and throughout the Modernist crisis. To restore continuity with elements of the mission of Jesus and of the early Church required discontinuity with some aspects of the Tridentine legacy. At the end of his papacy, Benedict would, however, offer a yet more damning perspective on interpretations of the Council at variance with his own.

In his final address to the clergy of Rome on February 14, 2013, Pope Benedict XVI suggested that the Second Vatican Council had been misrepresented by the mass media, and the world had in large part been deluded. Benedict juxtaposes in stark terms, two greatly contrasting interpretations of the Second Vatican Council: the "Council of faith" and the "Council of the journalists." Benedict asserts, "There was the Council of the Fathers—the real Council—but there was also the council of the media. It was almost a Council apart, and the world perceived the Council through the latter, through the media."[78] Hence, Benedict argues that the actual Ecumenical Council was accompanied by a fabricated "council," as it were, a false impression of the Council, disseminated by the media. Furthermore, this "council" conjured up by the media served as the lens through which the world perceived the actual Council. Benedict asserts, "Thus, the Council that reached the people with immediate effect was that of the media, not that of the Fathers."[79] Benedict attributes a host of ecclesial problems to the council of the media.

> We know that this Council of the media was accessible to everyone. Therefore, this was the dominant one, the more effective one, and it created so many disasters, so many problems, so much suffering: seminaries closed, convents closed, banal liturgy . . . and the real Council had difficulty establishing itself and taking shape; the virtual Council was stronger than the real Council.[80]

Hence, Benedict blames an array of the Church's problems on a distorted view of the Second Vatican Council, as opposed to the Council itself—a sentiment not far removed from that of Pope Paul VI's "smoke of Satan" homily, but without explicit reference to the devil. Benedict accuses the journalists of promoting those elements present at the Council that were most positively disposed towards the modern world. "It was obvious that the media would take the side of those who seemed to them more closely

78. Benedict XVI, "Meeting with the Parish Priests."
79. Benedict XVI, "Meeting with the Parish Priests."
80. Benedict XVI, "Meeting with the Parish Priests."

allied with their world."[81] Thus, Benedict implies that a more reconciliatory stance on the part of the Church towards the modern world was, at least in part, a deceitful delusion conjured up by the media. The letter of the conciliar texts themselves, and in particular *Gaudium et Spes*, may however, tell a different story.

Again, a question arises as to whether Benedict's zeal for the letter of the conciliar texts and his ambivalence towards "spirit" underestimates the agency of the Holy Spirit within a dynamic, evolving Tradition. When Benedict asserts that "the virtual Council was stronger than the real Council," it should not be forgotten that the pontiff is speaking of an ecumenical Council of the Church, carrying supreme teaching authority with the highest level of ecclesiastical infallibility.[82] Yet, Benedict suggests, the ecumenical Council was less effective than fake news.[83]

CONCLUSION

This chapter identifies what may be an underestimated moment in the Church's relationship with modernity when a pope decried that the modern world, the sciences, and critical voices within the Church were influenced by a preternatural Satan. Pope Paul VI's "smoke of Satan" homily of June 29, 1972, and the Pontiff's remarks on Satan on November 15 of that same year, vaunted the Church's current teachings on Satan as though to dare his detractors to openly dissent and call for a reformulation of the doctrine.

Pope Paul VI's smoke of Satan homily, with its negative view of research and innovation, serves as a reminder that, while the Second Vatican Council ideated a dialogical stance in relation to the modern world and its insights, in a sense, the Modernist crisis had not been finally resolved. Pope Paul's concerns resembled those of Cardinal Ottaviani, the Council minority, as well as those of his predecessors, Popes Pius IX and Pius X. These men feared that dialogue with the modern world would lead to unwarranted accommodation and would compromise the prophetic spirit of the gospel.

The dialogical tone of the Council, for better or for worse, had empowered the faithful to speak out in the face of a magisterial pronouncement. The dissidence that followed the publication of *Humanae Vitae* signified a clash of expectations. Postconciliar popes, without directly rejecting the dialogical stance of the Council, did not, for the most part, promote it.

81. Benedict XVI, "Meeting with the Parish Priests."
82. Paul VI, "*Lumen Gentium*" 22; Sullivan, *Magisterium*, 56–57.
83. Benedict XVI, "Meeting with the Parish Priests."

St. John Paul II, noting the difficulties faced by Pope Paul VI, argued that just as the modern world changes, so must the Church's stance in relation to it. John Paul decisively steered the Church from a dialogical stance to a more assertive, Evangelical one.

Pope Benedict XVI, for his part, rejected interpretations of the Council that viewed it as transformative, instead asserting a hermeneutic of reform—a tweaking rather than a transformation. Nonetheless, no authoritative pronouncement of the Church has ever rescinded the teaching of the Second Vatican Council that the Church is called to engage in a frank exchange of ideas with the entire human family so as to benefit from the unfolding insights of modernity. And hence we press forward in candidly outlining our case for a reformulation of the doctrine of Satan.

9

Pope Francis on the Devil, Discernment, and Interpretations of Doctrine

Throughout his papacy, Pope Francis has regularly affirmed the teaching that the devil exists as a supernatural reality responsible for facilitating an array of human sins, including those associated with the scandal of clerical sexual abuse and the failure of Church authorities to respond appropriately.[1] Francis's references to the devil are scattered across a plethora of homilies, addresses and interviews, rather than presented in an organized treatise on the subject. It should therefore be noted that *Rebuking the Devil*, published by the USCCB, is not, despite the impression given by its cover, a book written by Pope Francis, but a compilation of the pope's remarks, annotated by an anonymous author with a clear commitment to affirming the ontological existence of the devil.[2]

It is in chapter 5 of the exhortation, *Gaudete et Exsultate*, that Francis presents his most expansive public reflection on the devil. In this context, the Holy Father reasserts his conviction that the devil exists as something beyond a myth or idea. Indeed, the pontiff goes so far as to propose that those who regard the devil as nothing more than a myth or idea, incur a

---

1. Rosica, "Why Is Pope Francis So Obsessed"; Laccino, "Pope Francis Satan Talk"; Faiola, "Modern Pope Gets Old School"; SanMartín, "Modern Pope Wants Rosary Prayer."

2. USCCB, *Rebuking the Devil*.

heightened susceptibility to the influence of evil.[3] Francis's association of beliefs about the devil with moral failure hold troubling implications for atheists, agnostics, and persons of faith, including some Catholics, who interpret doctrinal references to the devil in a figurative manner. It might be argued that Francis appears to attach a disproportionate degree of moral significance to an acceptance of the devil's existence.

So as to situate these observations in context, it should be noted that *Gaudete et Exsultate* bears the ecclesial status of an exhortation, the genre being characterized by a homiletic tone rather than that of a doctrinal declaration, a decree, or constitution.[4] The exhortation does not define doctrine but urges its readers to engage in personal spiritual discernment. In this regard, it is deeply influenced by St. Ignatius of Loyola's conviction that spiritual discernment can uncover the influence of good and evil spirits on one's thoughts and disposition.

Crucially, while refusing to equate the full reality of the devil with a mythical motif or concept, Francis does not, in *Gaudete et Exsultate*, impose a definitive account of the mode in which the devil exists, not invoking the designation of fallen angel or being as he did in his earlier, pre-papal ruminations on the subject.[5] Indeed, Pope Francis argues for the legitimacy of a variety of interpretations of doctrine and for the need to develop doctrine so that it can speak compellingly in its milieu.[6] This must apply to the matter of the devil as to any other area of Church teaching.

THE DEVIL AND TEMPTATION

Exhorting his readers to resist diabolical influence, Pope Francis sounds an apocalyptic note, employing the metaphor of a battle.[7] Lending support to a warfare perspective on the universe, Gregory Boyd, in his major work on Satan, challenges what he dubs a "blue-print" view of Divine Providence wherein every eventuality is imagined to be in keeping with God's will.[8] Whereas the blue-print perspective seems to indict God for the inclusion of evil and suffering in the divine plan, the warfare perspective, or the "battle" as Pope Francis puts it, arguably exonerates the Deity of direct responsibility for such affliction.

3. Francis, *"Gaudete et Exsultate"* 60–161, 166, 170.
4. Sullivan, *Creative Fidelity*; Sullivan, *Magisterium*.
5. Bergoglio and Skorka, *On Heaven and Earth*, 8.
6. Francis, *"Gaudete et Exsultate"* 42–44, 168.
7. Francis, *"Gaudete et Exsultate"* 158.
8. Boyd, *Satan and the Problem of Evil*.

Francis rallies his audience to resist a common foe, the inhuman devil who subjects humanity to temptation. "We need strength and courage to withstand the temptations of the devil and to proclaim the Gospel."[9] While the pontiff regards temptation as, in at least some instances, instigated by the devil, not every Christian account of temptation requires reference to the agency of a third-party tempter. An alternate view of temptation could appeal to a tension between human appetite and conscience. It could cite St. Augustine's account of vice as rooted in a disordering of desires that are in and of themselves good, a loss of priority in the face of some overwhelming attraction.[10]

Pope Francis argues that "the devil does not need to possess us" in order to exert evil influence.[11] The pontiff contends that the devil can facilitate a wide array of sins, including fear of failure, bitterness, despair, hyperefficiency, idolizing money, hypocrisy, exclusion of the poor, marital and domestic conflict, defamation, divisiveness, and gossip.[12] Granted, Pope Francis does not suggest that absolutely every instance of temptation can be directly attributed to diabolical agency. Nonetheless, while deemphasizing what might be regarded as sensational displays of diabolical prowess such as possession, the Holy Father argues that banal failings may reflect demonic influence. The question arises as to the extent to which habitual, venial sin is prompted by diabolical agency as opposed to the fallen nature and free will of a human being. While the Catechism argues that the Fall of humanity was facilitated by the devil, it would be a very different matter to argue that each personal sin is directly influenced by Satan.

Having noted that Pope Francis envisages the devil as facilitating a plethora of human failings, the pontiff insists that the spiritual battle facing Christians is not simply a conflict with human weakness, individual or collective, but with an inhuman reality. Indeed, it might be argued, Francis's argument is more anthropological than demonological, serving in large measure to distance the ultimate source of evil from human volition.

> We are not dealing merely with a battle against the world and a worldly mentality that would deceive us and leave us dull and mediocre, lacking in enthusiasm and joy. Nor can this battle be reduced to the struggle against our human weaknesses and

---

9. Francis, *"Gaudete et Exsultate"* 158.
10. Augustine, *City of God*, 10.
11. Francis, *"Gaudete et Exsultate"* 161.
12. USCCB, *Rebuking the Devil*, 51–85.

proclivities (be they laziness, lust, envy, jealousy or any others). It is also a constant struggle against the devil, the prince of evil.[13]

Refusing to envisage the spiritual battle as a conflict with human persons, Francis's position is clearly delineated from polemical narratives that invoke the motif of the battle so as to demonize other humans. Indeed, Francis's references to a supernatural tempter serve to discourage polarization among humans or, by the same token, excessive self-reproach. Francis references to the "world" and a "worldly" mentality evoke a dualistic, Johannine ring and suggest that the battle against the devil is not a battle against the collective sins of humanity as manifested in systemic or institutional evil. Francis regards the reality of the devil as distinct from systemic evil and capable of instigating it.[14]

Striking a somewhat triumphalist note, Pope Francis remarks of temptation, "This battle is sweet, for it allows us to rejoice each time the Lord triumphs in our lives."[15] Francis then envisages Jesus' jubilation whenever humans prevail in the struggle against inhuman evil, suggesting "Jesus himself celebrates our victories."[16] This curious spurt of triumphalism implies the character of a pep talk, designed to bolster human determination to resist temptation. Overall, the pontiff's references to the devil seem less inclined to instill fear than to sound a note of encouragement to stand united and morally resolute in the face of a common, inhuman enemy.

ARE SKEPTICS REGARDING A SUPERNATURAL DEVIL MORE SUSCEPTIBLE TO SIN?

Francis makes what appears to be an uncharacteristically judgmental assertion when he suggests that those who understand the devil as existing only as a mythical motif or a concept without a referent are consequently more prone to moral failure. The pontiff argues that such an understanding of the devil weakens one's capacity to withstand diabolical influence. "Hence, we should not think of the devil as a myth, a representation, a symbol, a figure of speech or an idea. This mistake would lead us to let down our guard, to grow careless and end up more vulnerable."[17] From Francis's perspective,

---

13. Francis, "*Gaudete et Exsultate*" 159.
14. USSCCB, *Rebuking the Devil*, 85.
15. Francis, "*Gaudete et Exsultate*" 158.
16. Francis, "*Gaudete et Exsultate*" 159.
17. Francis, "*Gaudete et Exsultate*" 161.

models of the devil as nothing more than a figurative construct may arise from diabolical trickery, lulling humanity into dangerous complacency.[18]

In his published conversations with Rabbi Abraham Skorka, Jorge Bergoglio, the future Pope Francis insists that the devil exists as a being and posits that the devil seeks to trick humanity into denying its existence, remarking "Maybe his greatest achievement in these times has been to make us believe that he does not exist, and that all can be fixed on a purely human level."[19] The pontiff's position is reminiscent of a line from Charles Baudelaire's prose poem *The Generous Gambler*, wherein Baudelaire remarks, "*La plus belle des ruses du diable est de vous persuader qu'il n'existe pas,*" that is, "The devil's finest trick is to persuade you that he does not exist."[20]

Intensifying his account of the moral life as a battle and exhorting spiritual vigilance, the pontiff quotes St. Paul's injunction to "stand against the wiles of the devil" (Eph 6:11) and to "quench all the flaming darts of the evil one" (Eph 6:16). Pope Francis remarks, "These expressions are not melodramatic, precisely because our path towards holiness is a constant battle."[21] Whereas Francis in paragraph 161 regards those who do not realize that the devil exists as more than a myth or idea as being particularly vulnerable to succumb to temptation, in paragraph 162, he now predicts with a more fatalistic air, "Those who do not realize this will be prey to failure or mediocrity."[22] The metaphor of prey, drawn from the hunt, is reminiscent of the image of the "roaring lion" in 1 Peter 5:8, and the prospect of falling "prey" would seem to denote a surrender to sin itself rather than an experience of temptation that might be resisted. Francis has, after all, suggested that temptation itself, once resisted, can be an occasion for jubilation."[23] Hence, the Holy Father's remarks in this regard seem to associate beliefs about the devil with sin, and to dismiss those who do not share his position as particularly predisposed to sin.

IGNATIAN DISCERNMENT AND THE DEVIL

Pope Francis's references to the devil and its influence on humans reflect the writings of St. Ignatius of Loyola, the founder of the Jesuits. Ignatius's "Rules for Perceiving the Movements Caused in the Soul" and "Rules for

18. Francis, *"Gaudete et Exsultate"* 160–61.
19. Bergoglio and Skorka, *On Heaven and Earth*, 8.
20. Baudelaire, *Generous Gambler*, 61.
21. Francis, *"Gaudete et Exsultate"* 162.
22. Francis, *"Gaudete et Exsultate"* 162.
23. Francis, *"Gaudete et Exsultate"* 159.

the Discernment of Spirits" suggest that good angels, the devil and, arguably, other fallen angels exert external influence upon the movements of the soul.[24]

Francis proposes spiritual discernment as a means to a "supernatural understanding" of the devil, empowering moral vigilance and fortitude.[25] The pontiff suggests that discernment enables us to identify the source of new thoughts, attitudes, and moods, discerning whether they are "brought by God or an illusion created by the spirit of this world or the spirit of the devil."[26] Francis's demarcation of the "spirit of this world" from the "spirit of the devil" serves to once more emphasize that, for Francis, the devil is not a figurative personification of the cumulative sin of the world. Francis suggests that belief in the existence of a supernatural, inhuman devil can foment understanding in relation to the havoc wielded by evil. "It is precisely the conviction that this malign power is present in our midst that enables us to understand how evil can at times have so much destructive force."[27]

With possible applicability to intransigent stances within the Church, Francis notes that not only change but also resistance to change can be induced by evil. "At other times, the opposite can happen, when the forces of evil induce us not to change, to leave things as they are, to opt for a rigid resistance to change."[28] The pontiff encourages a critical disposition, reading the "signs of the times" so as to "test everything; hold fast to what is good (1 Thess 5:21)."

Francis entrusts the task of discernment to the individual, his stance on this matter being highly consistent with his emphasis on the primacy of personal conscience.[29] He speaks of discernment as a gift that can sensitize us to the movements of a unique personal relationship with God as might be explored through Ignatian discernment.[30] The Holy Father at one point describes discernment as uncovering a glimpse of "that unique and mysterious plan that God has for each of us, which takes shape amid so many varied situations and limitations."[31] Understood as such, discernment grants insight into a person's relationship with God rather than ontological truths such as the existence of the devil as a particular creature.

24. Ignatius, "Spiritual Exercises," 113–214.
25. Francis, *"Gaudete et Exsultate"* 166.
26. Francis, *"Gaudete et Exsultate"* 168.
27. Francis, *"Gaudete et Exsultate"* 160.
28. Francis, *"Gaudete et Exsultate"* 168.
29. Francis, *"Amoris Laetitia"* 37.
30. Francis, *"Gaudete et Exsultate"* 13, 170.
31. Francis, *"Gaudete et Exsultate"* 170.

Francis notes that spiritual discernment "does not exclude existential, psychological, sociological or moral insights drawn from the human sciences" but transcends them. For Francis, discernment is a grace that "includes reason and prudence" but "goes beyond them."[32] Hence, the pontiff argues that spiritual discernment can facilitate an engagement with mystery beyond that made possible by intellectual inquiry alone.

Warning against a contemporary manifestation of Gnosticism in Christian spirituality, Francis cautions against a smug intellectual elitism whereby "We can think that because we know something, or are able to explain it in certain terms, we are already saints, perfect and better than the 'ignorant masses.'"[33] Francis's injunctions against thinking of the devil as merely a myth, when read in context, are not an assertion that the attainment of hidden knowledge of the devil can in and of itself make some people more saintly than others, much less a suggestion that some people, perhaps regarded as psychics or sensitives, have a supernatural understanding that is denied others. Rather, Francis suggests that any perspective, whether it arises from doctrinal integralism or from the uncritical acceptance of a scholarly perspective, can be absolutized so as to become a form of Gnosticism that leads to a self-assured moral complacency.

INTERPRETING ST. IGNATIUS'S REFERENCES TO THE SPIRITS

For the most part, St. Ignatius attributes the experience of gladness and joy to God and his angels and experiences of sadness and disturbance to "the enemy."[34] The enemy, according to Ignatius, insidiously undermines our happiness and consolation, facilitating discouragement and temptation to surrender. St. Ignatius also cautions that an evil angel can impersonate a good one by instilling a false sense of consolation.[35] With the benefit of modern psychological insights into human motives, moods, emotions, hormones, the functions of the brain, and the formative effect of life events, we might call into question Ignatius's and Francis's attribution of discouragement, depression, or temptation to the agency of an evil spirit.

Illustrating the prevalent zeitgeist in the West, when a priest-exorcist interviewed on public television in Ireland in 2019 raised the possibility that, in some cases, thoughts of suicide might be influenced by evil spirits,

---

32. Francis, *"Gaudete et Exsultate"* 170.
33. Francis, *"Gaudete et Exsultate"* 145.
34. Ignatius, *Spiritual Exercises,* 329.
35. Ignatius, *Spiritual Exercises,* 332.

the public response was largely one of outrage.[36] The exorcist's point arguably implied diminished culpability on the part of those who killed themselves while unable to exercise the freedom required for a sin to be deemed as mortal. To many within his contemporary audience, however, this point seems to have been lost. Some of the indignation in question may have arisen in response to any association whatsoever of suicide and mental illness with the demonic, while some resented its association with sin, a category just as obsolete from some secular perspectives. While not all interpreters of the *Spiritual Exercises* would agree that a devil is responsible for the movements of the soul, Pope Francis is insistent on the point.

Ignatius's reference to a diabolical agent who visits desolation upon humanity serves, to some degree, to emphasize that God does not send desolation our way—though God does permit it.[37] While asserting that Christ rejoices when we resist temptation, Pope Francis has adamantly rejected any suggestion that God leads us into temptation. The pontiff has addressed this point in relation to the conventional English translation of the sixth petition of the Our Father which implores God not to lead us into temptation, and hence could be interpreted as implying that it is conceivable that God might do so.[38] The prospect of God handing a person to Satan for a Job-style loyalty test, or of God's Spirit leading a person to a desert encounter with Satan, seems laden with the residue of a morally ambiguous, monist model of God rather than the God of ethical monotheism. On the contrary, for Ignatius, for Francis, and for much of the Christian Tradition from Patristic times onward, references to the devil serve to defend God, and at times humanity, from imputations of blame in relation to evil and suffering.[39]

No doubt, Ignatius's references to the agency of good and evil angels, including the "enemy," reflect the saint's sixteenth-century interpretation of scripture. While Ignatius clearly did not have access to the findings of the historical-critical method as applied in modern biblical scholarship, Hemult Gabel posits that Ignatius diligently drew upon the exegetical resources available to him.[40] Gabel further suggests that "It was a foreign idea to Ignatius to invoke a spiritual experience that somehow went beyond what intellectual reflection and rational efforts could yield. He set all that he experienced spiritually within the theological knowledge of his time."[41]

36. Monaghan, "Fr. Pat Collins."
37. Ignatius, *Spiritual Exercises*, 324.
38. Harris, "Pope Francis Says Our Father Is Poorly Translated."
39. Russell, *Satan*, 27–28.
40. Gabel, "Ignatian Contemplation and Modern Biblical Studies," 45.
41. Gabel, "Ignatian Contemplation and Modern Biblical Studies," 45.

In Gabel's view, St. Ignatius is not suggesting that discernment can disclose ontological truth that is inaccessible to theological reflection. Pope Francis, on the other hand, while acknowledging a role for intellectual inquiry, including scriptural exegesis, does suggest that discernment can disclose truth that is inaccessible through study.[42]

It would appear that from the outset, Ignatius assumes the existence and influence of good and bad angels as envisaged in Catholic doctrine. For Ignatius, the manner in which evil spirits assert influence upon the excitant is a matter for discernment, whereas their existence is a given. Nonetheless, Ignatius's use of varied terms to describe evil influences may suggest a degree of nuance regarding their precise identity. Ignatius refers intermittently to the "enemy," "evil spirit," and "evil angel," raising a question as to whether Ignatius is alleging any certainty as to the specific identity of the spiritual assailant. Just as Catholic doctrine affirms the ontological existence of the devil, so it affirms the existence of a multitude of inhuman evil spirits, that is, demons or fallen angels.[43] Indeed, the categories of the diabolical and the demonic are ambiguously intertwined in Christian discourse under a general assumption that lesser demons, as it were, ultimately further the devil's agenda. This ambiguity should occasion pause for thought with regard to the question as to whether it is possible to discern the existence and influence of a singular devil, as opposed to some junior hellion or the realm of evil in a more amorphous sense.

Roger Haight expounds upon the difficulties entailed in presenting Ignatius's Spiritual Exercises in their current form to a diverse and often quite sophisticated contemporary audience.[44] Language and assumptions drawn from the lexicon of a particular community of faith may be inhibitive to a broader audience. Haight's arguments may well apply to Pope Francis's rumination on discernment of spirits with its distinctly Ignatian flavor. References to the devil and evil spirits, especially if they appear to reflect supernaturalism, biblicism, or integralism can lose credibility for Ignatian spirituality and Christianity more broadly. Clearly, contemporary directors and exercitants of Ignatian discernment can draw upon modern biblical scholarship and a wide range of exegetical and hermeneutical approaches to enrich their discernment.[45]

---

42. Francis, *"Gaudete et Exsultate"* 166.
43. CDF, *Catechism of the Catholic Church* 393.
44. Haight, "Expanding the Spiritual Exercises," 3.
45. Gabel, "Ignatian Contemplation and Modern Biblical Studies," 45.

POPE FRANCIS'S INTERPRETATION OF SCRIPTURE IN RELATION TO THE DEVIL

Francis asserts of the devil, "He is present in the very first pages of the Scriptures, which end with God's victory over the devil."[46] Francis's allusion to Genesis as containing references to the devil would meet widespread exegetical objection on the grounds that the Adamic narrative itself, as opposed to a Patristic interpretation of it, includes no reference to the devil.[47] Nonetheless, Pope Francis's position on the devil is far more affable to the insights of modern biblical scholarship than was the 1975 CDF study *Christian Faith and Demonology* which denied that gospel references to demons reflected the historical context and worldview of their authors, and scoffed at the possibility that Jesus or the Evangelists might have referred to Satan or demons in a figurative manner.[48] In a remark that acknowledges the value of exegetical insights regarding the devil, Pope Francis comments that not all biblical references to the demonic denote a supernatural reality so much as maladies and miseries that had yet to be diagnosed in medical terms. "True enough, the biblical authors had limited conceptual resources for expressing certain realities, and in Jesus' time epilepsy, for example, could easily be confused with demonic possession."[49] Having acknowledged the possibility that biblical references to the demonic can denote natural evils, the Holy Father argues that such an interpretation does not necessarily account for every instance. "Yet this should not lead us to an oversimplification that would conclude that all the cases related in the Gospel had to do with psychological disorders and hence that the devil does not exist or is not at work."[50]

Francis's interpretation of Luke 10:18 proves central to his moral exhortation. "Jesus himself celebrates our victories. He rejoiced when his disciples made progress in preaching the Gospel and overcoming the opposition of the evil one: 'I saw Satan fall like lightning from heaven.'"[51] This text is not unanimously understood as a reference to a primordial fall of Satan so much as an expression of eschatological hope in the ultimate conquest of evil.[52] Nonetheless, the reference to Satan's inglorious ejection from

---

46. Francis, *"Gaudete et Exsultate"* 160.

47. Clifford and Murphy, "Genesis," 12; D'Aragon, "Apocalypse," 482.

48. Brown, *Introduction to New Testament Christology*, 41: Heaster, *Real Devil*, 244; Jeremias, *New Testament Theology*, 93.

49. Francis, *"Gaudete et Exsultate"* 160.

50. Francis, *"Gaudete et Exsultate"* 160.

51. Francis, *"Gaudete et Exsultate"* 159.

52. Gathercole, "Jesus' Eschatological Vision."

heaven reinforces Pope Francis's emphasis that the ultimate source of evil lies outside of human nature, highlighting the devil's inhuman nature as a disgraced denizen of the realm of disembodied spirits. This serves to refute Manichean tendencies to identify evil with the physical and bodily realms, suggesting that evil originates in the realm of pure spirit.

The verse holds further implications too. Rene Girard, in his work entitled *I See Satan Fall Like Lightning,* speaks of Satan as a force that impels scapegoating whereby some individual or group is demonized and blamed for the ills of an age—a form of demonization that Francis strenuously counteracts.[53] While Girard views the satanic scapegoating mechanism as unifying the human mob in common opposition to some designated human enemy, Francis's references to the devil seek to unify humanity in the face of an inhuman enemy, diverting our hostility away from human targets. In a sense, Pope Francis subverts satanic scapegoating, turning it against the devil.

WHAT DOES POPE FRANCIS MEAN BY "MYTH"?

While Francis may regard it as a diabolical illusion to equate the full reality of the devil with a mythic motif, his position need not be interpreted as completely dismissing the role of myth in expressing the reality of the devil. Richard Bell regards the devil as a noumenal reality, lingering on the fringes of waking consciousness and discoverable precisely through myth.[54] For Bell, the devil exists as more than a mythical motif but not as an ontological reality—much less a disembodied person.

When Francis rejects an equation of the devil with a mythic motif, much depends on the model of myth in question. Some of Francis's readers may, drawing upon a colloquial sense of the term as assumed in *Christian Faith and Demonology*, equate myth with fallacy. Rudolph Bultmann envisaged that the Kerygma could and should be demythologized. This Bultmanian account of myth as archaic and disposable packaging for the kerygma has arguably heightened the magisterium's suspicion of the term "myth" as applied to scripture and may be influential in Francis's references to the genre.[55]

By contrast, as we have seen, the model of myth advocated by David Tracy, Paul Ricoeur, Claude Lévi-Strauss, and Jean-Luc Marion, among others, distances the genre from figurative accounts of history, primitive science, or causal explanations of any kind.[56] These authors regard myth as

---

53. Girard, *I See Satan Fall Like Lightning,* 35–38.
54. Bell, *Deliver Us from Evil,* 173.
55. Bultmann, *Jesus and the Word,* 8; McBrien, *Catholicism,* 136.
56. Segal, "Myth and Ritual," 355; Lévi-Strauss, *Naked Man,* 556; Marion, "Erotic

a potent expression of existential truths and possibilities. From such a perspective, mythical references to Satan can express truths concerning freewill, evil, suffering, and enmity, but not truths of a historical or biographical nature. This vast disparity between various understandings of myth greatly complicates attempts to interpret Pope Francis's apparently dismissive references to the genre.

POPE FRANCIS ENDORSES DIVERSITY OF DOCTRINAL INTERPRETATION

It seems fair to argue that statements in *Gaudete et Exsultate* regarding the moral hazards of equating the devil with a myth or idea should be interpreted in light of the same document's more general remarks on the interpretation of doctrine. In his remarks on Gnosticism, Francis recognizes the difficulty of expressing and interpreting the deposit of faith, acknowledging "It is not easy to grasp the truth that we have received from the Lord. And it is even more difficult to express it."[57] This seems highly applicable to the matter of the devil. If Pope Francis regards those who think of the devil as a mythical motif or concept as susceptible to moral failure, this warning can be balanced with his injunction against imposing one interpretation of doctrine as absolute.

> So we cannot claim that our way of understanding this truth authorizes us to exercise a strict supervision over others' lives. Here I would note that in the Church there legitimately coexist different ways of interpreting many aspects of doctrine and Christian life; in their variety, they "help to express more clearly the immense riches of God's word."[58]

While by no means endorsing an indifferentist or relativist approach to doctrine, Pope Francis acknowledges the possibility that a number of valid interpretations may co-exist among the People of God. The pontiff acknowledges that doctrinal formulae, as opposed to the eternal truths they seek to mediate, form part of a dynamic, evolving tradition. "In effect, doctrine, or better, our understanding and expression of it, is not a closed system, devoid of the dynamic capacity to pose questions, doubts, inquiries."[59] Francis's

---

Phenomenon," 164; *God Without Being*, 22; Tracy, *Analogical Imagination*, 100; Ricoeur, *Symbolism of Evil*, 15.

57. Francis, "Gaudete et Exsultate" 42.
58. Francis, "Gaudete et Exsultate" 42.
59. Francis, "Gaudete et Exsultate" 44.

distinction between "doctrine" and "our understanding and expression of it" is reminiscent of Pope St. John XXIII's reminder on the eve of the Second Vatican Council that "The substance of the ancient doctrine of the deposit of faith is one thing, and the way in which it is presented is another."[60]

Francis's recognition of the desirability of reinterpreting and reformulating doctrine is entirely consistent with the position adopted by the CDF in *Mysterium Ecclesiae* that viewed doctrinal formulae as time-conditioned attempts to express eternal truths.[61] The 1973 declaration proceeded to approve a role for theologians in the exegesis and formulation of doctrine at the service of the Church.[62]

POPE FRANCIS ENDORSES THE POSSIBILITY OF DOCTRINAL DEVELOPMENT

Pope Francis in *Gaudete et Exsultate* recognizes the possibility of doctrinal development in light of the insights and concerns of a given milieu, proposing, with strong undertones of the opening sentence of *Gaudium et Spes,* that "The questions of our people, their suffering, their struggles, their dreams, their trials and their worries, all possess an interpretational value that we cannot ignore if we want to take the principle of the Incarnation seriously. Their wondering helps us to wonder, their questions question us."[63] Francis's position in this regard might be applied to the doctrine of the devil to suggest that it is not a closed question. Indeed, when the pontiff argued that the forces of evil can "induce us not to change, to leave things as they are, to opt for a rigid resistance to change," this might be applied to a dogged and integralist approach to the doctrine of Satan.[64]

CONCLUSION

Pope Francis, in *Gaudete et Exsultate*, argues that to think of the devil only in terms of a mythical persona or idea leads to a heightened susceptibility to diabolical influence—a position that may be resented by his detractors on this point. The Holy Father does not, however, positively mandate a particular account of the mode in which the devil exists. Rather, he rejects the

60. John XXIII, "*Gaudet Mater Ecclesia*."
61. CDF, *Mysterium Ecclesiae* 5.
62. CDF, *Mysterium Ecclesiae* 5.
63. Francis, "*Gaudete et Exsultate*" 44; Paul VI, "*Gaudium et Spes*" 1.
64. Francis, "*Gaudete et Exsultate*" 168.

Pope Francis on the Devil, Discernment, and Interpretations of Doctrine

position that the myth or idea of the devil lacks a referent, and leaves room for further theological reflection on the matter.

Francis's ruminations on diabolical influence reflect the writings of St. Ignatius of Loyola who believed that angels and demons affect the thoughts and moods of human persons. Interpreters of Ignatius differ as to whether they understand the saint to be referring to demons or spirits in the sense of ontological beings. Modern psychology and modern biblical scholarship can both challenge and enrich Ignatian spirituality in this regard.

Despite his strongly worded warnings regarding the devil, Pope Francis shows an openness to the insights of modern biblical scholarship that were harshly dismissed by Pope Paul VI and the CDF. Francis argues for ongoing discernment and the validity of diverse interpretations of doctrine so as to attend to the questions, doubts and insights of our time. His rather vehement injunctions on the subject of the devil may hence be regarded as his spirited contribution to an ongoing conversation and in that spirit, we press forward so as to explore what Jesus and the gospel writers might have meant by their references to Satan.

10

What Did Jesus and the New Testament Authors Teach about Satan?

"Without ever placing Satan at the center of his Gospel, Jesus nevertheless only spoke of him on what were clearly crucial occasions and by means of important pronouncements."[1] So states *Christian Faith and Demonology*, the 1975 study authored anonymously and sponsored by the Congregation for the Doctrine of the Faith. The study interprets gospel references to Satan as "important pronouncements" uttered by Jesus, tacitly dismissing the possibility that the Evangelists each addressed their presentation of Jesus' teachings to the concerns of their authorial context, and that their references to Satan may have reflected the challenges and conflicts current in their own situations.

The study also dismisses the possibility that Gospel references to Satan reflect the cultural assumptions of Jesus and the Evangelists. Initially acknowledging that Jesus belonged to a particular cultural context, the study immediately negates the significance of that observation, claiming that the earthly Jesus could not have been influenced by his culture:

> There is no disputing the fact that Christ, and even more so the Apostles, belonged to their times and shared the current culture. Nevertheless, because of his divine nature and the revelation

1. CDF, "Christian Faith and Demonology."

which he had come to communicate, Jesus transcended his milieu and his times: he was immune from their pressure.²

The present chapter appeals for a more circumspect stance in relation to the question of what the gospel writers meant by their references to Satan and demons and what Jesus himself may have thought and taught on the matter. Jesus was steeped in the Jewish scriptures and it is hence reasonable to argue that he was familiar with the motifs of Satan that we have discussed in relation to the Hebrew Bible. Since these models of Satan predate Patristic and Gnostic disputes about the devil, none of them equate with the "Christian" model of Satan promoted by the Council of Braga or the Fourth Lateran Council.

That is not to say, however, that Jesus added no new significance to the motifs of Satan that already featured in the Jewish imagination of his time. In a sense, the Jesus of the canonical gospels did transcend his culture, adding new layers of significance to old motifs and demonstrating a mythopoetic sensibility. Myth, as understood by Ricoeur, overflows with an abundance of meaning and engenders new interpretations. Yet it remains myth, not transposing itself into history.

THE SATAN OF THE GOSPELS AND THE DEMONIZATION OF JEWISH ADVERSARIES

As Philip Almond notes, "it would be wrong to seek a unified view of the Devil in the collection of works that make up the New Testament."³ Without imposing an unwarranted homogenization, it might, however, be observed that gospel references to Satan generally reflect the adversity experienced by the gospel writers and their communities." Given that the Hebrew origins of the word "Satan" denote enmity and evoke an adversarial role rather than a particular being, it makes sense that New Testament references to Satan would reflect forms of adversity experienced by the sacred authors.⁴

Marianne Dacy notes the adversity that arose between the Jesus movement, composed in large part of Jews, and the broader Jewish community after the destruction of the temple in 70 AD.⁵ Tension between the Jesus movement and the wider Jewish community, within which it had existed for four decades, stemmed from disagreements concerning the messianic

2. CDF, "Christian Faith and Demonology."
3. Almond, *Devil*, 23.
4. Kelly, *Satan*, 3.
5. Dacy, *Separation of Early Christianity from Judaism*, 20–50.

identity of Jesus, the Resurrection, liturgical disputes, and the admission of gentiles into the ecclesial communities.[6] Also contributing to the estrangement, during the siege of Jerusalem, Jewish Christians had not fought alongside their coreligionists against the Romans.[7] Many commentators agree that by 80 AD, members of the Jesus movement had, in most places, been expelled from the synagogues.[8]

The gospel writers may have regarded their conflicts with the broader Jewish community as symptomatic of a cosmic struggle. Wilfred Harrington identifies an apocalyptic tendency to interpret strife on earth as a "repercussion of something already determined in a heavenly world."[9] On a similar note, Jon Levenson observes, "the enemies cease to be merely earthly powers . . . and become, instead or in addition, cosmic forces of the utmost malignancy."[10] The association of human enemies with cosmic forces of evil need not, however, imply their association with supernatural beings. Indeed, it may suggest that the cosmic forces of evil are well-served by bad actors of flesh and blood so that supernatural villains would be largely redundant.

MARK'S GOSPEL

Mark's Gospel reflects the conflict between the Jesus movement and elements within the wider Jewish community. To modern readers, it can seem as though the gospel indicts a large and undifferentiated Jewish mob for pressurizing the Romans to execute Jesus. That said, what may appear to modern readers as references to a ubiquitous, blood-thirsty crowd may have held far more specific connotations for early audiences more au fait with intra-Jewish conflicts of the time. As Dennis Hamm observes, when the passion narratives are read on their own terms, it is not all Jews but a certain stratum of Jewish leadership that is indicted for the killing of Jesus.

> A careful reading of the four gospels shows that it is not the people as a whole but certain religious leaders joined by a few others who are complicit in the Romans' execution of Jesus. There is no historical reason to doubt that this picture reflects reality. Pilate

---

6. Dacy, *Separation of Early Christianity from Judaism*, 20–50.

7. Bauckham, "Jews and Jewish Christians," 228–38.

8. Harrington, *Church According to the New*, 123; Rensberger, *Johannine Faith and Liberating Community*, 26.

9. Harrington, "Understanding the Apocalypse."

10. Levenson, *Creation and the Persistence of Evil*, 44; Pagels, *Origin of Satan*, 38.

What Did Jesus and the New Testament Authors Teach about Satan?   151

and certain Jewish leaders were flawed men, each party acting according to their own notion of "homeland security."[11]

Without reading into the gospels a mass condemnation of all Jews, these observations offer some indication of the intra-Jewish adversity that impacted the contexts within which the gospel authors operated. Such bitterness led to a degree of demonization and to the invocation of the motif of Satan.

MATTHEW'S GOSPEL

Matthew's Gospel, reflecting Mark and additional sources unknown to Mark, portrays the Pharisees as particularly opposed to the mission of Jesus. "But the Pharisees went out and took counsel against him, how to destroy him" (Matt 12:14). Matthew depicts the Pharisees and Jesus trading accusations of association with the demonic. Matthew portrays the Pharisees as slurring Jesus saying, "It is only by Be-el'zebul [sic], the prince of demons, that this man casts out demons" (Matt 12:24) and Jesus, for his part, as responding in kind, calling the Pharisees "children of hell" (Matt 23:15).

Elaine Pagels observes that Matthew's account of the temptation of Jesus in the desert depicts Satan as engaging in a mode of proof-texting associated with the Pharisees.[12] Such polemics may reflect post-diaspora competition between the Jesus movement and the Pharisees for the hearts and minds of Jews.[13] Matthew 13:39 speaks of the devil as sowing weeds in an apparent slur on those who, from the perspective of the sacred authors, compete with the sowing of the seed of the Word of God. Granted, this does not mean that Jesus did not during his earthly ministry experience conflict with Pharisees, but it highlights the difficulty in identifying pronouncements made by Jesus regarding Satan, distinguishing these from the later-breaking concerns of the gospel writers. The gospel writers are not being deceptive so much as interpreting obstacles to evangelization as enmity towards Jesus, risen and active through his Church.

LUKE'S GOSPEL

Luke's Gospel continues to demonize the Jewish people in an apparently broad, undifferentiated sense.[14] A literal reading of Luke could suggest that

11. Hamm, "Are the Gospel Passion Accounts Anti-Jewish?"
12. Pagels, *Origin of Satan*, 81.
13. Pagels, *Origin of Satan*, 38–39, 46–47.
14. Pagels, *Origin of Satan*, 89.

a large assembly of Jews, shares collective responsibility for Jesus' death. "They all cried out together, 'Away with this Man'" (Luke 23:18). It is widely considered that the author of Luke's Gospel wrote in the 70s AD, a period during which the followers of Jesus were being gradually excluded from the synagogues. Luke portrays Jesus himself being ejected from the synagogue in Nazareth (4:16–30) and in Capernaum (4:31–44), offering some inkling of the contemporary issues at stake. Again, this is not a question of deception so much as a theological point acknowledging the presence of the Risen Lord who moves in and through his suffering people, and perhaps a motivational tactic, reminding the expelled Christian Jews that Jesus encountered such rejection on his path to Resurrection.

JOHN'S GOSPEL

Authored after the expulsion of Christian Jews from the synagogues, John's Gospel more overtly associates Jews with Satan. In John 8:44, Jesus is cited as referring to the Jews as children of the devil, intensifying the vitriol of the Matthean epithet "children of hell" (Matt 23:15), "You are of your father, the devil; and you want to accomplish your father's desires." This heated spate emerges out of a dialogue that began on a cordial note and includes Jesus' assurance that the truth would set his hearers free (John 8:31–32). Should this association of Jewish people with the devil, as *Christian Faith and Demonology* seems to suggest, be regarded as an "important pronouncement" by Jesus? Or is it more akin to sectarian sparring on the part of the gospel writer, or, put more kindly, a pep talk for the benefit of Christian Jews still smarting from the experience of being ousted from their synagogue communities? It is noteworthy that even as they maligned other Jews with whom they were locked in conflict, the gospel writers did so in a deeply Jewish fashion, invoking a motif from the Hebrew scriptures to drive their point home.

John also depicts Jesus making a thinly veiled allusion to Judas as a devil. "Did I not choose you, the twelve? Yet one of you is a devil" (John 6:70–71). The text suggests that one of the twelve is not only influenced by or possessed by a devil but *is* a devil. Hence, the gospel writer applies the term "devil" to a human enemy rather than a supernatural being—in much the same way as the term *ha-satan* denotes an adversarial role in the Hebrew Bible. This should occasion pause for thought for those who insist that Jesus and the gospel writers must have thought of Satan as a particular supernatural being.

What Did Jesus and the New Testament Authors Teach about Satan? 153

While the Evangelists may have invoked the motif of Satan so as to demonize the temple leadership, the Pharisees, or Israel more generally, this does not, of course, preclude the possibility that Jesus spoke of Satan during his earthly ministry. These later-breaking developments do, however, raise questions as to whether we can regard all gospel references to Satan as originating on the lips of Jesus, how we can be certain as to what, if anything, Jesus pronounced about Satan, and how we can disentangle any such pronouncements by Jesus from post-Resurrection conflicts.

CHRISTIAN FAITH AND DEMONOLOGY'S INTERPRETATION OF MYTHICAL LANGUAGE

The anonymously-authored study on the devil published by the CDF in 1975 condemns an interpretation of gospel references to Satan as the figurative personification of an idea, an invented fable, or a primitive superstition, dismissing all three possibilities in one sweep.

> Satan, whom Jesus had confronted by his exorcisms, whom he had encountered in the desert and in his Passion, cannot be simply the product of the human faculty of inventing fables and personifying ideas, nor can he be an erroneous relic of a primitive cultural language.[15]

This sweeping rejection dismisses in one breath the figurative personification of ideas that stands worlds apart from the "invention of fables" and from primitive superstition. Much depends upon what one means by the term "idea." It might be argued that the representation of any being in narrative is mediated by an idea of that being, and that the idea is hence personified. That is to say, the persona within the narrative represents a phenomenal reality, a representation, more immediately than it does a noumenal one, the "person-in-themselves," as it were, prior to any mental representation. However, the disapproving context in which the author of *Demonology* invokes the term "idea," and the preceding phrase "cannot simply be," suggest a whimsical connotation to ideas as though to emphasize that they can be fanciful and delusional.

The author of *Demonology* implies that if gospel references to Satan can be regarded as a figurative representation, then Jesus was not thinking clearly. "Otherwise one would have to admit that in those critical hours the mind of Jesus, whose lucidity and self-control before the judges are attested to by the Scripture accounts, was a prey to illusory fantasies, and that his

---

15. CDF, "Christian Faith and Demonology."

word was devoid of all firmness."[16] The statement rings of emotional manipulation, accusing those who regard gospel references to Satan as symbolic as doubting Jesus' stability and reliability, as if to say "if you do not agree with me, then you apparently do not trust Jesus." More broadly, the statement implies that recourse to mythical language is indicative of "illusory fantasies." An alternate diagnosis, reflecting the remarks of Walter Wink, for example, might portray Jesus as someone deeply attuned to the imaginal realm and to the mythic tradition of his heritage, articulating deep truths in the language of myth.[17] Ironically, a study sponsored by the magisterium of the Catholic Church, resorts to the argument that one who employs figurative language in an endeavor to express religious truth must be deluded—an objection that might be more consistent with an empiricist critique of religion.

When *Demonology* ridicules the prospect that the biblical authors employed the motif of Satan in a figurative sense, this is inimical to exegetical clarity as well as charity. Todd Klutz decries the propensity to interpret biblical texts through the lens of pejorative, modern assumptions, regretting the "tendency to use a particular set of abstract categories of classification—ideas such as 'superstition,' 'magic,' and 'primitive mentality'—which, though employed in a spirit of scholarly analysis, carry a heavy load of ideological baggage that puts the interpreter in a position inimical to interpretative clarity."[18] The difficulty highlighted by Klutz is that a category such as "primitive mentality" is so pejorative as to bias all subsequent exegesis. Myth, however, does not have to be approached from the perspective that it is pre-science, pre-history, or superstition. The non-explanatory option offered by Ricoeur regards it as anything but primitive as it grapples with realities that confound conscious thought and propositional discourse.

Having hitherto referred to "fables" and "primitive cultural language," the study proceeds to refer to myth in a pejorative sense, chastising contemporary scholars who propose that

> the names of Satan and of the devil are only mythical or functional personifications, the significance of which is solely to underline in a dramatic fashion the hold which evil and sin have on mankind. They are only words, which it is up to our times to decipher, even at the cost of having to find another way of inculcating into Christians the duty of struggling against all the forms of evil in the world.[19]

16. CDF, "Christian Faith and Demonology."
17. Wink, *Human Being*, 40–41.
18. Klutz, *Exorcism Stories*, 6.
19. CDF, "Christian Faith and Demonology."

What Did Jesus and the New Testament Authors Teach about Satan? 155

The use of the word "only" before the adjective "mythical" prejudices the positions subsequently outlined so as to illustrate how powerful words can be. On the other hand, the word "only" serves to restrict the scope of the implied criticism to scholars who deny any underlying satanic reality whatsoever, other than a figurative personification of evil.

Demonology suggests that some scholars may regard scriptural references to the devil as something that it is "up to our times to decipher, even at the cost of having to find another way of inculcating into Christians the duty of struggling against all the forms of evil in the world."[20] The implication is that modern interpreters of myth might find more effective ways to express an underlying truth, having decoupled it from ancient, mythical terms. Yet, the endeavor to interpret myth does not necessarily reflect an intention to replace it with non-mythical formulations—if such is even possible. Rather, the motive can be to clear away the obfuscation of historicized misinterpretations so as to discover the poetic truths engendered by the text when it is recognized as myth.

Paul Ricoeur implies demythologization of this kind when he remarks that "We must never speak of demythization, but strictly of demythologizing, it being well understood that what is lost is pseudo-knowledge, the false logos of myth, such as we find for example in the etiological function of myth. But when we lose the myth as immediate logos, we rediscover it as myth."[21] Ricoeur argues that in order to interpret myth as myth, we must cease interpreting it as history, science or etiology. While the term *logos* carries an array of meanings, Aristotle used it to denote reasoned discourse whereas he used the term, *mythos* to denote plot.[22] This implies a distinction between narrative and propositional statements. Similarly, Jungian scholars and Karen Armstrong have drawn a distinction between mythos and logos to contrast mythical and logical thinking.[23]

Whereas Ricoeur regards demythologization as freeing myth of historicist expectation so that it can function as myth, the author of *Demonology* implies a "slippery slope" argument, fearful as to where demythologizing may lead. "Those . . . who are knowledgeable in the biblical and religious sciences wonder where this demythologizing process entered upon in the name of hermeneutics will lead." In defense of the author of *Demonology*, while some of Ricoeur's work on myth had been published by 1975, some

---

20. CDF, "Christian Faith and Demonology."
21. Olson, "Mythic Language of the Demonic," 12.
22. Rapp, "Aristotle's Rhetoric."
23. See Shelburne, *Mythos and Logos*, 1–14; Armstrong, *Battle for God*, xvi, xvii, 49, 447.

had not. The author therefore had limited access to Ricoeur's insights on myth, whereas much of Rudolph Bultmann's work on demythologizing had been published by that date.

It might be argued that Bultmann alienated the stewards of orthodoxy, Catholic and otherwise, in relation to the topic of Satan, quipping that "It is impossible to use electric light and the wireless and to avail ourselves of modern medical and surgical discoveries, and at the same time to believe in the New Testament world of daemons and spirits."[24] Bultmann's comment however, may be interpreted with regard to a concern for the credibility of the kerygma in modernity, and an endeavor to liberate existential truth from language that reflects a specifically first-century—that is, "New Testament"—understanding of demons and spirits. Interpreted as such, Bultmann's statement would not necessarily negate *all* understandings of demons and spirits—just obsolete ones, rooted in an ancient paradigm, that cannot speak effectively to the modern paradigm. That is not to argue that all New Testament perspectives on spirits and demons are necessarily obsolete. Indeed, they may be far more insightful and nuanced than literalistic interpretations in our time would have one believe. It is merely to extend some exegetical charity to Bultmann whose statement need not be construed as a complete denial of the reality of demons and other spirits.

Elsewhere, with reference to the influence of Zoroastrianism upon Second Temple Judaism, Bultmann referred to Satan as a "Persian intrusion into Judaism."[25] The language of "intrusion" as opposed to "influence," implies that there is something inherently suspicious in any syncretic cross-pollination in the development of a religious motif.[26] This suspicion of development may reflect Bultmann's low view of history. Curiously, Bultmann, like Harnack before him, shares with his more orthodox critics a suspicion of historical development as though it necessarily compromises authenticity.[27]

Having acknowledged that Bultmann's remarks on Satan and on myth may have provoked the ire of the author of *Demonology*, it remains the case that the study fails to constructively engage less incendiary biblical scholars who recognized the complex relationship between the gospel narratives and history in a narrowly factual sense, who propose models of myth as something more than primitive superstition, and who recognize that Satan may

---

24. Bultmann, "New Testament and Mythology," 5.
25. Bultmann, *Kerygma and Myth*, 5.
26. Bultmann, *Jesus and the World*, 8.
27. Harnack, *What Is Christianity?*, 234.

be a reality other than a being encountered by Jesus on specific occasions that are meticulously recounted in the gospels.

A PRONOUNCEMENT ABOUT SATAN IN THE LORD'S PRAYER?

Demonology asserts that the Sermon on the Mount includes important pronouncements by Jesus on the subject of Satan, interpreting the seventh petition of the Our Father as one such pronouncement on the matter.[28] It regards the petition for deliverance from evil as a reference to a personal Satan. "It was again against this adversary that he put his listeners on their guard in the Sermon on the Mount and in the prayer which he taught to his followers, the 'Our Father,' as is admitted today by a good many commentators, who are supported by the agreement of several liturgies."[29] This interpretation was to be reinforced, and more widely disseminated, in the 1992 Catechism which states, "In this petition, evil is not an abstraction, but refers to a person, Satan, the Evil One, the angel who opposes God."[30] The reference to Satan as an angel suggests a disembodied person, a pure spirit.[31] While it could be argued that hermeneutical charity should allow for the possibility that the Catechism invokes the motif of the angel in a figurative sense, a more literal intent is implied by the Catechism's explicit rejection of the possibility that the petition might regard evil as an "abstraction."[32]

While the author of *Demonology* argues that Jesus only speaks of Satan by means of important pronouncements, the question arises as to the extent to which the petition for deliverance from evil constitutes a pronouncement.[33] The Our Father is first and foremost a prayer of petition. In Matthew 6, it is preceded by an injunction issued by Jesus on the subject of prayer. "When you are praying, do not heap up empty phrases as the Gentiles do; for they think that they will be heard because of their many words. Do not be like them, for your Father knows what you need before you ask him. Pray then in this way" (Matt 6:7–9a). This injunction might be said to include a pronouncement on the nature of God, the divine Father who already knows our needs.

---

28. CDF, "Christian Faith and Demonology."
29. CDF, "Christian Faith and Demonology."
30. CDF, *Catechism of the Catholic Church* 2851.
31. CDF, *Catechism of the Catholic Church* 328.
32. Augustine, *Confessions*, 4.
33. CDF, "Christian Faith and Demonology."

If the Our Father conveys pronouncements, they are pronouncements on the subjects of God and on prayer of petition—not the devil. This, it might be argued, is consistent with allusions to Satan in the Hebrew Bible that always serve as to ultimately allude to some truth about God and God's relationship with humanity, more than to affirm the existence of a personal Satan.

The petitions, "lead us not into temptation" and "deliver us from evil" are related by the conjunction "but" so as to suggest an antithetic parallelism. The implication is that deliverance from evil is the alternative, perhaps the opposite, of being led into temptation. This reflects the residual influence of ancient images of God. The idea that God might lead someone into temptation evokes an ancient image of YHWH from whom evil, as well as goodness, was imagined to proceed.[34] This is reminiscent of the plight of Job whom God allows to be tempted by Satan, saying "Very well, he is in your power; only spare his life" (Job 1:6) or, as James Alison observes, Jesus led by God's Spirit to be tempted by Satan in the desert (Matt 4:1–11).[35] If the petition for deliverance from evil implies traces of the Joban worldview, the Satan associated with this view is a tempter, tester, and prosecutor who serves God's inscrutable will.[36] It may also reflect the residual influence of a morally complex image of God. This model of God was one that utilized Satan as an unsavory henchman, giving Satan permission to inflict horrendous suffering upon Job and his loved ones.

To the extent that Matthew 6:13 invokes a Joban model of Satan, it might be argued that the Satan in question inhabits the narrative arc of myth, rather than the cosmos beyond. As R. A. F. MacKenzie notes, "the greater part of Jb [sic] is in poetic form."[37] Its genre is not that of historical writing. Given the poetic register of language that characterizes the Book of Job, its invocation of Satan the tempter and tester seems to be intended as a figurative personification rather than reference to a particular person. Having earlier noted Joseph Fitzmyer's suggestion that St. Paul seems to have interpreted the Adamic myth in a historicized fashion, it may be disingenuous to assume that Jesus and the gospel writers exhibited a similar failure to recognize figurative writing and speech.[38] Bernard Batto remarks, "I doubt that any society in the historical period—and this includes not only the ancient Israelites but also the ancient Babylonians, Canaanites, Egyptians,

---

34. Volz, *Das Daimonische in Jahwe*; Nielson, *Satan*, 55.
35. Alison, "Deliver Us from Evil."
36. Kelly, *Satan*, 2–23.
37. MacKenzie, "Job," 511.
38. Fitzmyer, "Romans," 407.

What Did Jesus and the New Testament Authors Teach about Satan? 159

and Greeks—has been so unsophisticated that it accepted its myths in an unreflective and preconscious *naïveté*."[39] Furthermore, MacKenzie cites the existence of "forerunners" to Job in Egyptian and Mesopotamian literature, suggesting possible syncretism.[40] This might also imply that the narrative exemplifies a subgenre, perhaps identifiable as theodic narrative, rather than historical reconstruction.

Matthew's reference in the seventh petition of the Our Father to the *poneros* or "Evil One" may be further explored with reference to the other instances in which the gospel-writer utilizes this term in his account of the Sermon on the Mount. Whereas, *Demonology*, asserts that Jesus, in the Sermon on the Mount, put his listeners "on guard" against Satan, the Matthean author's uses of the term *poneros*, and the overall thrust of the sermon, suggest an allusion to evil in a general sense.[41]

Matthew 5:39 reads, "But I say to you, 'Do not resist one who is evil. But if anyone strikes you on the right cheek, turn to him the other also.'" Timothy Jackson observes that the term denoting "one who is evil" or "evil doer" in this verse is again *poneros*.[42] In this instance, the *poneros*, is depicted as striking the cheek—suggesting the act of an embodied human rather than a disembodied spirit. Furthermore, the injunction not to resist the "evil one" seems more likely to be intended to discourage violent retaliation against human adversaries than to advocate non-resistance in relation to Satan as a supernatural tempter. This begs the question as to whether we can, with any degree of certainty, insist that in the petition for deliverance from evil in Matthew 6:13, *poneros* denotes a particular disembodied being whereas in Matthew 5:39, it refers to human enemies. Matthew's reference in 5:39 to "one who is evil" paves the way for Jesus' command to enemy-love in Matthew 5:44, a command usually associated with human enemies. Hence, it might be argued that the term *poneros* personifies adversaries, or, even more broadly, adversity itself. Just as the Hebrew Bible invokes the term "satan" to denote adversaries of the human variety, Matthew's use of the term "Evil One" may do likewise—especially in the context of a sermon on how to treat others, including one's enemies.[43]

Noting that commentators in the East have, for the most part, historically, translated *poneros* in Matthew 6:19 as a masculine noun, while translators in the West have typically translated it in neutral form, Gerhard

---

39. Batto, *Slaying the Dragon*, 11.
40. MacKenzie, "Job," 511.
41. CDF, "Christian Faith and Demonology."
42. Jackson, *Priority of Love*, 124n37.
43. Pagels, *Origin of Satan*, 450.

Kittle and Gerhard Friedrich propose that "The petition then is probably a request for delivery from all evil, according to Jewish models."[44] The reference to Jewish models suggests the holistic, Semitic model of evil identified by Donald Senior, encompassing sickness and all that stands as an affront to human dignity.[45] Surely it is not beyond the bounds of possibility that Jesus, immersed in a Semitic, holistic worldview, when confronted with the specter of sick, impoverished, and excluded people, prayed for deliverance from evil in a holistic sense.

WHAT WAS JESUS' UNDERSTANDING OF SATAN?

While we cannot assume that every gospel reference to Satan represents an utterance on the part of Jesus, let alone an important pronouncement on his part, we can propose some inference into how Jesus may have understood the motif of Satan insofar as he was steeped in the traditions of the Hebrew Bible and other, extracanonical texts. Jesus may have been familiar with models of Satan as a "son of God," tempter and tester (Job 1:6–8), accuser (Zech 3:1), obstacle (Num 22:22), and adversary (2 Sam 24). These models of Satan depict a persona or role that is adversarial towards humanity, but not towards the Deity, whom it serves. There is, however, evidence in the gospels to suggest that Jesus and the Evangelists were also aware of the motif of a Satan fallen from God's good graces.

Jesus is likely to have been familiar with the motifs found in Isaiah 14, and Psalm 89, both of which describe the inglorious descent of heavenly beings, and the "Book of the Watchers" in *First Enoch* that refers to the fall of supernatural beings called Semihazah, Azazel, Mastema, Belial, and, notably, one "Satanail."[46] As Miguel de la Torre and Albert Hernandez suggest, Jesus may have known the *Enoch* narratives.[47] As such, he may have numbered the mythic Satan, among the fallen servants of YHWH. These tropes of fallen beings, however, seem to have been figurative representations of political turmoil and the fate of human tyrants, rather than assertions that supernatural beings were ejected from heaven.

Luke depicts Jesus asserting, in response to the success experienced by the apostles in driving out demons, "I saw Satan fall like lightning from Heaven: Behold I have given you power to tread on snakes and scorpions, and upon every power of the enemy" (Luke 10:18–19). Simon Gathercole

---

44. Kittle and Friedrich, *Theological Dictionary of the New Testament*, 914.
45. Senior, *Jesus*, 107.
46. See Orlov, "Watchers of Satanail."
47. Torre and Hernandez, *Quest for the Historical Satan*, 767.

What Did Jesus and the New Testament Authors Teach about Satan? 161

contextualizes this remark by the Lucan Jesus, noting that the disciples have just reported to Jesus their success as exorcists.[48] Gathercole doubts that the Lucan Jesus is seeking to trump their successes by saying that he witnessed the more impressive primordial fall of Satan. Such bragging would imply a reference to the pre-existing Logos and would be more Johannine than Lucan in character. Rather, Gathercole regards the reference to Satan's fall in Luke 10:18 as bolstering faith in the final defeat of evil at the *eschaton*.[49]

A COUNTERARGUMENT BASED UPON A HIGH CHRISTOLOGY

Demonology argues that Jesus, being divine, was not subject to the limitations of his culture. "Jesus transcended his milieu and his times: he was immune from their pressure."[50] Could it be argued, therefore, that Jesus, fully divine as well as fully human, had access to supernatural knowledge of the existence of an ontological Satan and demons, in a manner inaccessible to mere humans? Within the scope of the present work, I do not deny this as a possibility. We can never be certain as to what other minds know—even those that are human and not divine. However, it would be one thing for Jesus to have had access to a divine knowledge of supernatural beings, another thing for Jesus to have communicated this to his followers, and another thing yet for his followers to have, in turn, conveyed this to later generations.

If as *Demonology* argues, Jesus was immune from the pressures of his culture, he would have recognized that his human audience was not immune from such limitations and hence addressed his contemporaries in a manner that would be coherent to them. And if Jesus' original audience was culturally-bound, so too were the stewards of the oral tradition, and the New Testament writers. Without presuming to place any limitations upon the mind of Christ, the present work merely observes that when the New Testament texts present Jesus as referring to Satan, broadly speaking, these references reflect motifs drawn from the Hebrew Bible and extracanonical literature, or relate to conflicts between the Jesus movement and other groups within the heterogeneous fold of diaspora Judaism. This book interprets the biblical text and Christian Tradition—not the mind of Christ, what Jesus taught rather than what Jesus thought.

---

48. Gathercole, "Jesus' Eschatological Vision," 149.
49. Gathercole, "Jesus' Eschatological Vision," 149.
50. Gathercole, "Jesus' Eschatological Vision," 149.

CONCLUSION

This chapter proposes that Jesus' Jewishness, his immersion in Hebrew myth, and his propensity to reveal new layers of meaning in ancient symbols may have influenced anything he uttered with regard to Satan and demons. Whatever we believe about Satan, there is little reason to believe that Jesus and the gospel-writers were literalists who historicized and particularized the mythical motifs and narratives of their milieu.

When we examine the evidence, it is not at all clear what important pronouncements Jesus issued on the subject of Satan. This is not to deny that Jesus may have taught on the subject, but, rather, to question whether the gospels offer access to any such teachings. Gospel references to Satan are bound up with the polemics of their authorial contexts, particularly with regard to the demonization of the Pharisees, and the non-Christian Jews more generally. If Paul VI in his "smoke of Satan" homily invoked the motif of Satan so as to demonize forces that he believed to be inimical to the Church, so too, the Jesus movement of the first century invoked the term to demonize its theological opponents within the wider fold of Judaism—though not necessarily with reference to a supernatural being.

11

Interpreting Gospel References to Demons

If Jesus and the Evangelists drew upon their Jewish understandings of the motif of Satan, the same might be said of their references to demons. The 1975 study *Christian Faith and Demonology* rightly suggests that Jesus exhibited both "respect for the past" and "intellectual freedom."[1] It might thus be said that Jesus balanced *aggiornamento* with *ressourcement*, neither utterly transcending his culture nor entirely immune from its pressures. Jesus, as portrayed by the gospel writers, innovatively adapted elements of their Jewish heritage, attributing to them a new level of significance. The gospels indicate that Jesus often retained terminology drawn from his culture, ascribing it new meaning as is the case in relation to the Passover meal, baptism, the concept of "kingdom" and, arguably, demons and Satan. Hence, Jesus engaged creatively with his milieu and furthered the dynamic development of mythical motifs. As Ricoeur puts it, "the Christian fact is itself understood by effecting a mutation of meaning inside the ancient scripture."[2] Jesus may not have been rigidly limited by the contents of the Hebrew Bible, but his worldview was in large part formed by it, and he added new layers of significance to its motifs.

1. CDF, "Christian Faith and Demonology."
2. Ricoeur, "Preface to Bultmann."

When the gospels place allusions to demons upon the lips of Jesus, this does not necessarily endorse notions about demons already prevalent in his time, any more than Jesus' references to the messiah, the kingdom, or baptism were identical with previous understandings. Neither does it necessarily denote a new demonology as such. Rather, in the absence of specific propositions by Jesus on the nature of demons, his references to the demonic would appear to serve another end.

The Jesus of the synoptic gospels is propelled into ministry by the scandal of suffering, assuring afflicted people that God loves them, forgives them, and longs to make them well. Luke's Gospel introduces Jesus' public ministry in the words of the prophet Isaiah as an outreach to the poor, the captive, the blind, and the oppressed—including those oppressed by sickness of body, mind, and spirit. Hence, Jesus expels the afflictions that torment the reviled, marginalized people of his milieu, evoking the mythic motif of demons to show that maladies and social exclusion are not punishments from God, but are opposed to God's plan.

DEMONS AS SYMBOLS OF ALL THAT OPPOSES THE KINGDOM OF GOD

It is the exorcism narratives that are most instructive regarding Jesus' perspective on demons as related by the gospel writers. Donald Senior regards the exorcism stories as more concerned with the existential experience of suffering and God's healing power made manifest in Jesus than with an assertion of the ontological existence of demons. Senior advises against the retrojective imposition of modern assumptions upon the biblical text. "Americans in recent years have become curious about the world of the occult . . . but we should be careful not to too easily equate Jesus' exorcisms with our modern blend of superstition and fantasy."[3] In contrast to the sensationalized imagery of exorcism conveyed by Hollywood's special effects departments, Senior notes the miserable banality of evil as confronted by Jesus. "The biblical mindset . . . acknowledged that the power of evil had nudged its way into daily life. The biblical mind regarded sin and suffering and death as differing manifestations of the fundamental evil that afflicted the human world and set it in opposition to God."[4] Senior deglamorizes evil by relating it to the scandal of abject suffering.

---

3. Senior, *Jesus*, 107.
4. Senior, *Jesus*, 107.

> To get some sense of what the bible means by such evil, one has only to think of the impact of such chronic expressions of evil in our world today as the problem of drugs or violence, or the inequalities that have left millions starving throughout the world, or homeless and despairing people on the streets of the world's richest cities.[5]

Granted, Senior does not deny the possibility of what might be regarded as supernatural phenomena but emphasizes that the gospels document Jesus' exorcisms as the liberation of the most miserable, marginalized, and wretched of people as he took his proclamation of the kingdom into the darkest of cesspits, beyond comfort-zones and cultural boundaries. Jesus hence rejected smug assumptions that the most wretched of people were being punished for their own sins or the sins of their parents. James Kallas notes that whereas the pharisaic view regarded demoniacs as rogues who must have done something to open themselves to possession by parasitic, scavenging demons, Jesus recognized their undeserved suffering in the grip of realities that could possess people against their will.[6]

Far from issuing pronouncements about what we might now regard as supernatural demons or the devil, Jesus delivered a powerful message of divine compassion for suffering people. Raymond Brown observes that "some of the cases that the synoptic gospels describe as instances of demon possession seem to be cases of natural sickness. The symptoms described in Mark 9:17–18 seem to be those of epilepsy, while the symptoms in Mark 5:4 seem to be those of dangerous insanity."[7] What Brown asserts of some illnesses, Joachim Jeremias asserts more broadly, noting the terror that may have resulted from exposure to disturbed individuals who in the developed world would now most likely be institutionalized or, we might add, heavily medicated.

> Illnesses of all kinds were attributed to demons, especially the different forms of mental illness. . . . We shall understand the extent of the fear of demons better if we note that the absence of enclosed mental hospitals meant that illnesses of this kind came much more before the public eye than they do in our world. . . . There is nothing surprising in the fact that the gospels too portray mental illness as being possessed by demons. They speak in the language and conceptuality of their time.[8]

5. Senior, *Jesus*, 107.
6. Kallas, *Real Satan*, 66
7. Brown, *Introduction to New Testament Christology*, 41; Heaster, *Real Devil*, 244.
8. Jeremias, *New Testament Theology*, 93.

The "language and conceptuality" of the time does not have to be regarded as primitive and superstitious, that is, as a form of pre-science. Rather, it can instead be regarded as mythical, expressing the dark experiences that seem to defy propositional statements and causation.

DEMONS IN THE MYTHOLOGICAL STRUGGLE BETWEEN BINARY FORCES

Claude Lévi-Strauss posits that a characteristic of myth is its juxtaposition of binary opposites.[9] Within a biblical mindset, evil is more or less synonymous with chaos, and the binary forces represented by Jesus' confrontations with the demonic might be regarded as the imposition of divine order upon the chaos epitomized by shrieking, self-harming, and arguably insane demoniacs. Raymond Brown identifies the juxtaposed binaries of the gospel, asserting, "In Jesus' ministry, two kingdoms are pitted against one another. This is the logic of Mark 3:22–27: Jesus' expulsion of demons is not a case of Satan's kingdom divided against itself, but of God's kingdom versus Satan's."[10] John McKenzie notes such a juxtaposition of the power of Jesus and that of demons, and Jesus' triumph over them.

> The important feature of this and other exorcisms performed by Jesus is not whether he accepted the common belief; those who formed the Gospel traditions could not have represented him as speaking in terms other than those familiar to them. The important fact is that Jesus liberates men [sic] from the fear of demons; demons have no real power and are instantly subdued by a word from him.[11]

McKenzie argues that the important point is not so much Jesus' stance on the existence of demons as particular entities. It is rather that Jesus liberates people from the *fear* of demons. The gospel narrative does not, upon most readings, liberate its hearers from susceptibility to experiences of suffering, but, as McKenzie suggests, it can liberate people from a fear of those forces, natural, supernatural, or whatever their nature, that underlie suffering.

Todd Klutz cautions against the imposition of modern categories in relation to the equivocal language of ancient text "whose vocabulary . . . was designed less for facilitating historical understanding than for winning

---

9. Lévi-Strauss, *Naked Man*, 556
10. Brown, *New Testament Essays*, 172.
11. McKenzie, "Gospel According to Matthew," 78.

ideological contests."[12] In a sense, the gospel texts are concerned with winning an ideological contest, as Klutz puts it, insofar as they are written from a perspective of faith to further a theological agenda on the part of those who are zealously convinced of Jesus' messianic identity and Resurrection, and who are engaged in competition with the pharisaic brand of Judaism. The Evangelists are more concerned with the identity and significance of Jesus, and his victory in the cosmic struggle, than with historical details in the modern sense. In a case in point, Carroll Stuhlmueller observes in the Lucan account of the Gerasene demoniac (Luke 8:26–37) some ambiguity regarding the alleged location of the event and remarks, "This fluctuation of the name of the locality and other details in the story should caution the reader against trying too hard to reconstruct what really happened."[13] This suggests that the author is more concerned with the expression of theological meaning than with historical accuracy.

Daniel Harrington regards the miracle accounts of the gospel, and by extension, the exorcism narratives, as signs that the Kingdom of God was overtaking creation. The sacred authors were not, in Harrington's view, asserting the occurrence of what today's readers would regard as supernatural phenomena. Harrington posits, "Those who preach and teach about Jesus' miracles need to help people today to appreciate the inclusive and flexible approach of the Bible towards 'signs and wonders' as opposed to the Enlightenment idea of the miracle as the suspension of the laws of nature."[14] Harrington's remarks underscore that the miracles of Jesus were written in a world that was imagined to be governed not by "laws of nature," but by God. Before a framework governed by laws of nature was absolutized some sixteen hundred years later, the miraculous was conceived in terms of a mastery over creation that could reflect only the power of the Creator.

James Dunn and Graham Twelftree also view the exorcism narratives as indicative of the struggle between the power of God and the power of evil, that is, "hostility to God," which the authors regard as "unified" rather than categorized within the framework of the biblical text.[15] Dunn and Twelftree regard New Testament references to demons as pointing to a broader power of evil, rather than disembodied spirits. "The absence of any fixed designation indicates that the New Testament writers had no clear conception of particular entities."[16] Hence, Dunn and Twelftree deny that the New Testa-

12. Klutz, *Exorcism Stories*, 6.
13. Stuhlmueller, "Gospel According to Luke," 139.
14. Harrington, *Gospel of Matthew*, 187.
15. Dunn and Twelftree, "Demon Possession and Exorcism."
16. Dunn and Twelftree, "Demon Possession and Exorcism."

ment teaches the ontological existence of demons in the manner developed by the later tradition. "A clear conceptuality of demons, therefore, does not emerge from the gospel evidence."[17]

Similarly, Torre and Hernandez note with regard to the New Testament, "The full concept of demons developed only later in the Christian faith tradition."[18] These authors support their position, pointing to the absence of any specific term for evil spirits in the Hebrew bible, and the connotations of the Greek term, *daimonian* as a derivative of *daimon*, that is, "god." Torre and Hernandez note in this regard that the New Testament epistles tend to demonize all non-Christian images of God. "In short, early Christians regarded all other gods as being in fact, demons, in league with the prince of lies, Satan."[19] Torre and Hernandez regard this as having been a "very dangerous dichotomy" between Christian faith and the faith of other communities.

Stuhlmueller notes a precedent in Israelite religion for this demonization of the gods of the nations, whereby, for example, the ancient Israelites had corrupted the name of the Philistine god, Baal as Baal'zebul, meaning "lord of the house" or possibly implying "lord of the flies" with connotations of a dung heap.[20] This demotion of deities to the status of demons reflects the process whereby monotheism emerged from henotheism, and violent, tribal deities were relegated in status. The relegated gods may still have been begrudgingly imagined to exist as ontological beings—or their relegation may have reduced their names to bywords for all that is ungodly—the intersection perhaps of theology and profanity. In any case, the gospel accounts of exorcisms do not identify the possessing demons with reference to the names of deposed Pagan gods, suggesting a very broad conception as to what counted as a demon. As for Baal'zebul, we will later explore the intriguing ambiguity that surround Jesus' reference to this name while skirmishing with the Pharisees.

DISTINGUISHING JESUS' VIEW OF DEMONS FROM A PHARISAIC MODEL

It would be simplistic to assume that Jesus and the Evangelists inherited just one unanimously accepted version of demons. Indeed, to speak of Jesus' "culture" or that of the gospel writers in the truest sense may be to refer

17. Dunn and Twelftree, "Demon Possession and Exorcism."
18. Torre and Hernandez, *Quest for the Historical Satan*, 57.
19. Torre and Hernandez, *Quest for the Historical Satan*, 57.
20. Stuhlmueller, "Gospel According to Luke," 145.

to a diverse and competing constellation of worldviews among which the Hebrew Bible, itself influenced by a plethora of cultures, held pride of place. As *Demonology* notes, while the Pharisees believed in the existence of spirits, the Sadducees did not, and Jesus could conceivably have adopted either view.[21] That said, it is not necessarily the case that Jews who believed in the existence of spirits, which could include human spirits and possibly angels, regarded demons as belonging to this category.

James Kallas points to a further disagreement among first-century Jewish versions of the demonic.[22] The author argues that the Pharisees regarded demons as weak, disunited, and fickle, suggesting that they roamed the world less like roaring lions than squealing rats. In contrast with this view of demons as lone scavengers, Kallas detects on the part of Jesus a view of the demonic realm as unified in its evil purposes and more formidable than the model assumed by the Pharisees. On Kallas's reading, Jesus recognized the demonic as organized chaos.

> Jesus becomes aware that while he and the Pharisees talk about the reality of the devil, they mean different things by that reality. For them, Satan and his forces are disunited. One can be used against another. And they are weak; they can be resisted by man's personal diligence, and the person who does end up in their grip is one who brought it on himself.[23]

Demonology alludes to this disunity that the Pharisees imagined to prevail among the demons, citing the manner in which the Pharisees accused Jesus of "casting out devils with the help of the prince of the devils" (Matt 12:25). Jesus responds that "Every kingdom divided against itself is laid waste, and no city or house divided against itself will stand" (Matt 12:27). This is interpreted by Kallas as referring to the coordinated unity of the demons. Jesus, in Kallas's view, recognized the threat posed by a unified kingdom of Satan.

> In direct opposition to that view, Jesus, however, must break with the Pharisees. He insists that Satan's power is not divided. There is no group of unrelated, fratricidal demons, one working against the other. On the contrary, he insists, Satan's hordes are welded together into a lethal kingdom. One cannot throw out another.[24]

21. CDF, "Christian Faith and Demonology."
22. Kallas, *Real Satan*, 66.
23. Kallas, *Real Satan*, 66.
24. Kallas, *Real Satan*, 66.

Jesus' remark that a house or kingdom divided against itself must inevitably fall may be a loaded comment given that the Pharisees and the Jesus movement were competing factions within a fragmented diaspora Judaism. There may be some thinly veiled innuendo that the kingdom of Satan is more united and stronger than a divided Judaism.

With further implications for the themes of unity and divisiveness, gospel references to demons emphasized the inclusive nature of Jesus' ministry so as to potentially alienate a Jewish audience. Richard Bell points to the manner in which the gospels depict Jesus performing exorcisms on gentiles, as implied in the narrative of the Gerasene demoniac of Mark 5:1–20, and breaking with the accepted Jewish ritual, utilizing pigs in lieu of a scapegoat.[25] Similarly, Todd Klutz, with reference to Lucan exorcism accounts, reinforces this point, viewing Jesus' exorcisms as "anti-rites" that flaunted Jewish conventions.[26] These considerations, because of their potential to alienate a Jewish audience, might be viewed in relation to the criterion of embarrassment so as to support the historicity of Jesus' ministry of exorcism, though not necessarily any specific exorcism account. Jesus' inclusive ministrations broke with convention and made him susceptible to the accusation of being aligned with demonic chaos rather than divine order.

SATAN AND BAAL'ZEBUL AS SEPARATE DEMONS?

Jesus' exchange with the Pharisees in Matthew 12 invokes the terms "Satan" and "Baal'zebul" in a manner that occasions pause for thought as to whether the gospel writer intended these names to denote distinct ontological realities. The narrative offers little indication as to the relationship between the two terms or the identity of the "ruler of demons." This is especially intriguing in view of Russell's suggestion that the classification of Satan as a demon is a Patristic development.[27]

Jesus names both Satan and Baal'zebul in rapid succession without making clear whether he regards these two terms as synonyms or as references to distinct motifs. "If Satan casts out Satan, he is divided against himself; how then will his kingdom stand? If I cast out demons by Be-el'zebul [sic], by whom do your own exorcists cast them out?" (Luke 11:18) The question arises as to why the Evangelist would present Jesus as referring to Satan and to Baal'zebul with the same breath. One possible solution is that the classification of Satan as a demon predates Tatian's insight, and Jesus

25. Bell, *Deliver Us from Evil*, 72–73.
26. Klutz, *Exorcism Stories*, 44–148.
27. Russell, *Satan*, 73–74.

uses the term "Satan" as a synonym for Baal'zebul. Alternatively, Jesus may have believed that Satan and Baal'zebul were two distinct demons, both with leadership roles in the demonic realm, and he mentions both for the sake of emphasis. A related possibility is that the gospel writer employs the two terms for stylistic purposes so as to construct a parallelism. It might also be argued that Jesus' close association of the two terms implies that they are figurative personifications of the realm of evil rather than two distinct ontological realities.

Given the heated context of Jesus' dispute with the Pharisees and the extremely unpleasant subject matter under discussion, the rattling off of the two names of Satan and Baal'zebul might be somewhat akin to a string of profanity which is often a proliferation of redundant terms so that there would be little to be gained in attempting to parse the significance of each expletive. The association of Baal'zebul with dung and flies may offer some indication of the colorful language involved. While the exact relationship between Baal'zebul and Satan, as intended by the Evangelist, remains somewhat unclear, the ambiguity points to the sense in which Christian conceptions of Satan are often a hybrid of previously independent traditions and that it cannot be safely assumed that every sinister-sounding motif in the Bible from the "Beast" to the "Anti-Christ" is a synonym for Satan as understood in Christian theology.

FROM SEMITIC HOLISM TO GREEK DUALISM

While Jewish perspectives varied on the existence of spirits in general and on the subject of demons, Hellenistic thought offered its own perspectives of which Jesus and the gospel writers may have been to some extent aware. Dunn and Twelftree note that first-century Hellenistic thought sometimes regarded "daimons" as ghosts of the human dead, a view refuted by Tatian who categorized the demons as fallen angels.[28] In contrast with this Hellenistic conception of daimons, the authors posit that Semitic thought regarded "spirits" as manifestations of evil rather than as intelligences.[29]

This juxtaposition of Semitic and Hellenistic perspectives points to the difficulties entailed by the fact that the gospels were written in Greek but reflect preaching and a subsequent oral tradition that was most likely mediated through Aramaic and littered with references to the Hebrew Bible. Whereas Jesus' ministry of preaching is likely to have been delivered in Aramaic, inspired by Hebrew narratives, and inevitably drew upon Semitic,

28. Russell, *Satan*, 73
29. Dunn and Twelftree, "Demon Possession and Exorcism."

holistic assumptions associated with the language, New Testament texts authored in Greek inevitably carry dualistic overtones.

The overriding consensus to be drawn from this survey of gospel references to Satan and to demons is that the New Testament authors envisaged the cosmos as locked in a struggle between the forces of good and evil, order and chaos. In the exorcism accounts of the gospels, Jesus shows that God is on the side of the sick, poor, and marginalized. As such, the gospels may invoke the motif of demons in a mythical sense. In light of Ricoeur's model of myth as a means of bringing to consciousness that which otherwise evades reflection, it might be said that demons serve as symbols expressing dark realities that totter on the verge of the unthinkable and inexpressible.

DID JESUS ISSUE PRONOUNCEMENTS ABOUT DEMONS?

These considerations beg the question as to what extent we can look to the gospels as a source of theological pronouncements made by Jesus on the existence of either demons or Satan. It might be argued that such spiritual cryptozoology is not the purpose of the gospels. The Second Vatican Council regards divine revelation as first and foremost the revelation of a personal God rather than the revelation of pronouncements. "In His goodness and wisdom God chose to reveal Himself and to make known to us the hidden purpose of His will (see Eph 1:9) by which through Christ, the Word made flesh, man might in the Holy Spirit have access to the Father and come to share in the divine nature (see Eph 2:18; 2 Peter 1:4)."[30] New Testament texts that refer to demons may first and foremost reveal truth about God and God's saving will. These texts reveal God's will that people be healed and made whole, distancing God's will from the theories of divine retribution that had further marginalized the sick and the poor. This may be the kind of truth conveyed by New Testament references to demons and exorcism.[31] In order to represent a cosmic struggle, the opposition had to be depicted in some manner. Gospel references to demons, however, may tell us little about Jesus' views on the existence of Satan or other disembodied beings.

New Testament references to demons constitute examples of mythical motifs functioning in an expressive rather than an explanatory manner. That is, the mythical motif of demons expresses existential truth in relation to the experience of suffering, madness, and marginalization. This is not to deny the reality of Satan and demons per se. Rather, it is to suggest that,

30. Paul VI, "*Dei Verbum*" 2.
31. McGill, "Diagnosing Demons and Healing Humans," 70–80.

in Semitic worldviews, unlike Western perspectives heavily influenced by Greek dualism and by the Enlightenment, reality is not necessarily confined to the categories of the historical, empirical, and ontological. Neither is it to say that all New Testament texts that refer to demons are primarily mythical by genre. Rather, it is to suggest that they draw upon mythical motifs, that is, in Ricoeur's terms, "a species of symbols developed in the form of narration and articulated in a time and space that cannot be coordinated with the time and space of history and geography."[32]

DID DEMONS ISSUE PRONOUNCEMENTS ABOUT JESUS?

While there is broad scholarly support for the position that gospel references to demons imply a cosmic conflict between the Kingdom of God and the kingdom of evil, demons also serve another, though not at all contradictory, literary purpose. While the Jesus depicted in the gospels may not have issued important pronouncements about demons, it might be said that they issued important pronouncements about him. As Daniel Saunders observes, the demons of the synoptic gospels announce the messianic identity of Jesus.[33] For example, in Mark's Gospel, the first creatures to imply that Jesus is the Son of God are the "mob" or "legion" of demons who possess the Gerasene demoniac (Mark 5:9). Somewhat ironically, the demons act as witnesses to Jesus divinely-appointed role if not his full divinity (Even if supernatural demons were, by virtue of their divinely-infused angelic knowledge, familiar with the Chalcedonian formula, the gospel-writers lacked such clairvoyance.) The demons of the gospels serve as mouth-pieces for chaos, acknowledging the bringer of divine order. Within a literalistic mindset, a denial that demons existed as particular beings, and recognized the true identity of Jesus, could be regarded as a blow to the testimony of the gospels concerning Jesus' identity. In another sense, this helps to explain the decision of the evangelists to include demons in their narrative and powerfully conveys that Jesus' life and teaching are a powerful threat to the forces of evil.

---

32. McGill, "Diagnosing Demons and Healing Humans," 71.
33. Saunders, "Devil and the Divinity of Christ."

CONCLUSION

Gospel references to the realm of the demonic reflect a theme of conflict, invoking the kingdom of malady and misery that is opposed to the Kingdom of God. The Jesus portrayed by the gospels seems more interested in ministering to suffering people than in issuing pronouncements about demons.

The question as to how exactly Jesus and the gospel-writers understood demons raises wider questions as to what cultural influences informed each gospel writer and Jesus himself. While the Hebrew scriptures provided a primary lens through which Jesus and the Evangelists would have viewed the world, these narratives were interpreted differently in various sects and schools of thought within Judaism. Hellenistic thought too would have had some degree of influence on the writing of the gospels, the oral tradition, and perhaps the teachings of Jesus. Related to this cultural interplay, the nuances of Aramaic, Hebrew, and Greek cannot but have influenced the New Testament's references to the demonic.

Whether understood as ontological realities or figurative personifications of sickness, chaos, and evil, the gospel writers present demons as defeated by Jesus. Even if demons are to be understood as symbolic personifications of evil and suffering, the gospels make clear that Jesus vigorously opposes their harassment of humanity—a point sadly lost on those Christian voices that have, in the course of history, tried to justify suffering in this life as though it is meted out as punishment from God for impoverished nations, hedonistic cities, and individuals both troublesome and troubled.

12

Towards a Less Dualistic Approach to Possession and Exorcism

Announcing his ministry to the blind, the oppressed, the poor, and the prisoner, Jesus, as depicted in Luke 4:16, reads from the scroll of the prophet Isaiah. This outreach to the most marginalized of people includes exorcisms—ostensibly a form of healing. The same gospel later presents Jesus as empowering his apostles to continue this outreach to suffering people. "Then Jesus called the twelve together and gave them power and authority over all demons and to cure diseases, and he sent them out to proclaim the kingdom of God and to heal" (Luke 9:1–2). These verses appear to distinguish power over demons from the curing of sickness, raising a question as to whether the gospel-writer considers illness and the demonic to be two separate matters. Alternatively, the sequential reference to authority over demons and authority over disease may be a stylistic embellishment, specifically a synonymous parallelism. A parallelism of this kind can be seen in Luke 4:18 where Jesus speaks of "release to the captive," rapidly followed by letting "the oppressed go free."

As we have noted, New Testament scholarship detects a holistic view of evil on the part of biblical authors who invoked the motif of demons so as to capture the insidious manner in which suffering, including sickness, infiltrates the human experience. This holistic perspective, wherein evil defies clear categorization, calls into question the existence of demons as disembodied persons, and reliance upon supernatural phenomena to serve as criteria for the diagnosis of demonic affliction.

The contribution of the present chapter is to argue that even if demons exist as distinct ontological beings, their agency may be vexingly intertwined with physical and mental illness as well as corrupted systems and structures. Modern theologies of sin and Catholic social thought have recognized that personal sin can be ambiguously entangled with social and systemic sin. If this is the case for human beings, it could be even more so the case for disembodied fallen beings, should they exist. Lacking embodiment, a pure spirit may be heavily reliant upon the manipulation and corruption of systems, structures, and processes in the social and the natural realms so as to pursue its malevolent ends. The interplay of personal and social sin may suggest the possibility of collusion between demonic agency and other forms of evil.

Furthermore, if the distinction between the natural and supernatural is largely a question of perspective, reflecting the degree to which human knowledge and understanding has evolved in a given epoch, then it may be conceivable that the demonic could work in and through what we regard as natural. If this is the case, demonic evil may not always be distinguishable from other causes of misery and injustice.

In light of a holistic model of evil, this chapter seeks to prompt a discussion of the criteria that guide pastoral responses to those who interpret their suffering as a form of demonic molestation, and, in particular, the authorization of a major exorcism. Towards this end, it critiques the pastoral implications of a rigid dichotomy between health and spiritual wellbeing which became tragically apparent in the case of the alleged possession of Anneliese Michel.

THE CASE OF ANNELIESE MICHEL

"I am so torn apart, unintegrated . . . strung out between two poles," lamented Anneliese Michel, who suffered and died, caught in an impasse between a world of science that regarded her as ill, and a world of religion that believed she was possessed by demons.[1] The case of Anneliese Michel, whose demise inspired the movie *The Exorcism of Emily Rose* (2005), raises a question as to how, or whether, demonic affliction can be distinguished from natural ailments.

---

1. Goodman, *Exorcism of Anneliese Michel*, 59, 221.

Anneliese was born in 1952 in Leibfing, Bavaria, West Germany to a Catholic family.² Her mother, Ana, had previously given birth to another child, Martha, out of wedlock.³ Martha died at the age of eight. John Duffey depicts Anna Michel as overly strict, forbidding her daughters to interact socially with boys.⁴ The effects of this upbringing may have resulted in internal conflict for Anneliese when, while at college, she fell in love with a fellow student.⁵

In 1968, Anneliese began to suffer convulsions that her doctors at a Würzburg psychiatric clinic diagnosed as symptomatic of grand mal epilepsy.⁶ Anneliese claimed to experience demonic voices, apparitions, and physical oppression.⁷ Her doctors subsequently diagnosed her with schizophrenia and dissociative personality.⁸ In 1975, having twice refused the request, Bishop Josef Stangl, at the recommendation of Fr. Adolf Rodewyk, SJ, authorized an exorcism to be performed by Fathers Arnold Renz and Ernst Alt.⁹ The two priests performed a concatenation of exorcisms over a ten-month period during which Anneliese appears to have gone without adequate food and basic medical care.¹⁰

Two analyses of the case conflict starkly in their interpretation of Anneliese's condition. Felicitas Goodman suspects that Anneliese was a deeply sensitive and pious person who experienced a trance-like state of consciousness, and was misdiagnosed with epilepsy and schizophrenia.¹¹ Goodman hypothesizes that Anneliese's epilepsy medication, Tegretol, impeded the efficacy of her exorcisms, and caused physical damage that led to her death.¹² John Duffey, on the other hand, argues that Anneliese was neurologically ill, that her alleged possession was a misdiagnosis, and that Anneliese died because of neglect on the part of her parents and exorcists.¹³ Notably, neither Goodman nor Duffey attribute Anneliese's affliction to invasion by demons

2. Goodman, *Exorcism of Anneliese Michel*, 59, 221.
3. Goodman, *Exorcism of Anneliese Michel*, 1, 59.
4. Duffey, *Lessons Learned*, 4.
5. Goodman, *Exorcism of Anneliese Michel*, 50–51.
6. Goodman, *Exorcism of Anneliese Michel*, 50–51; Hauke, "Theological Battle," 32–69.
7. Goodman, *Exorcism of Anneliese Michel* 31; Reints, "Exorcism of Anneliese Michel."
8. Hauke, "Theological Battle," 47; Duffey, *Lessons Learned*, xvi, 6.
9. Goodman, *Exorcism of Anneliese Michel*, 31.
10. Duffey, *Lessons Learned*, xvi.
11. Goodman, *Exorcism of Anneliese Michel*, 209.
12. Goodman, *Exorcism of Anneliese Michel*, 245–48.
13. Duffey, *Lessons Learned*, 15, 44, 79, 93, 124, 140, 161.

in the sense of ontological beings and Goodman's endorsement of exorcism is offered strictly on therapeutic grounds as a means to release the subject from a trance-like state.

The pastoral response to Anneliese's situation, on the part of the clergy and her parents, seemed to radically dichotomize her alleged demonic affliction and the medical conditions with which Anneliese had been diagnosed. Notably, no doctor was present during Anneliese's exorcisms.[14] Following her death in 1976, ostensibly from dehydration and starvation, Anneliese's parents and her two exorcists, Fathers Renz and Alt, were charged with negligent homicide.[15]

Anneliese's trauma coincided with the ecclesial polarization that erupted during the immediate aftermath of the Second Vatican Council. Goodman asserts that Anneliese "loathed" the reforms of the Council.[16] By all accounts, Anneliese would have resonated with Pope Paul VI's 1972 "smoke of Satan" homily demonizing challenges to the doctrinal status quo, and with his statement issued later that same year, reaffirming the Church's teaching that Satan is a creature rather than an abstract force.[17]

Anneliese seemed to view her suffering as bearing witness to the ontological reality of the devil as defended by Pope Paul VI and by the 1975 study *Christian Faith and Demonology*, published in the year before her death.[18] Also, coinciding with the years of Anneliese's ordeal, William Friedkin's 1973 movie, *The Exorcist*, was released in West Germany, according to some observers, unleashing a wave of obsession with the demonic.[19] Film critic, Mark Kermode recounts reports of mass-hysteria in the country, occasioned by the movie's release.

DIAGNOSING POSSESSION

In 1979, the Catholic bishops of Germany appointed a commission to study the subjects of demonic possession and exorcism.[20] This commission, in 1983, recommended that the Church's teaching on demons should be

---

14. Goodman, *Exorcism of Anneliese Michel*, 95–96, 198.
15. Duffey, *Lessons Learned*, xiv; Huake, "Theological Battle," 46.
16. Goodman, *Exorcism of Anneliese Michel*, 6.
17. Paul VI, "Mass on the Ninth Anniversary"; "Deliver Us from Evil."
18. Duffey, *Lessons Learned*, 61.
19. Kermode, "Devilish Deceptions."
20. Hauke, "Theological Battle," 3–8; Probst and Richter, *Exorzismus Oder Liturgie Zur Befreiung des Bösen*, 66.

reformulated so as to avoid anthropomorphic assumptions.[21] Conceding that demonic possession is a possibility, the commission proposed that there are no criteria by which to distinguish it beyond all doubt from illness.[22] Manfred Probst and Klemens Richter characterize the commission's report as arguing that "the power of evil does not manifest itself beyond the concomitant causality of natural causes" so that "it is not possible to individuate specific signs of sickness or other phenomena that prove by themselves a state of being overwhelmed by the power of evil."[23] Hence the commission challenged the existence of distinctive criteria for diagnosing demonic activity.

In 1999, the Congregation for Divine Worship and the Discipline of the Sacraments published a revised rite of exorcism.[24] The 1999 rite provided for a deprecatory option whereby the exorcist offers prayers of supplication to God for the deliverance of the afflicted person, by implication downplaying anthropomorphic assumptions entailed by directly addressing demons. However, the criteria for the authorization of a major exorcism were not significantly updated.

Cardinal Jorge Arturo Medina Estévez, who served as Prefect of the Vatican's Congregation for Divine Worship and the Discipline of the Sacraments when it published the 1999 edition of *The Rite of Exorcism*, cites the signs of possession as "speaking many words in unknown languages or understanding them; revealing distant or hidden things; displaying strength beyond one's condition, together with a vehement aversion to God, Our Lady, the saints, the cross and sacred images."[25] The 1614 *Rite of Exorcism* had listed these same signs.[26]

Indicating some degree of openness to the insights of modernity, the 1964 edition of the *Ritual Romanum* acknowledges developments in modern psychiatry and medicine, counseling that the exorcist "should not believe too readily that a person is possessed by an evil spirit; but he ought to ascertain the signs by which a possessed person can be distinguished from one who is suffering from some illness, especially one of a psychological nature."[27] While this injunction is commendable for the circumspection it

---

21. Hauke, "Theological Battle," 37.
22. Hauke, "Theological Battle," 38.
23. Probst and Richter, *Exorzismus Oder Liturgie Zur Befreiung des Bösen*, 6; Hauke, "Theological Battle," 38.
24. CDWDS, *De Exorcismis*.
25. Hauke, "Theological Battle," 38.
26. Paul V, "De Exorcizandis Obsessis A Daemonio."
27. Paul V, "De Exorcizandis Obsessis A Daemonio."

advocates, it still implies the existence of criteria by which possession can be distinguished from mental illness.

Cardinal Leon Joseph Suenens recognizes the need for updated criteria in relation to the grounds for the performance of exorcisms, suggesting "it would be advisable to revise the criteria of the Roman Rite—which goes back to 1614—or at least those that enable us to recognize a genuine demonic possession. Today these criteria are inadequate. They should be nuanced and studied in conjunction with natural parapsychological phenomena, such as telepathy, etc., which are in no sense diabolical."[28] Suenens recommends a more nuanced approach, informed by the insights of modernity, while noting that not all that is considered supernatural is diabolical. By the same token, perhaps not all that is diabolical is supernatural.

With implications for the question as to whether possession can always be distinguished from "natural" maladies, Fordham sociologist, Michael Cuneo's observation of some fifty exorcisms leads him to soberly report that he witnessed nothing that constituted unambiguous evidence of the demonic. "If something happened during an exorcism that defied rational explanation, that seemed to reek of supernatural evil, I was committed to reporting it . . . but nothing happened."[29] Implying the possibility of group suggestion, Cuneo recalls, "Occasionally I found myself in a situation where I was the odd man out. . . . Just about everyone else on hand would claim to have seen something extraordinary, and they'd be disappointed—confused and disappointed—that I hadn't seen it also."[30] Granted, Cuneo may have been "unlucky" but his study raises the question as to whether demonic activity can be distinguished beyond question from natural phenomena.

A POSSIBLE INTERPLAY OF THE DEMONIC AND ILLNESS

Our survey of modern exegetical insights into New Testament references to demons revealed a holistic, Semitic perspective whereby the demonic is associated with sickness and misery rather than a sensationalized realm of the supernatural. We noted Raymond Brown's observation that at least some of the cases presented by the gospel writers as demonic possession appear to be instances of natural sickness, and the contrast that Donald Senior strikes between Hollywood's sensationalized depictions of the demonic versus the pits of human misery into which the scriptures imply that Jesus would have

---

28. Suenens, *Renewal and the Powers of Darkness*, 139.
29. Cuneo, *American Exorcism*, 274.
30. Cuneo, *American Exorcism*, 274–75.

waded as he ministered to the most feared, misunderstood, and reviled outcasts of his milieu.[31] New Testament scholarship, reflecting the historical-critical method, tends to associate demons with "natural" maladies rather than with sensationalized criteria of possession such as inexplicable linguistic abilities or clairvoyance.

If demons exist as free-willed, disembodied creatures, it may be no less credible to posit that they operate in and through illness than that their malice causes distinctly supernatural symptoms. Writing in the third century, Origen posited such an ambiguous interplay of the natural and demonic in the transmission of epilepsy and lunacy.[32] Indeed, it might be argued, a rigid distinction between natural and supernatural symptoms implies a dualism that is ultimately a question of perspective. What was perceived as yesteryear's "supernatural" may be today's "natural," given an evolving understanding of natural causes. Once a phenomenon is scientifically explained, however, it need not cease to have religious significance. This line of reasoning has been invoked with reference to the divine, but it may also hold implications for the demonic. With reference to images of God, Dietrich Bonhoeffer laments,

> How wrong it is to use God as a stop-gap explanation for the incompleteness of our knowledge. If in fact the frontiers of knowledge are being pushed further and further back (and that is bound to be the case), then God is being pushed back with them, and is therefore continually in retreat. We are to find God in what we know, not in what we don't know.[33]

Demons and the devil can also be invoked as stop-gap explanations for a lack of knowledge, identified with the inexplicable. Alvin Plantinga, however, identifies the demonic with natural evil and proposes that if God does not inflict natural disasters on the world, the agency of invisible free-willed entities may be at work, and such entities may be what the tradition has called demons.[34]

What Plantinga allows for in relation to the suffering of the world, Cardinal Suenens surmises at the level of personal suffering, affirming the possibility of recognizing in the "possessed" subjects, cases of a psychic, parapsychological, or psychopathological nature, while accepting the hypothesis that there too, evil influences of a spiritual kind may play a role,

---

31. Brown, *Introduction to New Testament Christology*, 41; Senior, *Jesus*, 107.
32. Origen, "Commentary on the Gospel of Matthew."
33. Bonhoeffer, *Letters and Papers from Prison*, 311.
34. Plantinga, *Analytic Theist*, 16–48.

concomitantly or separately, and contribute to the morbid behavior."[35] Thus, Suenens allows for the possibility that demons might work through or alongside "natural" maladies. Suenens ventures that "The fact that a phenomenon can be explained according to our scientific categories does not allow us to rule out an interpretation belonging to another order or level of reality."[36]

There are indications of an endeavor within the international medical community to locate experiences of the demonic within a psychiatric framework. The World Health Organization has added "Possession Syndrome" to its official category of mental disorders, regarding it as a culture-bound syndrome, while the American Psychiatric Association recognizes possession as a kind of trance disorder.[37] Granted, both organizations adopt a phenomenological perspective, regarding allegations of demonic possession as reflecting personal or cultural convictions, without affirming the ontological existence of demonic intelligences. This identification of demonic possession as a psychiatric syndrome contributes towards a more holistic view of the demonic, recognizing its nuanced relationship with sickness.

CHARISMATIC PERSPECTIVES

Popular author and psychologist, Scott Peck, opines, "I used to think that Multiple Personality Disorder and possession were completely different things, different diagnoses. Now, given my experiences, it is quite clear to me that both can be operative simultaneously."[38] Peck's change of heart in this regard was influenced in part by the writings of Malachi Martin, a former Jesuit priest who operated a ministry of exorcism without the approval of a Roman Catholic bishop.[39] During an interview with Art Bell on the radio program *Coast to Coast* on April 4, 1997, Malachi Martin, though obsessed with supernaturalism, refers to demonic manifestation in the form of "ailments."[40]

Cuneo observes that Peck's acknowledgment of an ambiguous relationship between sickness and demonic affliction struck a chord with

---

35. Suenens, *Renewal and the Powers of Darkness*, 181.

36. Suenens, *Renewal and the Powers of Darkness*, 181.

37. See APA, *Highlights of Changes*, 10; WHO, "Trance and Possession Disorders"; Ferracuti et al., "Dissociative Trance Disorder" 525–39; Ross, "Possession Experiences in Dissociative Identity Disorder," 393–400.

38. Peck, *People of the Lie*, 192.

39. Cuneo, *American Exorcism*, 43–47; Martin, *Hostage to the Devil*, 12.

40. Bell, "Malachi Martin."

Charismatic Christians.[41] Barbara Schlemon, a pioneer of the Catholic Charismatic movement in the US, regarded Jesus' command to heal and to drive out demons as denoting that there can be a "demonic dimension to sickness."[42]

Gregory Boyd emphasizes that Jesus viewed sickness, not as a punishment from God, but as the "work of the enemy."[43] Boyd suggests that from a New Testament perspective, "all sickness and disease was considered a form of satanic oppression."[44] Michael Green notes that Luke 13:16 attributes a case of physical infirmity to the agency of Satan, while Matthew 9:32 attributes an instance of dumbness to demonic activity.[45] Luke 9:42 associates epilepsy with demons, and Matthew 12:22 attributes blindness to their influence. While emphasizing that not all illness should be attributed to demonic activity, Green tells of encountering a man whose epilepsy "seems to be of the type brought about by the enemy."[46]

David Pytches detects a holistic response to sickness on the part of Jesus, remarking that "Jesus did not divide man into two—a soul to be saved and a body to be left sick and unhealed."[47] Pytches advocates that the Church should continue Jesus' ministry of *sozo*, that is, a holistic deliverance of body, mind, and spirit.[48] Cuneo notes that Charismatics at times refer to lust, addiction, and anger as demons.[49] Such references seem to regard demons as something other than fallen, disembodied intelligences, and imply a broader understanding of the demonic. The author refers to a US priest, regarded as a pillar of the Catholic Charismatic movement, wondering whether this priest regarded demons as a "metaphor for psychological or emotional sickness, or old-fashioned sin."[50]

In citing these perspectives that posit an interplay of sickness, human sin, and demonic activity, a note of caution may be in order. It is one thing to identify sickness with that which is opposed to the Kingdom of God and to human life lived in abundance. It would be quite another to identify sick

---

41. Cuneo, *American Exorcism*, 142; Peck, *People of the Lie*, 62, 135–36.
42. Cuneo, *American Exorcism*, 98.
43. Boyd, *Constructing a Trinitarian Warfare Theodicy*, 36.
44. Boyd, *Constructing a Trinitarian Warfare Theodicy*, 37.
45. Green, *I Believe in Satan's Downfall*, 87.
46. Green, *I Believe in Satan's Downfall*, 87.
47. Pytches, *Come Holy Spirit*, 18.
48. Pytches, *Come Holy Spirit*, 18.
49. Cuneo, *American Exorcism*, 42.
50. Cuneo, *American Exorcism*, 42.

people as evil. To clumsily associate mentally ill people with the demonic could exacerbate their stigmatization and thus perpetuate social sin.[51]

MINISTERING TO DEMONS?

Without ruling out the possibility that disembodied spirits may exist and may at times impinge upon the lives of human beings, perhaps working in and through natural ailments, the traditional conception of Christian exorcism is grounded upon assumptions that too easily evade critical scrutiny and invite incredulity. We have already noted the manner in which Zoroastrianism influenced Second Temple Judaism, heightening its sense of cosmic dualism and contributing to the Judeo-Christian assumption, bolstered by the Patristics, that disembodied spirits are either angelic or demonic in the sense of morally pristine or else lost causes.[52] It is in view of such absolutism that demons have been regarded as beyond all help or hope—but can this be assumed with certainty? If embodied spirits come in shades of grey, why must we assume there exists no moral complexity in the world of disembodied spirits?

A 2016 television series entitled *The Exorcist*, produced by the Fox network and directed by Rupert Wyatt, depicted an alternative to the usual Hollywood clichés whereby macho exorcists battle a cackling demon—usually, for some reason, ensconced in a dark-haired girl in a white nightdress. The Fox production, however, portrays a fictitious community of nuns who exercise a ministry of deliverance with reconciliatory overtones. Tending to a violent demoniac, the nuns chant, "Fallen angel, you are loved" while in another scene a priest working with them addresses a demon, "Fallen angel, you are forgiven" and goes so far as to tell it, "Son of the morning, you are redeemed." This stands in stark contrast with traditional adjurations whereby the exorcist, in the name of Christ, commands demons to return to the pit of hell. There is nothing doctrinally unorthodox about the idea that God loves all creatures, including demons should they exist, but the bounds of orthodoxy are transgressed by the suggestion that a rite of deliverance should entertain the prospect that the demon might be redeemed.

While the prospect of extending compassion towards a demon, or praying for its wellbeing, is unorthodox, the hostile imperatives issued in the traditional forms of exorcism are deeply problematic on several fronts. The adjuration assumes that the demon is an ontological reality distinct

---

51. Senior, *Jesus*, 107.

52. Isbell, "Zoroastrianism and Biblical Religion"; Kronen and Menssen, "Defensibility of Zoroastrian Dualism," 185–205.

from the human person but, having noted Jung's references to the Satan or shadow dimension of the self, the boundaries of the self are not easily defined. If one accepts the reality of the subconscious, and perhaps a symphony of levels of consciousness, it might be argued that to distinguish that which is "within" the self from that which is "outside" of it is to invoke a very crude spatiotemporal metaphor. A pastoral implication of this all too often literalized metaphor may be a litany of prayers forcefully demanding that some dimension of the human person, rather than be integrated or healed, be put through hell with all the power of suggestion entailed by the rite.[53]

A related difficulty posed by spatiotemporal language is evident in the prospect of ordering a spirit, which does not by definition occupy space, to "depart" a human body as though it could be yanked out like a tapeworm—and then returned to hell, as if it had temporarily slithered out of a purportedly eternal state of being. The question arises as to whether the primary goal of exorcism is the healing of a human person or the "expulsion" of a demon. As opposed to the connotations of the term "deliverance" which refer to the aid rendered to the human victim, the term "exorcism" refers to the expulsion of the demon. Except in the 1999 deprecatory option, wherein the exorcist addresses God, traditional forms of the rite emphasize orders issued to the demon to "depart" its human host. However, if demons are not corporeal beings, the pastoral problem at hand has little to do with physical location. The metaphorical nature of the language of exorcism is too easily forgotten. When faced with the reality of a suffering person who believes their affliction to be demonic in nature, is the ultimate goal, we might ask, to mediate Christ's healing power or to order about disembodied spirits, adjuring them to return to hell? What would be lost by praying for the healing and wellbeing of all beings involved in the situation?

CONCLUSION

Exegetes adopting the historical-critical method detect in the New Testament a holistic view of evil whereby the demonic may become manifest in and through illness. This biblical perspective recognizes the capacity of evil to infiltrate and corrode everyday life, a far cry from a cinematic model of supernatural evil. So too, this holistic view of evil challenges the longstanding position of the magisterium that the symptoms of demonic affliction can, with reference to criteria that purportedly indicate the supernatural, be distinguished from the symptoms of natural ailments. A perspective associated with some contemporary Charismatic Christians, including

53. Jung, *Archetypes and the Collective Unconscious*, 153–54.

Catholic Charismatics, may reflect the biblical association of sickness and the demonic.

The Church's presentation of doctrine still insists that demons exist as free-willed creatures rather than only as mythical motifs. This need not, however, completely negate the holistic view of evil detected by New Testament scholarship. This chapter proposes that a recognition of the interplay between personal and social sin in the human realm raises a question as to whether the personal agency of demons, disembodied and hence incapable of the kind of physical agency enacted by humans, might collude with other forms of evil, including the social, systemic, and natural. Without dismissing the possible existence of demons as intelligent entities, evil may be experienced in a holistic manner, having "nudged" its way into the personal, social, and physical dimensions of daily life.[54]

If there are disembodied spirits involved in cases of demonic possession, the question seems at least worthy of theological reflection as to whether the prayer of the Church should speak of God's love for them and endeavor to bring them peace. While it is quite orthodox to suggest that God loves them, it is another matter to suggest that they can in any way be helped. But why not? A fatalistic gloating at the plight of the damned has become embedded in many forms of Christian theology and our next chapter will explore the scriptural roots, the logic, and the ethics of such condescension.

---

54. Senior, *Jesus*, 107.

13

Zeal for the Damnation of the Enemy Versus Enemy Love and Forgiveness

Whereas the satans of the Hebrew Bible enjoyed a divine mandate and even in the gospels, Satan maintains some degree of moral ambiguity, the Book of Revelation celebrates the casting of Satan into a "lake of fire and sulfur" (Rev 20:7–10). This apocalyptic image enthusiastically anticipates the demise of the forces of oppression as experienced by the author's community, invoking the imagery of a dragon, serpent, beast, and Satan. However, when Satan is thought of as a being rather than a mythical motif, Revelation is misinterpreted as though it somehow discloses the eternal damnation of a particular irreconcilable, irredeemable enemy of God as though human authors could be privy to such a situation. Such rhetoric perpetuates massive misunderstanding of Genesis, Revelation, and scripture in general. It also allows apocalyptic thinking to take a sinister turn.

When apocalyptic thinking degenerates so as to celebrate the evisceration of persons, even one person rather than of evil itself, such a vision contradicts Jesus' mandate to enemy-love and to limitless forgiveness. Yet this is the very vision that underpins doctrinal formulations that insist upon the eternal damnation of Satan and the other demons characterized as persons. The doctrine of an irredeemable Satan, who could not choose to repent even if it so wanted, reflects a distorted form of apocalyptic thinking that confuses the subjugation of evil forces with the torture of persons. It implicitly calls into question either God's salvific power or God's salvific will. Either God wills that Satan be given no further opportunity to repent—or God is unable to help a being trapped forever in the implications of its worst choice.

THE BOOK OF REVELATION DEMONIZES INSTITUTIONAL OPPRESSION

We have already noted that Gospel references to Satan reflect the intra-Jewish conflicts experienced by the gospel writers and not necessarily the utterances of Jesus. While the gospels reflect a mindset whereby conflict between human communities and institutions was thought to reflect a cosmic conflict, this is even more apparent in the Book of Revelation.[1] Revelation is apocalyptic in genre, authored in the midst of intense persecution by the Roman Empire, and envisaging a final standoff between the forces of good and evil. As Catherine Keller and Candida Moss both argue, Revelation, and apocalyptic literature more generally, seek to encourage the persecuted righteous to stand firm to the end, and to envisage the eventual obliteration of the forces of oppression.[2]

In the Book of Revelation, it is the Roman Empire rather than Jewish opposition that is vilified. While there exists broad scholarly consensus that the motif of "666," the mark of the beast, alludes to the Greek spelling of the name of the Roman Emperor, Neron Caesar, Revelation eagerly foresees the demise of oppressive forces rather than the destruction or torture of beings.[3] Revelation's figurative personification of an oppressive super-power finds something of a modern equivalent in Walter Wink's invocation of the motif of Satan as the "world-encompassing spirit of the domination system," as noted in our discussion of systemic evil.[4]

THE BOOK OF REVELATION'S APPEAL TO MYTHICAL MOTIFS

The motifs evoked in Revelation so as to signify systemic evil include re-patriated denizens of myth, now attributed a new layer of symbolic significance. While Henry Ansgar Kelly asserts that St. Justin Martyr was in the mid-second-century the first on record to explicitly identify the Adamic

---

1. Harrington, "Understanding the Apocalypse"; Levenson, *Creation and the Persistence of Evil*, 44; Pagels, *Origin of Satan*, 38.
2. Keller, *Apocalypse Then and Now* 1; Moss, "Roman Imperialism."
3. D'Aragon, "Apocalypse," 482.
4. Wink, *Theology for a New Millennium*, 27.

snake as Satan, the Book of Revelation seems at first glance to preempt such an association by several decades.[5] Verse 12:9 states, "The great dragon was thrown down, that ancient serpent, who is called the Devil and Satan, the deceiver of the whole world—he was thrown down to the earth, and his angels were thrown down with him."[6] While modern readers may assume that this verse directly identifies Satan with the talking snake of the Adamic narrative, Revelation 12 provides no indication that the author is invoking that particular myth. Jean Louis D'Aragon interprets the reference to a serpent as denoting the chaos monster, Leviathan, as described in Psalm 74:13, or Rahab as mentioned in Job 26:12 and Psalm 89:10. D'Aragon notes that serpents in the iconography of ancient Christianity were virtually synonymous with dragons.[7] Another arguable influence on the motif of the serpent, at least indirectly, is the Egyptian motif of Apophis or Apep as the enemy of the sun god Ra.[8] If this is the case, Revelation 12:9 may be an antecedent to, rather than an instance of, the association of the Adamic serpent with Satan.

Revelation's reference to the throwing down of the dragon-serpent-devil-satan evokes the motif of fallen beings, signifying the toppling of tyranny. This trope is evident in the morning star/Lucifer motif of Isaiah 14:15 that poetically signified the conquest of King Sennacherib of Babylon, and in Ezekiel 28 in its reference to the fall of the Prince of Tyre.[9] It was hence an established idiom to denote the downfall of tyranny. We have also noted that the intertestamental *Book of the Watchers* refers to a rogues' gallery of fallen beings and the tendency to depict turmoil in the earthly realm in terms of a cosmic conflict. The trope of Satan falling from heaven was, as we have noted, known to Jesus or at least to the writer of Luke's gospel, authored a decade or more before the Book of Revelation.[10]

Revelation's references to the serpent, the dragon, the devil, and Satan exemplify the manner in which the apocalyptic mindset appropriates mythical imagery in relation to a specific context characterized by oppression. As such, it is an early indication as to how the motif of Satan would be weaponized, albeit in this case quite understandably, on the part of oppressed people in fear for their lives.

---

5. Kelly, "Adam Citings before the Intrusion of Satan," 13.
6. Kelly, *Satan*, 176–79; Tertullian, *Adversus Marcionem* IV.38.2.
7. D'Aragon, "Apocalypse," 482.
8. Mark, *Set*.
9. Kelly, *Satan*, 196.
10. Gathercole, "Jesus' Eschatological Vision," 149.

SATAN AS DECEIVER OF THE WHOLE WORLD

The assessment in Revelation 12:9 that the "entire world" is deceived by Satan indicates a step in the gradual emergence of the Christian motif of Satan as the entity whose agency facilitates all evil—directly or indirectly. Equally well, the reference to the "whole world" may not carry cosmic overtones so much as an indictment of the Roman Empire.[11] As Catherine Keller notes, "world" in this context may represent a social construct, that is, the "known world" of the Roman Empire.[12] Hence, this statement may be a grim assessment of the moral status of a particular regime rather than a pessimistic view of the state of creation as a whole.

The First letter of John 5:19 makes a similar claim that "the whole world is in the power of the evil one." Luke Timothy Johnson regards this apparent alarmism as reflecting the author's exasperation with internal disputes about doctrine.[13] In this same letter, the term anti-Christ appears to refer to a human who preaches unorthodox doctrine rather than to a supernatural being.[14] Revelation 20:10 reiterates the association of the devil with deception and anticipates the fiery fate of supposed heretics and schismatics: "And the devil who had deceived them was thrown into the lake of fire and sulfur where the beast and the false prophet were, and they will be tormented day and night for ever and ever."

IMAGERY OF HELLFIRE: PURGING OR PUNISHING?

Revelation's allusion to a "lake of fire and Sulphur" raises the question as to why fiery imagery has become so ubiquitously associated with eternal punishment while there exist so many other terrifying prospects that could have been symbolically invoked in this context. T. J. Wray and Gregory Mobley note that the Gospels depict hell by recourse to the image of an unquenchable fire, an image at least in part inspired by Gehenna, the smoldering garbage dump outside Jerusalem, where child sacrifices had once been performed (Mark 9:43–48; Matt 13:40–43, 49–50; 25:41; Luke 16:19–26).[15]

These Gospel references to hell differ from Old Testament references to *Sheol* insofar as they hold judgmental connotations whereas *Sheol* was typically depicted as the dreary destiny of the dead more generally. That

---

11. D'Aragon, "Apocalypse," 469.
12. Keller, "Dis/Closing," 13
13. Johnson, *Writings of the New Testament*, 502.
14. Johnson, *Writings of the New Testament*, 502.
15. Wray and Mobley, *Birth of Satan*, 150.

said, the purpose of lighting a fire on a dump would be to sanitize and purge, burning away the fetid matter that would attract scavengers and spread disease. This could arguably suggest the purging flames of a purgatory-like state, rather than eternal punishment. In support of such an interpretation, the term employed in Matthew 25:41 and typically translated as "eternal" is *aeonios*, which may suggest "ages" rather than eternal in the sense of "without end."[16]

Not all commentators are convinced that Jesus' references to Gehenna as a place of fire reflect its use as a garbage dump. Noting that the earliest known references to a garbage dump on the location are medieval, Andrew Perriman posits that Jesus' remarks, or those of the gospel writer, are inspired by a string of Old Testament passages that imply corpses were disposed of at the site so that its name may have implied death.[17] Second Kings 23:10 and Jeremiah 7:31 associate Gehenna with human sacrifice, whereas Isaiah 66:24 suggest that the bodies of infidels were thrown there to rot. Perriman suggests that Jesus may have hence associated Gehenna with the prospect of judgment rather than a posthumous state of punishment.

Perriman notes Josephus's comment that, during the Siege of Jerusalem, corpses were flung out of the city into the surrounding valleys. While the siege postdated the death of Jesus by four decades, the gospel writers would have been painfully aware of it (while acknowledging that some critics may date Mark before 70 AD). If gospel references to Gehenna reflect the Siege of Jerusalem, they are laden with political and sectarian innuendo given the destruction of the temple and the resentment with which other Jews held Christians for not fighting in its defense.[18] The corpses that Josephus claims were disposed of in the valleys outside the city would have been, for the most part, those of non-Christian Jews who fought against the Romans. Granted, this is a speculative interpretation that goes beyond Perriman's remarks, but if there is anything to it, it suggests that gospel references to Gehenna were a very low blow, recounting the bloody demise of non-Christian Jews so as to envisage the fate of the wicked.

The reference in Mark 9:48 to the fire of hell as "unquenchable" might be interpreted as a warning against eternal damnation. However, it is one thing for a fire itself to be "unquenchable" and another to say that an object of purification cannot pass through it as gold is tested in fire (1 Peter 1:7). More telling yet, the reference to unquenchable fire in Mark 9:48 is surrounded

---

16. Salisbury, "Eternity Explained."
17. Perriman, "Was Gehenna a Burning Rubbish Dump?"
18. Bauckham, "Jews and Jewish Christians," 228–38; Perriman, "Was Gehenna a Burning Rubbish Dump?"; Josephus, *Wars of the Jews* V.12.3.

by hyperbolae that urges the sinner to amputate limbs and to gouge out eyes rather than be thrown into hell. The outlandish metaphors are awkwardly mixed as evident in the implication that there will be especially resilient worms that will apparently never die in the unquenchable fire. The important point is that the language is figurative and loaded with hyperbolae, most of which is not literalized in the Christian imagination, save for the supposed reference to eternity.

Another reference to unquenchable fire in Matthew 3:12 invokes the burning of chaff that has been removed from wheat that is taken to a granary. This might be interpreted to suggest the removal of the husk or expendable, external coating that surrounds that which is of value—arguably the stripping away and destruction of that which is not of a person's essence, the destruction of sin rather than of sinners.

Meghan Henning observes that, in the ancient world, the imagery of hellfire served a pedagogical purpose so as to influence behavior in the present, rather than to predict details of the posthumous state.[19] While New Testament authors may have intended their imagery of hellfire to serve an exhortative rather than a descriptive purpose, there is no denying that the prospect of the eternal fires of hell became well established in the Christian imagination and, indeed, Christian doctrine.

St. Augustine's *City of God* speaks of the eternal fires of hell but Augustine's purpose is to argue against annihilationism, that is, Augustine emphasizes that the fires of hell may burn forever but do not annihilate the sinner.[20] Again suggesting that the damned persist in being and are not annihilated, the Fourth Lateran Council taught that "all will receive, according to their deeds, good or evil, the former their everlasting glory with Christ, the latter their perpetual punishment with the devil."[21] Satan, in this context, is the cause célèbre in the case against annihilationism.

THE WAR IN HEAVEN: TRANSPOSING LANGUAGE FROM MYTH TO DOCTRINE

Revelation 12:7, in its reference to a war in "heaven" and a subsequent Fall of heavenly beings, highlights the vast differences between the manner in which terms function in myth as compared with later doctrinal formulae. That is, the notion of expulsion from heaven is essentially incompatible with a contemporary Catholic understanding of heaven as eternal friendship

---

19. Henning, *Educating Early Christians*, 218.
20. Augustine, *City of God* 21.
21. "Fourth Lateran Council" 8.17.

with God—a state of being that, by definition, cannot end. The Catechism teaches that those who are in heaven "live forever with Christ."[22] The motif of expulsion from heaven seems closer to the mythic motif of the loss of paradise associated with classic Christian interpretations of the Adamic myth. This point underscores the sense in which terminology used in the context of mythical narrative can hold connotations very different from that associated with its homonyms in doctrinal formulae. The trope of ejection from heaven gathers a degree of irony when combined with an insistence that the fallen angels are condemned in an eternal hell—as if this time, their state of being really is eternal.

As noted in our discussion of possession and exorcism, the tradition, for all of its rhetoric regarding the horrors of hell, has tended to regard it as a minimum security penitentiary whose inhuman inmates can abscond so as to infest, oppress, and possess humans—a breach that would seem to fall short of an omnipotent, omniscient and omni-benign Judge. None of this lends credibility to interpretations of scripture or doctrinal formulations that presume the actuality of an eternal hell populated by Satan and the damned. And so, we turn to the way in which the apocalyptic anticipation of the conquest of inimical forces has influenced the Church's teaching on the damnation of persons.

THE CATECHISM DESPAIRS OF SATAN'S REDEMPTION

The Catechism's presentation of the doctrine of Satan describes a personal being—a fallen angel that, because of its irrevocable choice to reject God, is beyond the possibility of repentance and subsequent salvation.[23] The Catechism asserts that the plight of Satan and the other demons, devoid of any hope of salvation, is an inherent consequence of their choice rather than a punishment imposed by God. "It is the *irrevocable* character of their choice, and not a defect in the infinite divine mercy that makes the angels' sin unforgivable. 'There is no repentance for the angels after their fall, just as there is no repentance for men after death.'"[24] This statement asserts that God's mercy is infinite. However, it describes the choice of the damned to reject God as not simply "unrevoked" but "irrevocable." This implies that they could not repent even if they wanted to—as if their free will has been nullified—at least in relation to this matter.

---

22. CDF, *Catechism of the Catholic Church* 1023.
23. CDF, *Catechism of the Catholic Church* 2851–52.
24. CDF, *Catechism of the Catholic Church* 393.

Affirming God's salvific will, the Catechism quotes 2 Peter 3:9, stating that "God does not want 'any to perish, but all to come to repentance.'"[25] This begs the question as to why the damned could not repent if they so wanted—and why God's infinite mercy could tolerate the situation in which a being could be damned and denied any further opportunity to repent and be reconciled. Given that Jesus mandated his followers to emulate a God of enemy-love and infinite forgiveness, this question holds practical implications for the attitudes and actions of Christians in relation to their human enemies.

In a world wherein religious motifs are manipulated to demonize the Other, the doctrine of an enemy who is beyond all hope of reconciliation is one that should be closely scrutinized. Even when the irreconcilable enemy is presented as a non-human, supernatural person, the prospect still looms that humans may be regarded as influenced by, or even embodying, this ultimate adversary. Indeed, this possibility has been tragically instantiated by the demonization, persecution, and slaughter of human persons throughout history. Such a doctrine is well-poised to undermine Jesus' teachings on enemy-love and infinite forgiveness, simply writing off adversaries as evil.

Granted, it might be argued that the damned are unable to repent since they do not exist in chronological time, wherein a change of heart or mind can transpire. They are, according to such a view, eternally putrefied in their choice to reject God. This suggests that God is subject to the limitations of time and is, after a determined point, unable to allow Satan and the other damned to repent.

NO OPPORTUNITY FOR REPENTANCE AFTER DAMNATION

The Catechism speaks of hell as "eternal separation from God," raising a question as to whether it is a banishment externally imposed by God, or whether it is self-imposed separation, chosen consciously or as the cumulative outcome of a lifetime of bad choices.[26] It might be argued that hell understood as an externally imposed punishment falls short of the standards for morally defensible punishment as applied in Catholic moral theology.[27] The imposition of eternity in hell achieves nothing in terms of restitution, rehabilitation, or even prevention since consignment to hell does not apparently, within the terms of Catholic doctrine, effectively protect society from

---

25. CDF, *Catechism of the Catholic Church* 1023.
26. CDF, *Catechism of the Catholic Church* 1035.
27. USCCB, "Responsibility, Rehabilitation, and Restoration."

ongoing harassment by the devil and other demons up to and including full-on possession. Its effectiveness as a deterrent is also questionable, especially in relation to demons who did not exist in time and could not have learned from the fate of demons who were damned "before" them. A view of hell as the natural consequence of a creature's choices, on the other hand, is not liable to such objections.

Charles Seymour identifies a "freedom view" of hell, regarding the condition as the natural consequence of a creature's choice rather than something externally inflicted by God.[28] The Catechism speaks of hell as the natural consequence of freely choosing to reject relationship with God, our neighbor, and significantly, the poor.[29] Our capacity to freely love God and neighbor must entail the possibility of rejecting this option—even forever. This is a very different prospect to that of a punishment externally imposed by God. Rahner's argument for the "fundamental option," proposes that at death, the cumulative effects of a life's choices add up to a fundamental choice for or against God.[30] Ron Highfield characterizes Rahner's position, remarking, "Hell's gate is locked from the inside."[31] Even if self-inflicted, however, the analogy of separation is difficult to reconcile with the sacramental worldview of Catholicism and a view of God as omnipresent.

ETERNAL SEPARATION FROM GOD AS A CHALLENGE TO THE SACRAMENTAL WORLDVIEW

We have noted that Origen and Augustine among others emphasized that Satan is not the personification of pure evil. Evil, for these thinkers, is a privation, whereas Satan is a divine creation whose being is inherently good—despite its corrupted character. Pure evil could not by its very nature repent and remain evil. Its identity as evil would in effect be annihilated. If, however, Satan is not simply the personification of pure evil, then why is it inconceivable that this creature of God might repent? If all hope is utterly denied, then it may be meaningless semantics to say that Satan is not pure evil personified, but, rather, a fundamentally good creation that has become corrupt. It would be incongruous to speak of an inherently good creation that is utterly devoid of hope. Indeed, if this were the case, Jeffrey Burton Russell would be right to reject the penchant, evident in Origen and

---

28. Seymour, "Hell, Justice and Freedom," 78.
29. Seymour, "Hell, Justice and Freedom," 78.
30. Rahner, *Foundations of the Christian Faith*, 93–106; "Theology of Freedom," 190–93; "Punishment of Sins," 92b–94b.
31. Highfield, "Freedom to Say No," 494; Rahner, "Punishment of Sins," 92b–94b.

Augustine for "packing the moral and the ontological into one hamper."[32] To argue that the positive existence of a thing by definition entails some degree of goodness is, for Russell, a conflation of the ontological and moral spheres.

The sacramental worldview essential to Catholicism is deeply invested in the possibility of finding God in *all* things.[33] According to the sacramental worldview, God co-exists in and through all of creation, not just the bits and pieces deemed good or holy. The question would hence arise as to whether Satan and the other damned are an exception to the sacramental principle that God exists in and through all things, including persons. If God, or grace as we might put it, exists in and through all things, including fallen persons, then no person can be utterly separated from God. A person may willfully oppose God, or be willfully impervious to God's presence, but neither scenario indicates the absence of God. The separation view of hell challenges belief in God's omnipresence in creation, limiting God to the kind of presence associated with created things that are to be found in one place but not in another. Being without grace rings of abstraction rather than actuality—or else we need to reevaluate the relationship between God and being so as to separate the two and argue that God is *a* being, thus undoing centuries of Christian theology so as to effectively baptize Zeus.

PERSONHOOD AS A RELATIONSHIP WITH THE DIVINE PERSONS

The prospect of a damned person who does not have an ongoing opportunity to repent holds implications not only for our image of God but also for our image of personhood. Ian McFarland proposes a model of personhood that could not apply to a Satan that is beyond any hope of redemption, as the Christian Tradition has, for the most part, upheld. McFarland suggests that personhood is defined by an ongoing and potentially salvific relationship with the persons of the Godhead. The Christian Tradition has broadly assumed that Satan, whether by its own choice or because of an external judgment, has lost all hope of such a salvific relationship.[34]

McFarland contends that the classification of personhood should not be contingent upon possession of cognitive abilities, biological viability, independence, or, indeed, any other attribute. McFarland proposes that "the basis of our 'personhood' is not any quality that we possess (whether in equal or in different measure), but simply the fact that God in Christ addresses us

32. Russell, *Satan*, 128.
33. Himes, "Finding God in All Things," 102.
34. McFarland, *In Adam's Fall*, x.

as persons—speaking to us in time the same Word spoken eternally within the Trinity."[35] Personhood might thus be understood as Christ's invitation for us to participate in the community of the Triune Godhead, that is, an invitation to *theosis*.[36] In this sense, the possibility of salvation is integral to personhood. If personhood is defined by a potentially salvific relationship with Christ, then it cannot be attributed to a Satan whose relationship with Christ is beyond the possibility of reconciliation.

Granted, the argument might be offered that Satan, prior to becoming evil, derived its personhood from Christ, and retains it just as it retains the nature of an angel, a "pure," that is, disembodied, spirit.[37] However, McFarland regards personhood as bestowed by Christ's ongoing address to us as persons, "Christ addresses us *as* persons—speaking to us in time."[38] McFarland's position suggests that a being is sustained in personhood by Christ's ongoing invitation to relationship, not an invitation that has expired.[39]

It might further be argued that McFarland's account of personhood applies only to humans as they exist in time and excludes pure spirits who exist in eternity. This would, however, contradict the longstanding designation of angels, fallen or otherwise, as disembodied persons, a position reiterated in the Catechism.[40] The Catechism in its exposition of the seventh petition of the Our Father specifically regards the devil as a person.[41] Further, if angels exist outside of time, their "choice" against God could not have been a change of mind whereby they tired of their angelic duties and rebelled. A change of mind requires the passage of time. The implication is that angels were created as part of the inherently good creation and their being is therefore good in itself, but as soon as they were created, they instantaneously chose against God. That is, their will was never exercised for good. This raises a question as to whether there can be freedom without time to choose.

The demons seem akin to hapless children who pulled rude faces while the wind changed, leaving them forever to be the gargoyles of the cosmos. Their imagined plight seems to accentuate the privileged status of humanity for whom God was willing to launch a rescue operation in the Incarnation. To be a child of God, it might be argued, will be more appreciated if God has

---

35. McFarland, *In Adam's Fall*, 106, 1152.
36. McFarland, *In Adam's Fall*, 106, 1152.
37. Tanner, *Decrees of the Ecumenical Councils*, 1:245.
38. McFarland, *In Adam's Fall*, x.
39. CDF, *Catechism of the Catholic Church* 392.
40. CDF, *Catechism of the Catholic Church* 330.
41. CDF, *Catechism of the Catholic Church* 2851.

turned his fatherly gaze from the urchins of creation. If, on the other hand, the Incarnation is understood as God's outreach to all of creation, or even all of sentient creation, it makes little sense that the demons are excluded. On this note, we now turn to the teachings of one who championed the most marginalized and troubled of persons.

JESUS' TEACHINGS ON ENEMY-LOVE

It seems reasonable to apply Jesus' teachings on enemy love to Satan, a term derived from the Hebrew word for enemy. From the strife of the Maccabean rebellion, to the tensions between Jewish Christians and the broader Jewish community, to the Roman persecution experienced by the author of Revelation, and later by the Patristics, the motif of the fallen Satan has been invoked so as to express the experience of engagement with the adversary—whether understood as human, supernatural, mythical, or institutional.

To accept that Satan and other demons are damned for all eternity, sets a precedent for accepting that human persons too may be beyond redemption, although, granted, we cannot know with certainty that this is the case for any human person. To write off the satanic or allegedly satanic in such a manner stands in stark contrast with the disposition that Jesus advocated in relation to the enemy.

New Testament scholar, Daniel Harrington, interprets Jesus' command to enemy love (Matt 5:43–48) as a mandate to emulate God's own disposition towards enemies. "This new demand is based, not on human nature, but on the example of God."[42] David Gill agrees, positing that while Jesus was not the first to teach enemy-love, his teaching is distinctive since in his rendition of the doctrine, "the primary motive is imitation of the Heavenly Father, whose daughters and sons the disciples are."[43] Likewise, John McKenzie observes that this passage exhorts Christians to exhibit "God-like providence as they vindicate their title of sons of God."[44] This suggests a God who practices enemy-love which, it might be argued, would include openness to reconciliation, never utterly foreclosing on this possibility.

Terrence Rynne contrasts Jesus' command to enemy-love with the sectarian attitudes that characterized the Qumran literature which counseled, "Members of the community are to love all the sons of light, each according to this lot among the Council of God, but to hate all the sons

---

42. Harrington, *Gospel of Matthew*, 871.
43. Gill, "Socrates and Jesus," 246–62.
44. McKenzie, "Matthew's Gospel," 73.

of darkness, each according to this guilt in the vengeance of God."[45] This injunction is characterized by apocalyptic imagery of light and darkness—epitomizing the tension between Jesus' command to enemy-love and the apocalyptic worldview that seeks the obliteration of the enemy, embodied or disembodied.

JESUS' COMMAND TO FORGIVE INFINITELY

With reference to Jesus' command in Matthew 18:21–35 to forgive seventy-seven times, Daniel Harrington argues that "Christians have no right to place any limit on forgiveness."[46] Concurring with Harrington, John McKenzie observes that to forgive seven times, would, according to a biblical mindset, have suggested the perfect degree of forgiveness, beyond which forgiveness would be excessive.[47] However, McKenzie argues, Jesus teaches that there is no limit on perfect forgiveness. The duty to forgive never ceases. Yet, the Catechism's position that a fallen being should be left eternally stranded with the consequence of an evil choice, deprived of the ability to repent, in effect places a limit on forgiveness. The Creator of the universe cannot plead impotence because of time or any other rules that govern some aspect of its creation. For God to tolerate such limitations on divine forgiveness would signify a point beyond which God chooses not to extend the possibility of salvation.

Granted, it might be argued that the mandate for infinite forgiveness applies to humans and not necessarily to God upon whose authority it is based. Fallible humans, it might be countered, must not withhold forgiveness since they can never fully know the heart of another, but the omniscient Deity is in a position to justifiably do so.[48] God alone, it might be argued, knows who is truly repentant. This argument breaks down, however, since infinite forgiveness and unconditional love cannot, by definition, be contingent upon repentance. Unconditional love and infinite forgiveness must, by definition, prevail regardless of what is known by the omniscient God.

An account of the plight of the damned, more consistent with infinite mercy, might lie in relation to the divine attribute of omniscience. Damned spirits, should they exist, may not be arbitrarily deprived of the free will that would enable them to accept God's love and end their state of hell, but an omniscient God would be agonizingly aware of a situation in which such

45. Rynne, *Jesus Christ, Peacemaker*, 70.
46. Harrington, "Matthew," 889.
47. McKenzie, "Matthew's Gospel," 95.
48. Worthington et al., "Interpersonal Forgiveness," 33.

a spirit would never choose to. The omniscient mind would be hence deprived of the hope that can persist in all other minds. Laboring under the grim realization that a creature will never accept God's loving forgiveness, God would be no less present in that creature than in a saint. God's love would infuse both beings—embraced in one instance and unrequited in the other.

The Christian mandate to exercise love and forgive enemies cannot be rooted in the nature of a God who is not infinitely willing to do likewise. This would seem to create an odd situation in which the Christian is mandated to forgive villains whom even God does not forgive, and in that sense, be more forgiving than God. However, even if one were to concede that divine forgiveness is dependent upon repentance, this could only reasonably apply to creatures that still have the opportunity to repent. Otherwise divine forgiveness expires with the ability to repent, and God's mercy is not infinite.

A TENSION BETWEEN GOSPEL PASSAGES: RECONCILIATION VERSUS ETERNAL PUNISHMENT

Admittedly, it would lack even-handedness to characterize the gospels as unambiguously championing reconciliation, forgiveness, and enemy love. Simon Joseph notes a tension between, on the one hand, conciliatory "wisdom" aphorisms in Matthew, espousing reconciliation and, on the other hand, sayings in that gospel that seem to reflect an apocalyptic perspective.[49] Both sets of sayings reflect Matthew's use of the "sayings gospel" known as "Q."[50]

Joseph asserts that Jesus' teaching on enemy-love appears to critique his own Jewish tradition and its more restricted stance on forgiveness.[51] However, it should be noted, Israelite religion and Judaism include the prophetic tradition that advocates reconciliation and peace. In a case in point, Isaiah's vision of the Peaceable Kingdom (Isa 11:1–9) might be regarded as highly consistent with Jesus' teachings on these matters as natural enemies, predators and prey, are depicted as existing in harmony.

Eschatological passages in Matthew include the parable of the thief (Matt 24:42–44; Q12:39–46), the parable of the unprepared servant (Matt 24:45–51; Q12:42–46), and the unexpected coming of the Son of Man (Matt 34:36–51; Q17:22–37). While some degree of tension exists in Matthew, and the Bible as a whole, between eschatological passages versus

49. Joseph, "'Love Your Enemies,'" 29–41.
50. Joseph, "Love Your Enemies," 29.
51. Joseph, "Love Your Enemies," 29

ones that foment reconciliation, the underlying difference may be more a question of tone and genre than of conflicting theologies.[52] These eschatological sayings do not despair of reconciliation or envisage the inevitable destruction of the enemy.

The Parables of the Kingdom exhort their audience to embrace reconciliation in the face of a pending judgment, more than they relish the inevitable destruction of an enemy. These eschatological passages stress the importance of reconciling one's life to the gospel before it is too late. But the "too late" may refer to death rather than to an eternal hell as later conceived in the reception histories of these texts. Interpreted thus, these parables, and the Q-sayings that undergird them, offer little support for a doctrine of irreconcilably damned enemies, and do not contradict Jesus' commands to enemy love and to infinite forgiveness, so much as they urgently underscore the importance of reconciliation with God and with neighbor in the present. They "light a fire" under their hearers, rather than consign them to eternal fires.

CONCLUSION

Apocalyptic literature, such as the Book of Revelation, sought to comfort persecuted communities, encouraging them to hold to the faith until, in the end, justice would be done, and the forces of oppression vanquished. However, when the apocalyptic is interpreted as eagerly anticipating the destruction of persons rather than forces, this fuels the ideation of an irreconcilable, irredeemable enemy of God. Such thinking is reflected in a doctrinal insistence upon the existence of Satan, demons, and damned human persons.

The motif of the irreconcilable enemy stands in tension with Jesus' teaching on enemy-love and unreserved forgiveness—especially if we regard such moral practices as emulating the God revealed in the teachings of Jesus. It would be one thing to say that Satan chooses not to repent. Forgiveness, salvation, reconciliation, and love cannot be forced upon a being, contrary to their will. It is a different matter, however, to argue that the inhuman spirits and the human dead, because they exist outside of chronological time, cannot choose to repent if they so willed. Such a situation could suggest that God's saving will is constrained by time, only able to operate in the temporal condition. An alternative argument is that God's mercy expires,

---

52. Tuckett, *Scriptures in the Gospels*, 3–26; Horsley and Draper, *Whoever Hears You*; Collins, "Cult and Culture," 38–61; Attridge, "Reflections on Research into Q," 223–34.

and God chooses not to extend the possibility of salvation to disembodied spirits that are fallen or to the human damned. Such a conclusion alleviates the unreasonable mandate imposed by Jesus to emulate a God of infinite mercy, and comfortably accommodates Christianity to the realities of a vengeful world.

To insist upon the actual existence of any irredeemable creature sabotages Catholicism's sacramental vision of creation. A God who is eternally separated from any creature can no longer be a God who is omnipresent. To speak of a "person," human or otherwise, as eternally damned also assails a Christian theology of personhood, rooted in the Trinity, whereby all persons are called to participate in the community of divine persons. Personhood is, from a Christian perspective, not defined in terms of abilities or moral stature, but rooted in an ongoing invitation from Christ. Within such a framework, an eternally damned person is an oxymoron—as is an omnipresent God of infinite mercy from whom some creatures are separated with no further opportunity for reconciliation. The doctrine of Satan as currently formulated by the Catholic Church represents an "out-clause," protecting Christians from the uncomfortable implications of committing their lives to enemy-love and unlimited forgiveness.

14

A Proposed Reformulation of the Doctrine of Satan

This chapter suggests a reformulated account of the doctrine of Satan so as to reflect the relationship between an omnipresent God of infinite mercy and free-willed, grace-infused though fallen persons. The genre of myth is well-positioned to express such mysteries precisely because it deals in possibilities and probes beyond where propositional discourse can assert certainty. While doctrine can never express poetic truth as powerfully as myth can do, a doctrinal formulation can explicitly recognize its own limitations by avoiding misplaced certitude and wild speculation.

Several contemporary reflections on the motif of Satan implicitly challenge the orthodox position that Satan exists as a supernatural being, yet offer little basis upon which to reformulate the doctrine. Relating the motif to the power of suggestion, they view the idea of Satan as a deceptive guise for evil. If evil is essentially nothingness, then any representation of it as an existent is ultimately misleading. This point may be of psychological interest but offers little basis for any doctrinal or theological formulation.

Even less helpful are references to Satan as an aberration of personhood, adding credence to the dangerous argument that personhood may be lost through misdeeds, implying Satan's ontological existence as a subpersonal monster, and hence perpetuating a spiritualized cryptozoology.

Such accounts seem to side-step the question of a constructive theology of Satan for our time.[1]

General reluctance to propose a constructive theology of Satan may reflect the reality that a coherent reformulation would by necessity challenge the literalism, dualism, and baseless speculation embedded in the Church's current exposition, and hence trigger smoke detectors in the hallways of orthodoxy.

Against such a backdrop, this chapter proposes one avenue to a coherent theology of Satan, making explicit what is already implicit in the doctrine as it ideates the possibility that even if a free-willed person might ultimately reject God, the Deity would nonetheless sustain that person in being in the state referred to as hell.[2] For all its punitive connotations, the trope of Satan's consignment to hell suggests that even if a creature were to use its free-will so as to irrevocably reject God's offer of friendship, God would neither actively destroy it, nor allow it to be annihilated as a consequence of its choices. Such is the possibility of Satan. Drawing upon mythical language, the doctrine can offer a powerful representation of enemy-love, and of God's unconditional sustenance of being.

SATAN DISTINGUISHED FROM PURE EVIL BY ITS BEING

The motif of Satan depicts a personal being, albeit a mythical one, and not pure evil in and of itself. "Evil is nothing," proposed St. Augustine, "since God makes everything that is, and God did not make evil."[3] Augustine parted ways with both his Manichean and Neo-Platonist influences by insisting that creation, though fallen, is essentially good.[4] For Augustine, no created thing or being is inherently evil.

While insisting upon the inherent goodness of creation, Augustine affirms the ontological existence of demons, including Satan, leading Frederick Coplestone to remark, "With evil non-existent and only a privation of goodness, it would seem that an invisible world of spirited beings such as demons and angels would also be non-existent, lacking a positive existence."[5] As Peter Finney notes, however, Augustine alleviates the apparent contradiction between his model of evil as a privation, and his

---

1. CDF, *Catechism of the Catholic Church* 2851
2. McGill, "Evolution of the Christian Motif of Satan."
3. Augustine, *Confessions*, 8.
4. Hick, *Evil and the God of Love*, 4.
5. Coplestone, *History of Philosophy*, 2:76.

acceptance of the ontological existence of the devil by insisting that Satan cannot be flatly reduced to the personification of pure evil.[6] Rather, in Augustine's view, affirmed by Braga I and Lateran IV, Satan retained a nature that was created good by God and is shared in common with the angels. "Not even the devil himself is evil, so far as its nature; but perversity makes it evil."[7] In Augustine's thought, it is Satan's very being, that is, its status as part of the inherently good creation, that distinguishes Satan from evil itself.

SATAN IN THE TENSION BETWEEN BEING AND NOTHINGNESS

It is the ontological reality of Satan, albeit within the narrative world of myth, that has in Christian thought, distinguished Satan from evil in itself. Several contemporary theologians, however, apparently influenced by the Patristic association of evil with non-being, and distancing themselves from the literalism of the magisterium's position, describe Satan as an illusory image of nothingness and, in effect, an attempt to represent pure evil. Their remarks, as we shall see, imply that Satan exists in the form of a void, masquerading as positive existence. A void cannot, by definition, be represented in the mind except by recourse to positive imagery so that the mind is tricked into thinking in terms of the existence of nothing as though it were a thing. However, to blur the distinction between, on the one hand, Satan as a mythical being and, on the other hand, the nonbeing of evil, is to strip the motif of Satan of the inherent goodness of created things so that Satan becomes a single-dimensional avatar for evil.

Paul Tillich directly equates Satan with nothingness—an abyss of negativity, utterly devoid of positive existence.[8] For Tillich, Satan is the figurative personification of pure evil, that is, a privation in being.[9] Such a single-dimensional avatar could no longer explore complexities in the God-creature relationship, so that there would be nothing but confusion to be gained by maintaining a doctrine of Satan as envisaged by Tillich.

Implying that Satan amounts to nothingness thinly veiled, Daniel Day Williams, asserts that "satan . . . is not a person. We personalize him as we participate in the demonic powers. He is the mask of the plunge toward annihilation."[10] Williams implies that the personal Satan is a façade that

---

6. Finney, "Empty Evil and the Positive Devil," 3.
7. Augustine, *Confessions*, 160.
8. Tillich, "Demonic."
9. Tillich, "Demonic."
10. Williams, *Demonic and the Divine*, 5.

conceals a descent into oblivion. Williams's metaphor is highly ambiguous in terms of the relationship it implies between Satan and annihilation. The reference to a mask suggests a façade so that Satan represents the illusion of a being, a hologram, as it were, projected from the abyss.

In a sense, Williams subverts Baudelaire's famous quip so as to imply that the devil's greatest trick has been to fool humanity into thinking it exists.[11] For Williams, it constitutes a form of participation in the demonic powers to regard Satan as a person, implying that to do so is to succumb to diabolical deception as we are gulled into thinking of nothing as though it were a thing. While this offers an interesting contrast to Pope Francis's argument that to view the devil purely as a myth or idea is to succumb to diabolical deception.[12]

While Williams speaks of Satan in terms of an illusion, the author attributes agency to the "demonic powers" in which, he imagines, humans can participate by succumbing to the illusion of Satan's positive existence. Hence, Williams offers some implication that the realm of the demonic may, unlike the figure of Satan, exist in some positive form. In this instance, Williams associates the demonic with deceit, perhaps self-deceit. While the demonic might be understood to denote negative impulses within the self, social systems, or creation more generally, even an assertion of the existence of supernatural demons is far more credible than claims about the singular existence and alleged curriculum vitae of an individuated Satan, named and all but baptized. It is in specific biographical claims about Satan that a healthy apprehension about the demonic crosses the bounds of credibility so as to imply a paparazzi's perspective on goings-on in the unseen realm.

Williams's motif of the plunge toward annihilation suggests Satan's antipathy towards being and a gravitation towards the privation of evil. There may be a Faustian undertone to Williams's analogy in this regard. Jordan Peterson has observed that the diabolical figure of Mephistopheles in Goethe's *Faust* holds as its credo that being is so tragic that it would be better if nothing existed at all.[13] "I am the spirit that negates / And rightly so, for all that comes to be / Deserves to perish wretchedly; / 'Twere better nothing would begin."[14] In Part II of *Faust*, authored a decade later, Mephistopheles returns to this nihilistic credo, declaring, "I'd rather have eternal emptiness."[15] Williams's analogy of the "plunge towards annihilation"

11. Baudelaire, *Generous Gambler*, 61.
12. Bergoglio and Skorka, *On Heaven and Earth*, 8.
13. Peterson, *Twelve Rules for Life*, 346.
14. Kaufmann, *Goethe's Faust*, 47.
15. Peterson, *Twelve Rules for Life*, 346.

represents the same sentiment that—"'twere better nothing would begin" and since it has begun, it should be concluded with all haste. Interpreted thus, the image of the "plunge towards annihilation" arguably carries undertones of suicide—with the caveat that in Christian thought, death does not result in utter annihilation.

While the metaphor of a suicidal person may carry some limited applicability to a Satan figure that has opted for the non-being of evil over the God who is the ground of being, it is fraught with pastoral risk and primed for the almost inevitable misinterpretation that all who commit suicide are damned—an assumption no longer supported by Catholic teaching—and a more insidious demonization of troubled souls. We have already noted the public response to Fr. Pat Collins's remarks on a possible connection between demons and suicide.[16]

Again, drawing upon the metaphor of the mask, Luther Link detects the nothingness that lies behind the faces we attribute to the devil, remarking, "The Devil is not a person. He may have many masks, but his essence is a mask without a face."[17] Link's assessment of the devil counteracts the literalization of myth whereby Satan is imagined to exist as a personal being beyond the narrative arc of myth and attributed a "face," as it were, in the sense of personal identity. Link's assertion finds support in a theological anthropology such as that of Ian McFarland who defines personhood in terms of relationship with the persons of the Triune Godhead, an understanding of personhood that would exclude an eternally damned Satan.[18]

On a similar note, Joseph Ratzinger asserts, "If one asks whether the devil is a person, then one must in an altogether correct way answer that he is the Un-Person, the disintegration and corruption of what it means to be a person. And so, it is particular to him that he moves about without a face and that his inability to be recognized is his actual strength."[19] Ratzinger is by no means denying the reality of Satan. Rather, he denies the devil's personhood while defending the doctrine of Satan against Herbert Haag's broad assertion that it is untenable for moderns to believe in Satan.[20] Though the comment that Satan lacks a face may imply a ubiquitous quality, a lack of particularity and personality, Ratzinger questions the mode rather than the fact of Satan's existence.

16. Monaghan, "Fr Pat Collins."
17. Link, *Devil*, 15.
18. McFarland, *In Adam's Fall*, 106, 1152.
19. Boeve and Mannion, *Ratzinger Reader*, 44.
20. Haag, *Abschiedvom Teufel*, 45; Ratzinger, "Abschiedvom Teufel?," 221–30.

Han Urs von Balthasar, for his part, speaks of the "non-person-hood" of the devil, suggesting that a propensity for love and relationship is integral to the definition of a "person" in the full sense.[21] Walter Kasper argues that "The Devil is not a personal figure, but a self-dissolving mal-figure, an entity that perverts itself into a mal-entity; he is a person in the manner of a mal-person."[22] Granted, Kasper refers to Satan as an entity, implying positive existence. On the other hand, Kasper's reference to a "self-dissolving mal-figure" suggests an entity that fades from being.

While calling into question a model of Satan as a particular person who exists beyond the narrative arc of myth, it is important to retain a sense of Satan's identity as a mythical person. Attempts to cast Satan as a non-person, obfuscate the significance of the doctrine of Satan for persons. Depictions of Satan as an aberration run the risk of implying a monster, that is, an evil entity that exists beyond the world of myth, and in doing so they objectify Satan, losing sight of the significance of the motif for all free-willed creatures.

This brief survey of contemporary references to Satan reveals little or nothing of theological significance, instead offering psychological observations regarding the difficulties entailed by attempting to think about evil if evil in itself is nothingness. The motifs of a "mask of nothingness" or the "un-person" have little to say about the mystery of God and God's relationship with the world. They are largely devoid of pastoral relevance—beyond the pastoral minefield entailed by Williams's innuendo of suicide.

Also fraught with pastoral danger is the concept of the "non-person," primed for application to the most reviled and marginalized of human persons so as to justify their execution on the grounds that they have abdicated their personhood as a consequence of their immoral choices. These contemporary theological references to Satan read as attempts to lend some fleeting intellectual respectability to a doctrine that, in its current formulations, has lost theological credibility. While moving beyond literalism and superstition, they strip the doctrine of theological relevance so that it becomes at best an intellectual curiosity—itself a mask for nothingness.

There is however an alternative—an account of Satan that is not dependent upon literalist misinterpretations of myth and that expresses an all-too real dimension of the Creator-creature relationship. This book began by arguing that the Catechism's presentation of the doctrine of Satan reflects a hermeneutical problem—a misinterpretation of myth, its narratives and

21. O'Connor, "Von Balthasar and Salvation"; Balthasar, *Dare We Hope That All Men Be Saved*, 144–46.

22. Kasper and Lehmann, "Teufel, Dämonen, Besessenheit"; Beinert and Fiorenza, *Handbook of Catholic Theology*, 173.

characters abducted from the world of mythos and relocated in the world of logos. If the problem is hermeneutical in nature, so is the solution. It is hermeneutics that holds the key to a profound and understated dimension of the doctrine of Satan. The genre of myth has long expressed the motif of Satan and enabled its development in ancient Israelite religion, Judaism, and Christianity. So too, it is the genre of myth that points to the theological and pastoral relevance of the doctrine of Satan in our time.

MYTH AS THE BEARER OF POSSIBLE WORLDS

Ricoeur suggests that myth can express both potentialities and actualities that characterize the experience of being human in the world, expressing this realm in terms of a narrative one. As such, the author recognizes in myth a capacity to express the "possible" as well as the actual.[23] Richard Kearney observes that "Ricoeur identifies a rich plurivocity of 'possible'— epistemological, moral, historical, practical, poetical, ontological, and eschatological."[24] Ricoeur is concerned with the identification of what Aristotle refers to as "poetic truth." Distinguishing between historical and poetic truth, Aristotle states that "it is not the poet's function to describe what has actually happened, but the kinds of thing that might happen."[25] This is the kind of truth that Ricoeur detects in myth.[26]

Aristotle regarded poetic truth as of greater philosophical import than historical truth because it holds universal relevance, dealing with what might happen to any person, as opposed to what actually happened to particular persons. "For this reason poetry is something more philosophical and more worthy of serious attention than history; for while poetry is concerned with universal truths, history treats of particular facts."[27] If myth can be regarded as an expression of that which is universally possible, this holds implications for the manner in which mythical language is adopted in doctrinal formulations.

Walter Wink captures this sense in which the imagination of the possible is crucial to the religious sensibility. With reference to Feuerbach's dismissal of religion as the product of imagination, Wink remarks, "He was unable to grasp the positive meaning of his insight . . . the realm of imagination, or what I prefer to call, following Henry Corbin, the imaginal

23. Stewart, "Hermeneutics of Suspicion," 306.
24. Kearney, *Passion for the Possible*, 50.
25. Aristotle, *Poetics* IX.
26. Aristotle, *Poetics* IX.
27. Aristotle, *Poetics* IX.

realm, produces a third kind of knowing, intermediate between the world of ideas, on the one hand, and the world of sense perception, on the other."[28] Wink regards this imaginal realm, situated between the realm of ideas and the realm of action, as an arena in which possibilities may be rehearsed. In myth, possibilities are actualized upon an imaginal stage so that, as Wink suggests, "We perceive the action as if it were staged on the physical plane but it is not."[29] As Corbin proposes, "This intermediate world of images and archetypes can be known only by the 'transmutation of inner spiritual states into outer states, into vision-events symbolizing these inner states.'"[30] Myth is rooted in "vision-events," but these are events that are played out in the forum of the possible, and have not necessarily transpired in the realm of actuality, and of the particular.

One might object to the argument that myth facilitates an envisioning of possibilities, countering that myths have long been regarded as an expression of human limitations—the maddening chasm between our aspirations and our abilities. As Bronislaw Malinowski observes, the myths of the Ancient Near East seek to reconcile human beings to the limitations inherent in their human condition, such as being mortal and fallible.[31]

In a case in point, the Yahwist school of authors, whose influence may be detected in the Book of Genesis, display a concern for the limitations of human capacities in relation to the rightful role of the Deity.[32] The Adamic narrative, the Babel narrative, and the non-biblical myth of Gilgamesh reinforce the boundaries that define the experience of being human. These texts seek to reconcile readers to their bounded reality, offering cautionary tales regarding attempts to transgress the boundaries that define what it means to be human.

While, at first glance, this concern for limits may appear to stand in tension with myth's rehearsal of the possible as identified by Ricoeur, these are two sides of the same coin. The juxtaposition of aspiration and restriction yields a creative tension that engenders the possible. The possible is identified in terms of its delineation from the impossible. If a narrative reminds the reader of mortality, it also provokes a wistful pondering on what it might be like to be immortal. To gaze upon the horizon is to let one's view rest upon a limit, a line beyond which we can see no further. If,

---

28. Wink, *Human Being*, 40–41; Seiple and Weidmann, *Enigmas and Powers*, 105–6; Corbin, *Creative Images in the Sufism of Ibn 'Arabi*, 174.

29. Seiple and Weidmann, *Enigmas and Powers*, 106.

30. Seiple and Weidmann, *Enigmas and Powers*, 106.

31. Malinowski, *Magic, Science and Religion*, 72–124; Segal, *Myth and Ritual*, 358.

32. Melvin, "Divine Mediation and the Rise of Civilization," 10.

as CS Lewis famously quipped, all things were translucent and our view encountered no limits, then we could see nothing at all.[33] Hence, it might be said, Malinowski's insight that myth expresses the experience of human limitations is the corollary of Ricoeur's insight that myth serves as a probe into the possible.

Ricoeur's characterization of myth as a bearer of the possible, suggests that the genre is particularly well-suited to engage the mystery of evil. Karl Simms notes that Ricoeur regards evil as a possibility rather than as an external force, much less an ontological Satan. "Evil is not an external metaphysical force that is presented to God as an object. It is not, for example, a 'satan' if Satan means a kind of other person who brings evil into the world. Evil is a possibility which man is born with—whether he realizes this possibility or not is up to him."[34] The present work proposes a model of Satan that is not "a kind of other person" so much as the real possibility that any person might ultimately reject God.

SATAN AS INDICATIVE OF A REAL POSSIBILITY

Our exegesis of satanic motifs in the Hebrew Bible and extracanonical literature suggests possibilities in the God-human relationship, potentialities that may or may not exist in actuality. In keeping with the evolution of the mythic motif of Satan, I propose that Satan exists in the form of a *possibility*.

The suggestion that Satan exists as a possibility rather than an actuality is by no means to suggest that Satan is impotent and innocuous. The power of that which *might* be is all too evident in the airports of the world as millions of passengers are subjected to security procedures driven by the possibility of what a tiny percentage of passengers might do, and when people exercise social distancing and go to considerable inconvenience because of the possibility that another person may be contagious with a virus. To speak of Satan as existing in the realm of the possible is not to relegate Satan to the realm of the unreal. The possible exerts powerful influence over the actual.

A SOTERIOLOGICAL POSSIBILITY: GOD'S UNCONDITIONAL SUSTENANCE OF BEING

If myth is characterized by a capacity to depict possible worlds, and if the mythical motif of Satan has long served to probe possibilities in the

33. Lewis, *Abolition of Man*, 80–81.
34. Simms, *Paul Ricoeur*, 203.

Creator-creature relationship, the motif may continue to do so with regard to soteriological possibilities. Specifically, the doctrine of Satan has provided a means of speaking about the condition of hell that may exist as a potentiality rather than an actuality.

Hans Urs von Balthasar contends that it falls short of the salvific will of God, and hence of Christian hope, to pray only for one's own salvation or that of certain individuals.[35] On the other hand, von Balthasar rejects the presumptuousness of universalism, identifying such thought as a form of predestination.[36] For von Balthasar, it remains a possibility, rather than a foregone conclusion, that any human person is actually damned for all eternity. Citing Hans Jurgen Verweyen, von Balthasar argues that if we love unreservedly as Christ calls us to, we should not despair of anyone, fatalistically accepting their condemnation.[37]

Significantly, von Balthasar rejects the possibility of the *apokatastasis*, that is, the redemption of Satan and the other demons.[38] It might be argued that it is integral to the Christian motif of the fallen Satan that it represents a prospective scenario wherein there is no possibility of a creature repenting so as to receive God's mercy. It is precisely the rigid intransigence of the mythic Satan that illustrates the ultimate expression of God's unconditional love, sustaining in being that creature that will never accept God's mercy and friendship. To hope for an *apokatastasis*, on the other hand, is to presume that at least one being is in actuality experiencing the state of hell, and that either it is God who is keeping the creature there or that God will override the creature's free will.

The Church does not presume that it can know with certainty that any human person is in the state of being known as hell. As Richard McBrien interprets it, "Neither Jesus, nor the Church after him, ever stated that persons actually go to hell or are there now. He—as does the Church—restricts himself to the *possibility*."[39] McBrien's assertion regarding the Church's teachings on hell may be substantiated by reference to the documents of Vatican II, among other ecclesial sources. The Council's *Declaration on the Church's Relations with the Non-Christian Religions* asserts the possibility that non-Christians may be saved, and Pope St. John Paul II's encyclical, *Redemptoris Missio* argues that Christ wills the salvation of all people, and that

---

35. Balthasar, *Dare We Hope?*, 74.
36. Balthasar, *Dare We Hope?*, 93.
37. Balthasar, *Dare We Hope?*, 78.
38. Balthasar, *Dare We Hope?*, 174–90.
39. McBrien, *Catholicism*, 1152.

this is a realistic possibility.⁴⁰ Even in the cases of those villains of history, reviled by humanity, the Church cannot say for certain that God's love has not ultimately prevailed. It is one thing to reject images of God, mediated through human language and concepts. It would be quite another thing to reject the Beatific Vision. Still, if humanity has been endowed with genuine free will, it must be conceivably possible to do so, and hell must remain a real possibility.

Paragraph 1035 of the Catechism affirms that humans who die in a state of mortal sin are dispatched to hell, but the Church cannot assume that anyone has in fact died without repenting, or has possessed the knowledge, freedom to act, and by extension, the sanity required in order to be culpable for mortal sin.⁴¹ The only "persons" that the Church could say, with certainty are in hell, are Satan and the other demons. If, however, Satan and the demons do not exist as beings in the cosmos beyond the narrative arc of myth, then they may serve as imaginal probes into the possibility of hell. Hence, the mythical motif of Satan, and of the other demons, would serve to illustrate a prospective situation, a logical possibility in view of the reality of free will, and of the reality that love cannot be coerced, even by God. Reference to damnation, in this sense, signifies what Wink calls a "vision event" rehearsing possibilities.⁴² Hell, it might be said, exists as a possibility to the extent that a genuinely free creature could forever refuse God's invitation to friendship. As Ratzinger surmises "Christ inflicts pure perdition on no one. In himself he is sheer salvation. Anyone who is with him has entered the space of deliverance and salvation. Perdition is not imposed by him, but comes to be wherever a person distances himself from Christ."⁴³

The Catechism suggests that the plight of the demons, devoid of hope of salvation, is an inherent consequence of their choice rather than a punishment imposed by God.⁴⁴ The situation of Satan and the demons, as depicted in mythical language, hence illustrates a possibility for human persons. We speak of the mythic persona of Satan in a situation in which we should not speak of any particular human person—that is, the situation of forever refusing friendship with God. The truth of the doctrine of Satan may hence represent a potentiality rather than an actuality—a poetic truth that could potentially pertain to any creature capable of mortal sin.

40. Paul VI, "*Nostra Aetate*" 1. See also chapter 2 in John Paul II, "*Redemptoris Missio.*"
    41. CDF, *Catechism of the Catholic Church* 1035.
    42. Wink, *Human Being*, 40–41; Seiple and Weidmann, *Enigmas and Powers*, 174.
    43. Ratzinger, *Eschatology*, xxi.
    44. CDF, *Catechism of the Catholic Church* 393.

In a curious sense, the doctrine of Satan is a statement of faith in God's unconditional love. Even if a creature were to reject God, and if there was utterly no hope of that creature recanting and seeking reconciliation, God would continue to sustain that creature in being. As soon as a God of unconditional love endows creatures with genuine freedom, there must then be the possibility of Satan—a creature that chooses to forever turn its back on God but whom God will not surrender to oblivion.

Interpreted in this way, the motif of Satan may not be an avatar of doom so much as an assurance that God's grace will always stand between persons and oblivion. Paul Tillich, who identifies Satan as nonbeing, chillingly proposes that our relationship with nonbeing may be more intimate than we care to acknowledge. Tillich remarks that "nonbeing is a part of one's own being."[45] Tillich suggests that we experience anxiety at the prospect that our being might one day be subsumed by nonbeing.[46] Whereas fear is an anticipation of specific phenomena, that is, anticipating in the mind prospective situations, anxiety, according to Tillich, is the anticipation of something more vague, awful and formless. "Anxiety has no object, or rather in a paradoxical phrase, its object is the negation of every object."[47] Ultimately, all anxiety reflects the prospect of losing our very being. "The only object is the threat itself, but not the source of the threat, because the source of the threat is 'nothingness.'"[48]

Tillich's insight may express an existential implication of the model of evil as nothingness. The concept of oblivion evokes anxiety in the face of the ultimate unknown. At 3am, when the realization sets in that each breath and heartbeat may mark a count-down to death and oblivion, this powerfully illustrates the terrifying influence that a possible scenario can exert upon our actual situation in the present. Contra Tillich's direct equation of Satan with nothingness, the figure of Satan, perhaps counter-intuitively, suggests an assurance that God will sustain a creature in being even if that creature willfully rejects God in favor of nonbeing. Ultimately, there is no "plunge into annihilation"—no ultimate suicide.[49]

---

45. Tillich, *Courage to Be*, 38.
46. Tillich, *Courage to Be*, 36.
47. Tillich, *Courage to Be*, 36.
48. Tillich, *Courage to Be*, 35.
49. Williams, *Demonic and the Divine*, 5.

A Proposed Reformulation of the Doctrine of Satan   215

DIVINIZED CREATURES SUSTAINING SATAN IN LOVE

While a creature that exercises its free will so as to forever reject God would exclude itself from theosis or divinization, the doctrine of theosis holds curious implications for the damned, should such beings exist in actuality. Granted, this may sound counterintuitive since the tradition has speculated that theosis applies to human beings with no mention of angels, fallen or otherwise. The International Theological Commission offers an account of theosis, stating that "human beings are called to participate in the life of God and to share in 'the divine nature' (2 Peter 1:4) through Christ, in the Spirit."[50] The Catechism too presents theosis as pertaining specifically to humanity.

> The Word became flesh to make us "partakers of the divine nature": "For this is why the Word became man, and the Son of God became the Son of man: so that man, by entering into communion with the Word and thus receiving divine sonship, might become a son of God." "For the Son of God became man so that we might become God." "The only-begotten Son of God, wanting to make us sharers in his divinity, assumed our nature, so that he, made man, might make men gods."[51]

This same sentiment is expressed ritually in the Mass, though perhaps seldom recognized. While mixing the water and wine, the priest prays, "Through the mixing of this water and wine, may we come to share in the divinity of Christ who humbled himself to share in our humanity."[52] "Divinity" within the sacramental worldview of Catholicism, does not relate to an uber-being that exists in the same manner as lesser creature-beings. Rather, the divine exists in and through all things as expressed in the words of Eucharistic Prayer I, addressed to the God in whom "we live and move and have our being" (Acts 17:28).[53] Surely, then, divinization, within the sacramental worldview, means participation in omnipresent divinity. Therefore, there is a sense in which divinization must hold significance for any damned being, including Satan, should such exist.

If the divine is omnipresent then, by definition, it cannot exclude presence in even one damned creature. If humans become divinized by adoption, the divinity into which they are adopted is not that of a Zeus who exists as a discrete being and the greatest among many but, rather, the

---

50. ITC, "Theology Today" 98.
51. CDF, *Catechism of the Catholic Church* 460.
52. ICEL, *Roman Missal.*
53. ICEL, *Roman Missal.*

omnipresent God who exists in and through all of creation, infusing every part of the sacramental universe.[54] In this manner, humans who have been divinized would be present in and through all of creation, including Satan, sustaining Satan in enemy love.

Such metaphysical speculation regarding the relationship between divinized persons and Satan may find support in the experience of unrequited love in the here and now. An applicable example may be that of the parent of a self-harming child who seeks to sustain their child for all his destructive choices and behaviors, willing it to live and thrive. In this sense, the possibility of Satan is replete with implications for the saved. If there are any damned persons, within the sacramental vision of creation, the divine does not forsake them but is co-present in them. Therefore, divinized persons are present in and through the damned—not sequestered in some hedonistic heaven so as to gloat from afar.

From the perspective of a futuristic realized eschatology, that which is not yet must inform that which already is. While theologians have rightly emphasized the vocation of the human person to be a co-creator with God, it might be argued that the human vocation includes a share in the work of each of the divine persons of the Triune Godhead so that humans are called to be co-creators, co-redeemers, and co-sustainers. The vocation to sustain one another and the wider environment in being need not only be thought of as a posthumous task endowed with the full realization of theosis, but a mandate in the here and now to sustain one another, and particularly those tottering closest to the brink.

LITURGICAL IMPLICATIONS

A reformulation of the doctrine of Satan would not require a massive overhaul of liturgical invocations of the devil in the Rite of Baptism or in the Renewal of Baptismal Promises. The reality may be that many Catholics already interpret these references to Satan in a figurative manner. In time, allusions to Satan as the prospect of God's beloved creature that scorns its Maker could be added to the canon of prayers, devotions, and liturgies, but such is by no means necessary for doctrinal reform.

One liturgical practice that would need to change would be overly confident, dogmatic homilies that speak of Satan, hell, and damnation as though the preacher personally saw Satan fall like lighting and has the photos to prove it. So too would exegetically unsound homiletic references to the snake of Eden and the beast of Revelation need to be exorcised from the

---

54. Lane, *Experience of God*, 29; Himes, "Finding God in All Things," 141.

liturgy. On the other hand, there exist biblical passages that might be newly evoked so as to support some of the theological principles underlying our proposed reformulation of the doctrine of Satan.

THE REFORMULATED ACCOUNT OF SATAN AND THE SENSUS PLENIOR

A model of Satan as the object of God's unreciprocated, sustaining love can be detected in the *sensus plenior* attainable through a canonical exegesis of the scriptures, that is, a reading with the benefit of hindsight and in the context of the entire canon. Gleaning in the text that which was not explicitly intended by the human author or discernable through historical-critical exegesis, traces of the intransigent Satan sustained in being by God may be glimpsed in the parables of the prodigal son, the lost sheep, the lost coin, and the pearl of great price. In each instance, the parable wistfully narrates God's passionate pursuit of that which is lost—with no trace of fatalistic defeatism.

The motif of Satan as the creature who rejects God's ongoing love may also be detected in the narrative of the rich young ruler of Matthew 19 who asked what he must do to inherit eternal life before walking away from Jesus, and the misnamed "bad thief" of Luke's Passion Narrative. Both these narratives seem poised to make theological points about the offer of salvation rather than to report particular conversations verbatim. Neither involve the imposition of punishment by Jesus and both end on a note of cautionary implication rather than a direct assertion as to whether the one who ostensibly rejected Jesus was in fact damned. Perhaps it is Wisdom 11:24–26 that most explicitly captures the relationship between the recalcitrant creature and the unconditional Sustainer of being.

> For you love all things that exist, and detest none of the things that you have made, for you would not have made anything if you had hated it. How would anything have endured if you had not willed it? Or how would anything not called forth by you have been preserved? You spare all things, for they are yours, O Lord, you who love the living.

CONCLUSION

This chapter completes our argument that the Church's presentation of the doctrine of Satan, founded as it is upon mythical language, should continue to develop as the "bearer of possible worlds," expressing possibilities in the

Creator-creature relationship. The Satan revealed by myth exists as a probe into the soteriological possibility known as hell, that is, the real possibility that a creature might use its free will to forever reject God, yet still be sustained in being by God. Ultimately, the doctrine of Satan may express a truth concerning God's unconditional sustenance of being.

A second contribution of the chapter is its recognition that a Satan stripped of ontological existence, albeit within the narrative arc of myth, is a Satan stripped of the grace that infuses being. Such a Satan is close to a uni-dimensional avatar, denoting evil in and of itself, and devoid of the moral complexity that has long allowed the motif to function as an exploratory device, probing into the complexities of humanity's relationship with the Creator. If Satan is merely the figurative personification of pure evil, that is, a mask for nothingness, then there is little point in retaining the doctrine and to do so is to invite misunderstanding and literalism.

While the state of hell has been associated with punishment, it can also be viewed as a natural and self-inflicted consequence of the exercise of free-will. Love of God cannot be forced and if free-will is genuine, there must be the possibility of rejecting God. The doctrine of Satan can denote the conceivable possibility that a free-willed creature could reject God and endure to tell the tale. It is only in view of such a possibility that love for God is truly voluntary and is hence genuine love. If God endows creatures with genuine free will, and unconditionally sustains them in being, then, by necessity, there must exist the possibility of Satan.

15

The Satan of Satanism: Validating Doctrine through Behavior

This chapter turns to a model of Satan within a non-Christian movement so as to consider the exhortative purpose served by the motif, that is, its role in influencing behavior as opposed to making an ontological truth claim. The doctrine of Satan as embraced by the Church of Satan (COS) exemplifies George Lindbeck's approach to doctrine as a language game, that is, a symbol system that orders behavior within a particular community.

The point of relevance to our discussion of the Catholic presentation of the doctrine of Satan is that, whether acknowledged or not, the doctrine serves to impact human behavior. Our proposed reformulation of the doctrine can continue to exhort lived discipleship, driven by love rather than by fear, and ultimately inspired by an image of God rather than the image of a hypothetical damned being.

THE ATHEISTIC SATANISM OF THE CHURCH OF SATAN

The Church of Satan (COS), founded by Anton LaVey, is an atheistic movement that views the doctrine of Satan as a regulating symbol through which to order behaviors and attitudes.[1] The term "doctrine" in this sense is at

1. Church of Satan, "Eleven Satanic Rules of the Earth."

least applicable to the extent that fields such as philosophy and economics employ the word without theological connotations, though one might venture that an atheistic assertion expresses beliefs about God and is, in that sense, theological. The COS website states that "Satanists do not believe in God, Satan, Heaven or Hell" and "Satan to us is a symbol of pride, liberty and individualism, and it serves as an external metaphorical projection of our highest personal potential. We do not believe in Satan as a being or person."[2] Indeed, the website of the COS encourages people who claim to have encountered a supernatural, ontological Satan or other demons to seek psychiatric treatment.[3] While the COS account of Satan holds implications for beliefs about God, it is not primarily theological so much as a philosophical motif and as a psychological archetype signifying a vision of human fulfillment.

THE POWER OF THE PICTURE

The fact that the COS so vehemently distances its references to Satan from ontological claims may be motivated by a desire to disassociate itself from imagery of Satanism as promulgated by Hollywood. The COS strives to distinguish its brand of Satanism from "devil worship" in which Satan is invoked as a supernatural being. Rather than a being to be worshipped, Satan, for the COS, is a concept to be explored.

> "Satan" is, to us, a symbol rather than an anthropomorphic being, although many members of the Church of Satan who are mystically inclined would prefer to think of Satan in a very real, anthropomorphic way. Of course, we do not discourage this, because we realize that to many individuals a picture, a well-wrought picture of their mentor or their tutelary divinity is very important for them to conceptualize ritualistically. However, Satan symbolically is the teacher: the informer of the whys and the wherefores of the world. And in answer to those who would label us "Devil worshippers" or be very quick to assume us to be Satan worshippers, I must say that Satan demands study, not worship, in its truest symbology. We do not grovel; we do not get down on our knees, genuflect, and worship Satan.[4]

---

2. https://www.churchofsatan.com.
3. https://www.churchofsatan.com.
4. https://www.churchofsatan.com.

The Satan of Satanism: Validating Doctrine through Behavior   221

Having clarified that Satan is, for the COS, a symbol, this statement acknowledges that many members of his movement "would prefer to think of Satan in a very real, anthropomorphic way." This comment in no way endorses, even begrudgingly, a belief in Satan as an ontological reality. Rather, the COS recognizes the power of a "well-wrought picture" that can enable one to "conceptualize ritualistically," that is, to think in a manner informed by symbols. The COS's acknowledgment of symbolic power stands in marked contrast with the low view of symbol implied by the magisterium of the Catholic Church in its repeated dismissal of figurative personification and myth.[5] Consider the contrast between the COS testimony to the power of the picture and Pope Pius XII's dismissive reference to "myths or other such things, which are more the product of an extravagant imagination," Pope Pius VI's references to "a pseudo-reality, a conceptual and fanciful personification," *Christian Faith and Demonology*'s reference to "illusory fantasies," and its suggestion that if Jesus spoke of Satan in a mythopoetic sense, he must have lacked firmness of mind.[6] Pope Francis too has underestimated the power of the picture, associating a figurative interpretation of the motif of Satan with complacency and moral carelessness.[7]

It may be somewhat ironic that a tradition that does not espouse belief in a God, heaven, hell, or supernatural realm, recognizes the power of symbol and the form of truth it mediates far more readily than modern popes have been willing to do. Little defense can be provided by a "slippery slope" argument that to regard Satan in figurative terms might lead some to also call into question the existence of God. The question of the reality of Satan is in no way equivalent to the question of the reality of God. The model of God who is omnipresent in the sacramental universe cannot be reduced to a supernatural being and is better described as the ground of all being. The Councils of Braga I and Lateran IV established this capital difference between the reality of God and the reality of the devil, jettisoning the Gnostic view that Satan existed as an evil deity.[8]

---

5. Paul VI, "Deliver Us from Evil"; CDF, "Christian Faith and Demonology"; CDF, *Catechism of the Catholic Church* 2851; Francis, *"Gaudete et Exsultate"* 161.

6. Pius XII, *"Humani Generis"* 39; Paul VI, "Deliver Us from Evil"; CDF, "Christian Faith and Demonology."

7. Francis, *"Gaudete et Exsultate"* 161.

8. Lane, *Experience of God*, 29; Himes, "Finding God in All Things," 141; Russell, *Satan*, 220, 225; First Council of Braga; Lateran IV, "Canons" 1.

SATAN AS A SYMBOL OF ETHICAL EGOISM

Whereas the Christian motif of Satan has, in its various forms and guises, symbolized evil, damnation, temptation, and the fallen state of creation, and, as suggested by the present work, God's unconditional sustenance of being, the COS symbol of Satan represents and celebrates the willful human ego. "Man has always created his gods" posits the COS website, "rather than his gods creating him." The online exposition of COS doctrine proceeds to explain that the church regards gods as the externalization and personification of psychological or external, natural forces. "All Gods are thus externalized forms, magnified projections of the true nature of their creators, personifying aspects of the universe or personal temperaments which many of their followers find to be troubling."[9] The comment reflects a Feuerbachian position, regarding the divine as nothing more than a projection of human attributes.[10]

LaVey unashamedly identifies the egoism at the heart of the COS worldview, remarking "We are simply carnal self-worshippers looking to enjoy our lives to the fullest."[11] The COS website describes Satan as the "avatar of carnality, justice, and self-determination."[12] Essentially, the COS invokes the motif of Satan as a symbol for a worldview characterized by hedonism and self-interest. As LaVey remarks, "Satan represents indulgence instead of abstinence."[13] Magus Peter Gilmore characterizes the COS ethic as to "live to maximize the Good for myself and those I value. At all times I remain in control of my pursuit of pleasure. I am an Epicurean."[14]

James Lewis observes that LaVey's *Nine Satanic Statements* borrow from Ayn Rand's philosophy of Ethical Egoism.[15] Rand's encapsulates her theory of ethics, declaring, "Every man is an end in himself. He exists for his own sake, and the achievement of his own happiness is his highest purpose."[16] LaVey shares in this ethical egoism, professing "Since our philosophy is self-centered, each Satanist sees himself as the most important person in his life."[17] Somewhat paradoxically, the COS commitment to egoism is enshrined in a communal code as evidenced in its "Nine Satanic

9. https://www.churchofsatan.com.
10. Wink, *Human Being*, 40–41; Seiple and Weidmann, *Enigmas and Powers*, 105–6; Corbin, *Creative Images in the Sufism of Ibn 'Arabi*, 174.
11. https://www.churchofsatan.com.
12. https://www.churchofsatan.com.
13. https://www.churchofsatan.com.
14. Gilmore, "What, the Devil?"
15. Lewis, "Diabolical Activity," 8.
16. Rand, *For the New Intellectual*, 123.
17. https://www.churchofsatan.com.

Statements" and "Eleven Satanic Rules of the Earth," its shared symbol system, and culture.[18]

A SUBVERSION OF BIBLICAL MOTIFS OF SATAN AND LUCIFER

Satan as a symbol of Ethical Egoism finds little basis in biblical motifs of Satan and Lucifer. It may reflect an imaginative interpretation of Revelation 12:7–13 that speaks of a war in heaven, thus suggesting insubordination before God. However, the Satan thrown down in the Book of Revelation symbolizes the fall of Roman oppression, an institution that would be diametrically opposed to the libertarianism of the COS.

The falling star motif that evolved separately to that of Satan before being conflated with it, further fuels the trope of an insubordinate Satan, cast out of heaven for being a strong individual and refusing to submit to divine tyranny. Saint Jerome's Vulgate employed the Latin name "Lucifer," literally "light-bearer" to signify the biblical and extracanonical motif of the "fall of the day star."[19] This motif is based upon Isaiah 14:15 and Ezekiel 28 in their respective references to the fall of the King of Babylon and the Prince of Tyre.[20] Its originators never intended the motif to denote admiration for a rebel so much as mocking contempt for deposed tyrants.

Granted, Patristic speculation regarding the fall of Satan provides some basis for the COS motif of Satan as a symbol of egoism. Tatian equated Satan with Zeus, the leader of the pagan gods, and speculated that Satan was cast out of heaven for refusing to worship the one true God.[21] Irenaeus posited that Satan fell because he first envied God and then envied humanity, created in the image of God, and hence orchestrated the fall of humanity.[22] It may be John Milton's *Paradise Lost*, however, that most clearly depicts the motif of the rebellious, prideful Satan who refuses to submit to a despotic God.[23]

18. https://www.churchofsatan.com.
19. Almond, *Devil*, 46.
20. Kelly, *Satan*, 196.
21. Russel, *Satan*, 74–75.
22. Russel, *Satan*, 80–81.
23. Milton, *Paradise Lost*, 206–469. Forsyth, *Satanic Epic*.

THE CHURCH OF SATAN AND SCIENCE OF MIND

The closest thing that the COS has to a body of doctrine is LaVey's *Satanic Bible*. This is a collection of teachings assembled by LaVey and with little or no relation to the Bible or any ancient texts. Given that the COS is an atheistic movement, it does not of course regard the *Satanic Bible* as revealed from any transcendent source.

James Lewis locates the genesis of the COS as a metaphysical religion akin to science of mind movements.[24] These groups purport to offer a means of self-improvement, appropriating the language of science and of religion. Lewis detects among these movements a tendency to look with disdain upon religions that cite divine revelation as a basis for their authority.[25] Adherents of the COS and of other "science of mind" religions pride themselves on the scientific basis of their teachings.[26] As Sentes and Palmer observe, however, this appeal to science is a ploy for credibility that lacks any clear scientific basis. These authors comment that such movements "articulate themselves, often with a popular fluency, in the discourses of the natural science and seek to justify their beliefs by means of para—or pseudoscientific investigation or argument."[27]

A CULTURAL-LINGUISTIC APPROACH TO DOCTRINE

COS references to Satan exemplify doctrine functioning so as to impel behavior within a given community, with no presumption that it corresponds to ontological truth—a function of doctrine that fascinated George Lindbeck. Writing from a Lutheran perspective, Lindbeck views the Bible as yielding a regulatory framework for all facets of life. To be religious, for Lindbeck, is to interiorize a set of skills, behaviors, and thought-patterns developed within a particular community.[28] Doctrines for Lindbeck serve as regulations for thinking and acting within a particular worldview rather than necessarily serving as affirmations of objective truths.

Lindbeck's approach to doctrine is distinctively postliberal insofar as it views doctrinal truth as native to a particular faith community, rather than universally binding. The author envisages a community of faith adopting narratives as lenses through which to view reality, a form of interpretation

---

24. Lewis, "Diabolical Activity," 8.
25. Lewis, "Diabolical Activity," 8.
26. Lewis, "Diabolical Activity," 8.
27. Sentes and Palmer, "Presumed Immanent."
28. Sentes and Palmer, "Presumed Immanent."

to which Lindbeck refers as "intratextuality," and the meaning derived from this view of reality as determining a way of life within that community.[29] Lindbeck is consistent, not offering any pretense of totalizing objectivity either in the process of interpreting sacred texts or in the nature of the truth derived from the process. There is hence a degree of relativism in Lindbeck's approach to biblical interpretation and doctrine.

Lindbeck describes his approach to doctrine as "cultural linguistic."[30] It is cultural insofar as it is concerned with life within the culture of a particular community or tradition. It is linguistic to the extent that doctrine, in this view, functions somewhat like the rules or grammar system of a particular language. In Lindbeck's cultural linguistic view, doctrine functions as a kind of moral and spiritual grammar within a given religious culture.[31] In this regard, Lindbeck is influenced by what Wittgenstein called "language games," that is the structure and internal logic of any given language.[32]

Lindbeck believes in the incommensurability of doctrines, doubting that the doctrine of any given faith community can be directly equated with that of another community as though both are expressions of a common, underlying universal human experience or objective reality.[33] As such, Lindbeck's position differs from what he terms "expressivist" approaches that view the doctrinal formulations of any given tradition as the attempt to articulate a universal truth that other faith communities also attempt to articulate in their own way.[34] When a Methodist minister is invited to give a "benediction" this may signify for her the bestowal of a simple blessing, whereas a Catholic priest may show up with the Blessed Sacrament encased in a monstrance—but more profoundly, Lindbeck's principle of incommensurability calls into question what faith communities mean by shared terms as foundational as that of "God," "faith," "good," or "Satan."

In a sense, Lindbeck's assertion regarding the incommensurability of religious language is a derivative of the "other minds" problem in epistemology, an "other faiths" problem as it were. How can we ever know what another faith community really means by a given doctrine? As we have seen, the term "satan" exists as a homophone reflecting connotations as varied as a member of the celestial court, a creator-demiurge, a fallen angel, and

---

29. Lindbeck, *Nature of Doctrine*, 122.
30. Lindbeck, *Nature of Doctrine*, 32.
31. Sentes and Palmer, "Presumed Immanent," 68–69.
32. Lieber, "On What Sort of Speech Act," 232–67.
33. Lindbeck, *Nature of Doctrine*, 68–69; Cheetham, *Ways of Meeting*, 20; Rigby et al., "Nature of Doctrine and Scientific Progress," 687.
34. Lindbeck, *Nature of Doctrine*, 68–69.

a common noun signifying human enemies. Each of these tropes of Satan functioned within some strand of tradition or "language game" within which it was loaded with assumptions concerning God and the world.

AN AMBIGUOUS RELATIONSHIP BETWEEN DOCTRINE AND ONTOLOGICAL TRUTH

Lindbeck distinguishes his cultural linguistic approach to doctrine from a propositionalist approach that views doctrine as necessarily signifying ontological truth.[35] The author thinks of truth as internal coherence, in his terms the "intrasystematic truth" of doctrine for the community of initiates privy to the religion's internal grammar.[36] Lindbeck regards intrasystematic truth of this kind as a necessary condition for the ontological truth of a doctrine, though by itself, no assurance of it.[37] So, one might argue, if a presentation of the doctrine of Satan contradicts more central tenets of a belief-system, for example God's infinite mercy and omnipresence, then that presentation of the doctrine of Satan is incongruous within the belief system. In Lindbeck's terms of reference, such a doctrine of Satan is not intrasystematically true and cannot hence be ontologically true.

Lindbeck is also concerned with "categorial truth," that is, the extent to which a doctrine is validated by a way of life rather than by some pre-existing fact.[38] In a case in point, Lindbeck remarks with reference to the biblical doctrine of God, "The primary focus is not on God's being in itself, but how life is to be lived, and reality construed in light of God's character as an agent as this is depicted in the stories of Israel and Jesus."[39] If Lindbeck can speak of the doctrine of God in such terms, it may be reasonable to propose that he would not hesitate to do so with reference to the doctrine of Satan, regarding the doctrine as concerned with "how life is to be lived" rather than the being of a particular creature.

Jordan Peterson advances a similar concern for the lived implications of belief when, in response to the question as to whether he "believes in God," he responds that to say with any integrity that one believes in God means that one lives as though God is real. ""It doesn't mean to state it; it means to act it out. And unless you act it out, you should be very careful

---

35. Lindbeck, *Nature of Doctrine*, 113–14.
36. Lindbeck, *Nature of Doctrine*, 64–65, 68–69, 80, 101.
37. Lindbeck, *Nature of Doctrine*, 68–69.
38. Lindbeck, *Nature of Doctrine*, 51.
39. Lindbeck, *Nature of Doctrine*, 68–69, 121.

about claiming it."[40] Peterson contrasts this with an attitude that God may be real in the same way that some distant artifact in the world may exist, but have no bearing on day-to-day life.[41]

Because Lindbeck emphasizes the regulative function of doctrine, it would be easy to caricature his approach as denying that doctrinal propositions correspond to any particular ontological truth whatsoever. At times, Lindbeck comes extremely close to saying as much, as when he proposes that "Meaning is constituted by use of a specific language, rather than being distinguishable from it."[42] David Cheetham recognizes this impression but clarifies that Lindbeck is not completely rejecting a correspondence theory of truth. Cheetham observes, in relation to Lindbeck's intratextual approach to religion that

> to assume that it presupposes a rejection of any kind of correspondence theory of truth, or that a full-blown anti-realism is being advanced, is a misrepresentation. Instead, the intratextual position seems to be a form of critical realism, maintaining that reality is mediated more *thickly* through a particular tradition's conceptual scheme."[43]

Consistent with Cheetham's interpretation, Lindbeck states that "there is nothing in the cultural-linguistic approach that requires the rejection (or the acceptance) of epistemological realism and the correspondence theory of truth."[44]

DOCTRINE WITHOUT A BASIS IN ONTOLOGICAL TRUTH AS DECEPTIVE?

Avery Cardinal Dulles sounds a note of caution as to the implications of emphasizing a regulatory role for doctrine, functioning as the rules of a Wittgensteinian language game, while being evasive as to its ontological claims. Dulles cautions that "the depiction of language as a set of convenient symbols used according to the conventional rules of a 'language game' is deceptive. . . . To substitute grammatical debates about the things meant is to obfuscate the necessary connection between meaningful language

---

40. Peterson, "Who Dares Say He Believes in God."
41. Peterson, "Who Dares Say He Believes in God."
42. Lindbeck, *Nature of Doctrine*, 68–69, 113–14.
43. Cheetham, *Ways of Meeting*, 20.
44. Lindbeck, *Nature of Doctrine*, 68–69.

and reality."[45] Dulles develops this criticism with relation to the doctrine of Christ. "If we are to worship, speak and behave, as though the Son of God is God himself, is this not because the Son really and ontologically is God, whether anyone believes it or not?"[46] Dulles's remarks raise the question as to what extent theological truth must be rooted in ontological truth, that is, the existence of things and beings, and in objective truths that in some sense exist independent of the extent to which they are recognized.

We earlier noted the argument that Pope Paul VI's 1972 affirmation of Satan's existence as a particular being was not an ontological claim, but rather an exhortation to adhere to a Catholic tradition of representing Satan in a given way. If so, then, in terms of Dulles's observation, Paul VI was being somewhat deceptive—or at least equivocal. Why, after all, should believers be pressurized to think in terms of a certain image if it does not necessarily correspond to ontological reality? Viewed in a dim light, the regulatory purpose played by doctrine in the cultural linguistic model is manipulative. Viewed more sympathetically, it could involve an open admission that the doctrine in question is not necessarily tethered to ontological truths—and is not universally binding.

LINDBECK'S CURIOUS ALLUSION TO THE "SATAN OF SATANISM"

While Lindbeck seldom refers to specific faith communities while outlining his approach to doctrine, he does make a curious reference to the "Satan of Satanism." Judging by his passing remark, Lindbeck was thinking in terms of theistic Satanism that shares with many Christians, Jews, Muslims, and other people of faith, belief in the devil as an ontological reality. Lindbeck utilizes the term "cognitivist" in this context to denote an ontological truth claim. "When one thinks of religions in a cognitivist fashion they are always at least meaningful enough to be false, and the more diabolical can contain some glimmers of truth even if it be no more than the belief that there is a devil."[47] Lindbeck suggests that if Satanists posit the existence of the devil, from the cognitivist perspective, their teachings would be true in relation to this claim, if indeed the devil exists as an ontological reality.

Somewhat cryptically, Lindbeck then remarks, "On a categorial interpretation, in contrast, beliefs about the Satan of Satanism might be neither

---

45. Dulles, "Postmodernist Ecumenism"; Lieber, "On What Sort of Speech Act"; Wittgenstein, *Tractatus Logico-Philosophicus*.

46. Dulles, "Postmodernist Ecumenism."

47. Linbeck, *Nature of Doctrine*, 50.

true nor false, but like those regarding a square circle, nonsensical (though horrendously so)."[48] Lindbeck suggests that it may make little sense to think of Satanists faithfully bearing witness to their doctrine of Satan by the way they live. Further, he implies that the Satan of Satanism is a self-contradictory idea. Granted, given his reference to the cognitivist truth claim that there is a devil, the author appears to be thinking in terms of theistic Satanism. As such, Lindbeck suggests that it may be nonsensical to think of theistic Satanists behaving in a manner that is consistent with their devotion to the devil. Repugnant as such behavior might be, it is not obvious why it would be impossible and would not, from a categorical perspective, indicate the truth of the beliefs in question. Whereas Lindbeck suggests that it would undermine the categorial truth that "Christ is Lord" if a crusader made this declaration while smashing in the skull of a Muslim, it might equally well be argued that it would bolster the categorial truth of the statement that "Satan is Lord" if a theistic Satanist were to make this declaration while committing some evil act.[49] If, however, an atheistic Satanist made this same declaration while committing an evil act, this would offer an exceptionally clear instance of categorial truth precisely because it is asserted without any ontological truth claim and is consistent with the vile behavior that accompanies it.

On a categorial interpretation, COS Satanists may self-validate the model of Satan as a guiding symbol to the extent to which they practice the Ethical Egoism that they preach. As Paul J. DeHart remarks with reference to Lindbeck's delineation of categorial truth, "The only test of categorical [sic] truth is the living of the pattern itself, the ongoing test of the religious symbol system's ability to provide illumination and orientation for life and account for anomalous experiences."[50] Hence, if COS members live in a manner consistent with their symbol of Ethical Egoism, then, on a categorical basis, their doctrine of Satan, far from nonsensical is, in Lindbeck's categorial sense, true.

RELEVANCE TO CATHOLIC CHRISTIANITY

When the COS advises those who believe they have experienced the harassment of the devil or demons to seek psychiatric help, it may be a sobering thought that within that movement's terms of reference, this advice would seem to pertain to Pope Francis who detects the agency of the devil underlying the full array of human sins. Granted, the COS injunction to seek

48. Dulles, "Postmodernist Ecumenism," 51.
49. Lindbeck, *Nature of Doctrine*, 63–69.
50. DeHart, *Trial of the Witnesses*, 84; Vaino, *Beyond Fideism*, 72.

psychiatric help may be born of encounters with those who claim experiences of the demonic far less credible than the Holy Father's diagnosis of diabolical activity. Also, it might be argued that the injunction reveals a closed-minded naturalism, failing to acknowledge there may be more things in hell and earth than are dreamt of in its philosophy. How, after all, we might ask, is the existence of demons or other disembodied entities falsifiable?

The relevance of these ruminations for Catholic doctrine is that as the COS appeals to the motif of Satan so as to condition moral behavior, the Christian tradition has, from its perspective, done likewise. While the COS holds up a motif of Satan as a positive example of how to live, the Christian tradition utilizes its motifs of Satan as counterexamples. In both cases, the motif is laden with exhortative power. We have seen that Pope Francis appeals to the motif of Satan in the context of *Gaudete et Exsultate*, subtitled *Apostolic Exhortation on the Call to Holiness in the World*. More generally, through the centuries, Christian preaching about Satan has not had as its primary objective the delivery of lessons in demonology but the moral exhortation of humans. Satan has served a pedagogical function as the cautionary tale of a disobedient creature, eternally damned for its choice against God.

If the doctrine of Satan were to be reformulated so as to emphasize God's unconditional sustenance of even the most recalcitrant being, it could serve as both a positive and antithetical inspiration to discipleship. Continuing to serve as a negative example, its exhortative power, however, would no longer be rooted in fear of punishment so much as in a recognition of the unconditional love of God. Sane adults do not honor loving relationships out of fear of punishment as though to say that one would consider having an affair because one's spouse is a forgiving person and would not exact punishment of some kind. A relationship with God that is driven by fear of punishment is hardly a relationship at all. The exhortative power of the model of Satan as the prospective being that forever rejects a loving relationship with God is rooted not in fear of externally imposed punishment but in the pain of unrequited love, rejection, and broken-heartedness.

In another sense, our proposed model of Satan positively exhorts discipleship insofar as it is not only an image of the intransigent figure of Satan, but portrays a tragic tableau depicting Satan in relation to God and the God-infused creation. It suggests a God who is the antithesis of Ethical Egoism, a God who is so other-centered as to overflow the boundaries of selfhood and be present in and through all things, a God whose commitment to being is unconditional so that it continues to hold Satan in being with the love of a broken-hearted parent for their self-destructive child. As such, our proposed image of Satan serves not so much to encourage speculation into the possibility that one or more persons have rejected God so as to instead choose a personal hell, but to cast light upon a dimension of God. In that sense, it is a truly theological image. On at least one point, the COS is right "because we realize that to many individuals a picture, a well-wrought picture of their mentor or their tutelary divinity is very important for them to conceptualize ritualistically."[51]

CONCLUSION

The manner in which the COS refers to Satan asserts no underlying ontological reality but rather a symbol that expresses a way of life within a particular community. The Satan of Satanism is, in this sense, a binding part of the grammar of a particular language group. It is an example of doctrine functioning explicitly in the cultural linguistic sense envisaged by Lindbeck. While Lindbeck would argue that doctrine in general functions in this way across the spectrum of religious traditions, the case of Satan in COS teaching is an exceptionally clear instance of doctrine functioning at the categorial level, divorced from ontological claims.

The COS invocation of the symbol of Satan offers a powerful indication of how a motif can symbolize and bolster a way of life, without insisting upon any underlying ontological reality. While the COS presents the motif of Satan as an exemplar of desirable behavior, the Christian tradition has presented its versions of Satan as a counterexample of how a person should behave.

The reformulated doctrine of Satan as proposed in this book could continue to instill a way of behaving, of living out a relationship with God. Its exhortative power would no longer lie in the threat of externally imposed punishment, but in the pain of broken relationships, and the dreadful prospect of choosing to forever refuse the invitation to love. Positively, it suggests a God of unconditional enemy-love, and calls forth from humanity forgiveness, boundless compassion, and regard for the one from whom we can expect nothing but rejection.

51. https://www.churchofsatan.com.

Bibliography

Abbot, Walter, ed. *The Documents of Vatican II*. New York: Guild & America, 1966.
Alberigo, Giuseppe, and Joseph Komonchak, eds. *The Formation of the Council's Identity: First Period and Intersession October 1962–September 1963*. Vol. 2 of *History of Vatican II*. Maryknoll, NY: Orbis, 1997.
Alison, James. "Deliver Us from Evil." Paper presented at the Metropolitan Center for Mental Health and the Metropolitan Institute for Training in Psychoanalytic Psychotherapy, New York City, April 30–May 1, 2005. Online. http://jamesalison.com/deliver-us-from-evil.
Allen, James P. *The Ancient Egyptian Pyramid Texts*. Atlanta: SBL, 2015.
Almond, Philip. *The Devil: A New Biography*. New York: Cornell University, 2014.
American Psychiatric Association (APA). *Highlights of Changes from DSM-IV-TR to DSM-V*. Arlington: American Psychiatric, 2013. Online. www.dsm5.org/Documents/changes%20from%20dsm-iv-tr%20to%20dsm-5.pdf.
Anselm. "Proslogion." In *St. Anselm: Basic Writings*, edited by S. N. Deane, 49–79. La Salle: Open Court, 1962.
Aquinas, Thomas. *The Summa Theologica*. Translated by the Fathers of the English Dominican Province. New York: Benziger, 1947. Online. http://www.ccel.org/a/aquinas/summa/FP/FP055.html#FPQ55OUTP1.
Argan, Glen. "Vatican II: When Cardinal Ottaviani's Microphone was 'Turned Off' During Debate on the Liturgy." *Western Catholic Reporter*, November 1, 2012. Online. http://catholicismpure.wordpress.com/2012/11/01/vatican-ll-when-cardinal-ottavianis-microphone-was-turned-off-during-debate-on-the-liturgy/.
Aristotle. *Poetics*. Translated by S. H. Butcher. Online. http://classics.mit.edu/Aristotle/poetics.1.1.html.
Armstrong, Karen. *The Battle for God: A History of Fundamentalism*. New York: Ballantine, 2001.
Attridge, Harold. "Reflections on Research into Q." *Semeia* 55 (1991) 223–34.
Augustine of Hippo. *The City of God*. Translated by Marcus Dods. New York: Random, 2000.
———. *Confessions*. Translated by R. S. Pine-Coffin. London: Penguin, 1961.

Balthasar, Hans Urs von. *Dare We Hope That All Men Be Saved?* Translated by David Kipp and Lothar Krauth. San Francisco: Ignatius, 1988.

Barr, James. "Revelation through History in the Old Testament and in Modern Theology." In *New Theology No. 1*, edited by Martin Marty and Dean Peerman, 67–68. New York: MacMillan, 1964.

Barron, Robert. *The Priority of Christ: Towards a Postliberal Catholicism*. Grand Rapids: Baker, 2007.

———. "Yves Congar and the Meaning of Vatican II." *Word on Fire*, June 29, 2012. Online. https://www.wordonfire.org/resources/article/yves-congar-and-the-meaning-of-vatican-ii/445.

Batto, Bernard. *Slaying the Dragon: Mythmaking in the Biblical Tradition*. Louisville: Westminster John Knox, 1992.

Bauckham, Richard. "Jews and Jewish Christians in the Land of Israel at the Time of the Bar Kochba War, with Special Reference to the Apocalypse of Peter." In *Tolerance and Intolerance in Early Judaism and Christianity*, edited by G. N. Stanton and G. G. Stroumsa, 228–38. Cambridge: Cambridge University Press, 1998.

Baudelaire, Charles. *The Generous Gambler*. Translated by Louis Varese. London: New Directions, 1947.

Bechtel, Lyn. "Rethinking the Interpretation of Genesis 2:4 (B)–3:24." In *A Feminist Companion to Genesis*, edited by Athayla Brenner, 77–117. Sheffield: Sheffield Academic, 1993.

Beinert, Wolfgang, and Francis Schüssler Fiorenza. *Handbook of Catholic Theology*. New York: Crossroads, 1995.

Bell, Art. "Malachi Martin." *Coast to Coast*. Las Vegas, NV: KDWN, April 4–5, 1997. Online. https://www.coasttocoastam.com/show/exorcisms-demonic-possession.

Bell, Richard. *Deliver Us from Evil*. Tübingen: Mohr Siebeck, 2007.

Benedict XVI. "Meeting with the Parish Priests and the Clergy of Rome." Address given February 14, 2013. Online. http://www.vatican.va/holy_father/benedict_xvi/speeches/2013/february/documents/hf_ben-xvi_spe_20130214_clero-roma_en.html.

———. "To the Roman Curia Offering Them His Christmas Greetings." Address given December 22, 2005. Online. http://www.vatican.va/holy_father/benedict_xvi/speeches/2005/december/documents/hf_ben_xvi_spe_20051222_roman-curia_en.html.

Bergoglio, Jorge, and Abraham Skorka. *On Heaven and Earth*. New York: Image, 2010.

Bokenkotter, Thomas. *A Concise History of the Catholic Church*. New York: Doubleday, 2004.

Bonhoeffer, Dietrich. *Letters and Papers from Prison*. Edited by Eberharde Bethge. New York: Touchstone, 1997.

Boyd, Gregory. *Constructing a Trinitarian Warfare Theodicy*. Downer's Grove, IL: InterVarsity, 2001.

Brown, Raymond. *The Gospel According to John*. Anchor Bible Commentary 29. Garden City: Anchor Bible, 1966.

———. "Hermeneutics." In *The Jerome Biblical Commentary*, edited by Joseph Fitzmyer et al., 616–19. Englewood Cliffs: Prentice Hall, 1968.

———. *Introduction to New Testament Christology*. New York: Associated Sulpicians of the US, 1994.

———. *New Testament Essays*. Milwaukee: Doubleday Religion, 1965.

———. "The Pater Noster as an Eschatological Prayer." *Theological Studies* 22 (1961) 175–208. Online. http://www.ts.mu.edu/readers/content/pdf/22/22.2/22.2.1.pdf.

———. "The Qumran Scrolls and the Johannine Gospel and Epistles." In *New Testament Essays*, by Raymond Brown, 10–11. New York: Paulist, 1965.

———. *Responses to 101 Questions on the Bible*. New York: Paulist, 1990.

Brown, Raymond, and Sandra Schneiders. "Hermeneutics." In *The New Jerome Biblical Commentary*, edited by Raymond E. Brown et al., 1146–65. New Jersey: Prentice Hall, 1990.

Brown, Truesdell. "Euhemerus and the Historians." *Harvard Theological Review* 39.4 (1946) 337–40.

Brown, Yaakov. "Genesis 16: Sarai, Avram, Hagar & Y'sh'mael." *Beth Melek* (blog), March 9, 2016. Online. https://www.bethmelekh.com/yaakovs-commentary---15081497151214931513-1497150615111489/genesis-16-sarai-avram-hagar-yshmael.

Brueggemann, Walter. *Reverberations of Faith: A Theological Handbook of Old Testament Themes*. Louiseville: John Knox, 2002.

Bruun Kofoed, Jens. "'Adam *What* Are You?' The Primeval History Against the Backdrop of Mesopotamian Mythology." *Hiphil* 3 (2005). Online. http://ww.see-j.net/hiphil/ojs-2.3.3-3/index.php/hiphil/article/view/30/30.

Bultmann, Rudolph. *Jesus and the Word*. New York: Scribner's, 1958.

———. "New Testament and Mythology." In *Kerygma and Myth: A Theological Debate*, edited by Hans Werner Bartsch, 5. Translated by Regina Fuller. London: SPK, 1960.

Campbell, Joseph. *The Power of Myth*. New York: Doubleday, 1988.

Carroll, James. *Practicing Catholic*. New York: Houghton Mifller Harcourt, 2009.

Carus, Paul. *History of the Devil and the Idea of Evil*. New York: Gramercy, 1996.

Cassirer Ernst. *Language and Myth*. Translated by Susan Langer. New York: Harper & Brother 1946.

Cazeneuve, Jean. *Lucien Lévy-Bruhl*. New York: Harper, 1972.

Chardin, Pierre Teilhard de. *The Phenomenon of Man*. 2nd ed. New York: Harper Colophon, 1975.

Cheetham, David. *Ways of Meeting and the Theology of Religions*. Farnham: Ashgate, 2013.

Church of Satan. "Eleven Satanic Rules of the Earth." Online. https://www.churchofsatan.com/eleven-rules-of-earth.

Clayton, John Powell. *The Concept of Correlation: Paul Tillich and the Possibility of Mediating Theology*. Berlin; New York: de Gruyter, 1980.

Clifford, Richard, and Roland Murphy. "Genesis." In *The New Jerome Biblical Commentary*, edited by Joseph Fiztmyer et al., 8–43. New Jersey: Prentice Hall, 1990.

Collins, John. "Cult and Culture: The Limits of Hellenization in Judea." In *Hellenism in the Land of Israel*, edited by John J. Collins and Gregory E. Sterling, 38–61. Notre Dame: University of Notre Dame Press, 2001.

Congar, Yves. *The Meaning of Tradition*. New York: Hawthorn, 1965.

Congregation for Divine Worship and the Discipline of the Sacraments (CDWDS). *De Exorcismis et Supplicationibus Quibusdam*. Editio Typica. Vatican City: Vatican, 1999.

Congregation for the Doctrine of the Faith (CDF). *Catechism of the Catholic Church.* Vatican City: Libreria Editrice Vaticana, 1997. Online. http://www.vatican.va/archive/eng0015/_index.htm.

———. "Christian Faith and Demonology." In *L'Osservatore Romano* [English], July 10, 1975. Online. http://www.vatican.va/roman_curia/congregations/cfaith/documents/rc_con_cfaith_doc_19750626_fede-cristiana-demonologia_en.html.

———. *Mysterium Ecclesiae.* Vatican City: Holy See, 1973.

Connor, James. "Original Sin: Contemporary Approaches." *Theological Studies* 29.2 (1968) 215–40.

Cook, David. "Can God Take Responsibility for Evil and Still Be Good?" *Testamentum Imperium* 2 (2009). Online. http://www.preciousheart.net/ti/2009/14-026_Cook_God_Responsibility_Evil.pdf.

Coplestone, Fredrick. *A History of Philosophy.* Vol. 2. Westminster: Newman, 1962.

Corbin, Henry. *Creative Images in the Sufism of Ibn 'Arabi.* Princeton: Princeton University Press, 1969.

Cox, Christof. "On Evil: An Interview with Alenka Zupancic." *Cabinet Magazine* 5 (2001). Online. http://www.cabinetmagazine.org/issues/5/alenkazupancic.php.

Cross, Richard. *The Metaphysics of the Incarnation: Thomas Aquinas to Duns Scotus.* Oxford: Oxford University Press, 2005.

Cuneo, Michael. *American Exorcism: Expelling Demons in the Land of Plenty.* New York: Doubleday, 2001.

Cunningham, Lawrence. "Four American Catholics and their Chronicler." *Horizons: The Journal of the College Theology Society* 31 (2004) 113–17.

Dacy, Marianne. *The Separation of Early Christianity from Judaism.* New York: Cambria, 2010.

Daly, Gabriel. "Creation and Original Sin (Paragraphs 268–421)." In *Commentary on the Catechism of the Catholic Church*, edited by Michael J. Walsh, 82–112. Collegeville, MN: Liturgical 1994.

———. *Transcendence and Immanence: A Study in Catholic Modernism and Integralism.* New York: Oxford University Press, 1980.

Daneels, Godfried. "Vatican II—An Unprecedented Event, A Council Like No Other." *The Tablet* (blog), October 25, 2012. Online. http://www.thetablet.co.uk/blogs/394/24.

D'Aragon, Jean Louis. "The Apocalypse." In *The New Jerome Biblical Commentary*, edited by Joseph Fitzmyer et al., 467–93. Englewood Cliffs: Prentice Hall, 1990.

Day Williams, Daniel. *The Demonic and the Divine.* Minneapolis: Augsburg Fortress, 1990.

DeHart, Paul. *The Trial of the Witnesses: The Rise and Decline of Postliberal Theology.* Oxford: Blackwell, 2006.

Denzinger, Henry. *Enchiridion Symbolorum.* 31st ed. Rome: Herder, 1960.

Donavon, Daniel. *Distinctly Catholic: An Exploration of Catholic Identity.* New York: Paulist, 1997.

Duffey, John. *Lessons Learned: The Anneliese Michel Exorcism: The Implementation of a Safe and Thorough Examination, Determination and Exorcism of Demonic Possession.* Eugene, OR: Wipf & Stock, 2011.

Dulles, Avery. *Church and Society.* New York: Fordham University Press, 2008.

———. "Karl Rahner on *Humanae Vitae.*" *America Magazine*, September 28, 1968. Online. http://www.americamagazine.org/content/article.cfm?article_id=10722.

———. *Models of Revelation*. New York: Orbis, 1992.

———. "Postmodernist Ecumenism." *First Things*, October 2003. Online. http://www.firstthings.com/article/2003/10/the-church-in-a-postliberal-age.

Dumm, Demetrius. *A Mystical Portrait of Jesus: New Perspectives on John's Gospel*. Collegeville, MN: Liturgical, 2001.

Dunn, James. "Demythologizing—The Problem of Myth in the New Testament." In *New Testament Interpretation: Essays in Principles and Methods*, edited by I. H. Marshall, 288–92. Exeter: Paternoster, 1979.

Dunn, James, and Graham Twelftree. "Demon Possession and Exorcism in the New Testament." *The Churchman* 94.3 (1980) 210–25. Online. https://churchsociety.org/docs/churchman/094/cman_094_3_dunn.pdf.

Faiola, Anthoni. "A Modem Pope Gets Old School on the Devil." *Washington Post*, May 10, 2014. Online. https://www.washingtonpost.com/world/a-modern-pope-gets-old-school-on-the-devil/2014/05/10/f56a9354-1b93-4662-abbb-d877e49f15ea_story.html

Ferracuti, Stefano, et al. "Dissociative Trance Disorder: Clinical and Rorschach Findings in Ten Persons Reporting Demon Possession and Treated by Exorcism." *Journal of Personality Assessment* 66.3 (1996) 525–39.

Finney, Peter. "Empty Evil and the Positive Devil in Augustinian Philosophy." Online. http://www.ignaciodarnaude.com/espiritualismo/Finney,Empty%20evil%20and%20positive%20devil%20in%20Augustinian%20philosophy.html.

Firmin, Alfred. "La Définition de la Religion." *Revue du Clergé Français* 18 (1899) 193–209.

———. "La Théorie Individualiste de la Religion." *Revue du Clergé Français* 17 (1899) 202–15.

———. "Les Preuves et L'économie de la Revelation." *Revue du clergé français* 22 (1900) 126–53.

———. "L'idée de la Revelation." *Revue du Clergé Français* 21 (1900) 250–71.

Fitzmyer, Joseph. *The Interpretation of Scripture: In Defense of the Historical-Critical Method*. New York: Paulist, 2008.

———. "Romans." In *Anchor Bible*, edited by Joseph Fitzmyer, 291–331. New York: Doubleday, 1993.

Forsyth, Neil. *The Satanic Epic*. Princeton: Princeton University, 2003.

"The Fourth Lateran Council." In vol. 1 of *Decrees of the Ecumenical Councils*, edited by Norman Tanner, 244. London: Sheed and Ward, 1990.

Foy, Vincent. "*Humanae Vitae* and Canada Forty Years After." *Social Conservatives United*, June 7, 2008. Online. http://www.catholicculture.org/culture/library.

Francis. "Amoris Laetitia." Post-Synodal Apostolic Exhortation given April 2016. Online. http://www.vatican.va/content/dam/francesco/pdf/apost_exhortations/documents/papa-francesco_esortazione-ap_20160319_amoris-laetitia_en.pdf.

———. "Gaudete et Exsultate." Apostolic Exhortation given March 19, 2018. Online. http://w2.vatican.va/content/francesco/en/apost_exhortations/documents/papa-francesco_esortazione-ap_20180319_gaudete-et-exsultate.html.

Frazer, James, ed. *The Golden Bough: A Study in Magic and Religion*. London: Wordsworth, 1993. Online. http://www.sacred-texts.com/pag/frazer.

Frei, Hans. *The Eclipse of Biblical Narrative*. New Haven: Yale University Press, 1974.

Gabel, Hemult. "Ignatian Contemplation and Modern Biblical Studies." *The Way* 44 (2005) 37–49.

Gallagher, Michael Paul. "A Reflection on Rublev's Icon of the Trinity: Show Atheists the Trinity." *The Tablet* 24.1 (1998) 104.

Gathercole, Simon. "Jesus' Eschatological Vision of the Fall of Satan: Luke 10:18 Reconsidered." *Zeitschrift für die neutestamentliche Wissenschaft* 94.3–4 (2003) 143–63.

Gilkey, Langdon. "Cosmology, Ontology, and the Travail of Biblical Language." *The Journal of Religion* 41.3 (1961) 194–205.

Gill, David. "Socrates and Jesus on Non-Retaliation and Love of Enemies." *Horizons* 18 (1991) 246–62.

Girard, Rene. *I See Satan Fall Like Lightning*. Maryknoll, NY: Orbis, 2001.

Goodman, Felicitas. *The Exorcism of Anneliese Michel*. Eugene, OR: Wipf & Stock, 1981.

Graffy, Adrian. "The Story of *Dei Verbum* Part Two: Drama in the Council." *Pastoral Review*, February 27, 2013. Online. http://thepastoralreview.org/index.php?option=com_content&view=article&id=116:the-story-of-dei-verbum-part-two-drama-in-the-Council&catid=42:marchapril-2013&Itemid=66.

Greeley, Andrew. *The American Catholic: A Social Portrait*. New York: Basic, 1977.

———. *The Catholic Myth: The Behavior and Beliefs of American Catholics*. New York: Scribner's, 1990.

Green, Joel B., et al., eds. *Dictionary of Jesus and the Gospels*. Downers Grove, IL: InterVarsity, 1992.

Green, Michael. *I Believe in Satan's Downfall*. Seven Oaks: Hodder and Stoughton, 1981.

Guinan, Michael. "Adam, Eve, and Original Sin." *Catholic Fidelity*, December 6, 2007. Online. https://www.catholicfidelity.com/adam-eve-and-original-sin-by-michael-guinan.

Gunkel, Hermann. *The Legends of Genesis*. Chicago: Open Court, 1901. Online. https://sacred-texts.com/bib/log/index.htm.

Gutiérrez, Gustavo. *A Theology of Liberation: History, Politics, and Salvation*. Edited by John Eaglson. Translated by Caridad Inda. Maryknoll, NY: Orbis, 1988.

Haag, Herbert. *Abschiedvom Teufel* [*Farewell to the Devil*]. Einsiedeln: Benziger, 1969.

Hague, Dyson. "The Doctrinal Value of the First Chapters of Genesis." In vol. 8 of *The Fundamentals*, edited by A. C. Dixon et al., 74–89. Los Angeles: BIOLA Book Room, 1917. Online. https://online.flippingbook.com/view/444508/2.

Haight, Roger. "Expanding the Spiritual Exercises." *Studies in the Spirituality of Jesuits* 42 (2010) 1–43. Online. https://jesuits.org/Assets/Publications/File/Studies_Summer_2010_42-2.pdf.

Hamm, Dennis. "Are the Gospel Passion Accounts Anti-Jewish?" *Journal of Religion and Film* 8.1 (2004). Online. http://www.unomaha.edu/jrf/2004Symposium/Hamm.htm.

Hanahoe, Edward. "Ecclesiology and Ecumenism, Part II." In *American Ecclesiastical Review*, November 1962, 328.

Hannenberg, Edward. "*Dei Verbum*." In *Vatican II: The Essential Texts*, edited by Norman Tanner, 79–89. New York: Image, 2012.

Harlow, Daniel. "After Adam: Reading Genesis in an Age of Evolutionary Science." *Perspectives on Science and Christian Faith* 62.3 (2010) 179–95. Online. http://www.asa3.org/asa/pscf/2010/pscf9-10harlow.pdf.

Harnack, Adolf von. *What Is Christianity?* London: Williams and Norgate, 1904.

Harrington, Daniel. *The Church According to the New Testament: What the Wisdom and Witness of Early Christianity Teach Us Today*. Oxford: Sheed & Ward, 2001.

———. *The Gospel of Matthew*. Collegeville, MN: Order of St. Benedict, 19910.

———. "Paul's Use of the Old Testament in Romans." Paper presented at Boston College School of Theology and Ministry, March 15, 2009. Online. http://www.ejournals.bc.edu/ojs/index.php/scjr/article/download/1536/1390.

Harrington, Wilfred. "Understanding the Apocalypse." *Scripture from Scratch*, November 1999. Online. http://web.archive.org/web/20130203072133/http://www.americancatholic.org/Newsletters/SFS/an1199.asp

Harris, Elise. "Pope Francis Says Our Father Is Poorly Translated." *Catholic News Service*, December 8, 2017. Online. https://www.catholicnewsagency.com/news/pope-francis-says-our-father-is-poorly-translated-38348.

Hauke, Manfred. "The Theological Battle over the Rite of Exorcism, 'Cinderella' of the *New Rituale Romanum*." *Antiphon* 10.1 (2006) 32–69.

Hayward, John. "The Uses of Myth in an Age of Science." *New Theology* 7 (1970) 59–77.

Healy, Nicholas. "*Communio*: A Theological Journey." *Communio* 33 (2006) 117–30.

Heaster, Duncan. *The Real Devil: A Biblical Exploration*. South Croydon: Carelinks, 1977.

Hebblethwaite, Peter. *Paul VI: The First Modern Pope*. New York: Paulist, 1993.

Hellwig, Monika. *What Are the Theologians Saying Now?* Westminster: Christian Classics, 1992.

Henning, Meghan. *Educating Early Christians through the Rhetoric of Hell*. Tübingen: Mohr Siebeck, 2015.

Hick, John. *Evil and the God of Love*. San Francisco: Harper & Row, 1977.

Highfield, Ron. "The Freedom to Say 'No'? Karl Rahner's Doctrine of Sin." *Theological Studies* 56 (1995) 485–505.

Himes, Jonathon, et al., eds. *Truths Breathed through Silver: The Inklings' Moral and Mythopoeic Legacy*. Newcastle: Cambridge Scholars, 2008. Online. http://www.mythsoc.org/reviews/truths-breathed-through-silver.

Himes, Michael. "'Finding God in All Things': A Sacramental Worldview and Its Effects." In *As Leaven in the World: Catholic Perspectives on Faith, Vocation, and the Intellectual Life*, edited by Thomas Landy, 91–104. Franklin: Sheed and Ward, 2001.

Horsley, Richard, and Jonathan Draper. *Whoever Hears You: Prophets, Performance, and Tradition in Q*. Harrisburg, PA: Trinity, 1999.

Ignatius of Loyola. "The Spiritual Exercises." In *Ignatius of Loyola: Spiritual Exercises and Selected Works*, edited by George E. Ganss, 113–214. New York: Paulist, 1991.

The International Commission on English in the Liturgy (ICEL). *The Roman Missal*. 3rd ed. Washington, DC: United States Catholic Conference of Bishops, 2011.

International Theological Commission (ITC). "Theology Today: Perspectives, Principles, and Criteria." Online. https://www.vatican.va/roman_curia/congregations/cfaith/cti_documents/rc_cti_doc_20111129_teologia-oggi_en.html.

Isbell, Charles David. "Zoroastrianism and Biblical Religion." *Jewish Bible Quarterly* 34.3 (2006). Online. https://jbqnew.jewishbible.org/assets/uploads/343/343_persian11.pdf.

Jackson, Timothy. *The Priority of Love: Christian Charity and Social Justice*. Princeton: Princeton University Press, 2003.

Jeremias, Joachim. *New Testament Theology*. London: SCM, 1972.

John XXIII. "*Gaudet Mater Ecclesia*." October 11, 1962. Online. https://jakomonchak.files.wordpress.com/2012/10/john-xxiii-opening-speech.pdf.

———. "*Mater et Magistra*." Encyclical given May 15, 1961. Online. http://w2.vatican.va/content/john-xxiii/en/encyclicals/documents/hf_j-xxiii_enc_15051961_mater.html.

———. "*Pacem in Terris*." Encyclical given April 11, 1963. http://www.vatican.va/content/john-xxiii/en/encyclicals/documents/hf_j-xxiii_enc_11041963_pacem.html.

John Paul II. "Message to Participants in a Study Session of the Pontifical Academy of Sciences." November 29, 1996. Online. http://www.vatican.va/content/john-paul-ii/en/messages/pont_messages/1996/documents/hf_jp-ii_mes_19961129_pont-accad-scienze.html.

———. "Reconciliation and Penance." Post-Synodal Apostolic Exhortation given December 2, 1984. Online. http://www.vatican.va/holy_father/john_paul_ii/apost_exhortations/documents/hf_jp-ii_exh_02121984_reconciliatio-et-paenitentia_en.html.

———. "*Redemptor Hominis*." Encyclical given March 4, 1979. Online. http://w2.vatican.va/content/john-paul-ii/en/encyclicals/documents/hf_jp-ii_enc_04031979_redemptor-hominis.html.

———. "*Redemptoris Missio*." Encyclical given December 7, 1990. Online. http://www.vatican.va/holy_father/john_paul_ii/encyclicals/documents/hf_jp-ii_enc_07121990_redemptoris-missio_en.html.

———. "*Sollicitudo Rei Socialis*." Encyclical given December 30, 1987. http://www.vatican.va/holy_father/john_paul_ii/encyclicals/documents/hf_jp-ii_enc_30121987_sollicitudo-rei-socialis_en.html.

Johnson, Luke Timothy. *The Real Jesus: The Misguided Quest for the Historical Jesus and the Truth of the Traditional Gospels*. New York: HarperCollins, 1996.

Josephus. *The Wars of the Jews*. Translated by William Whiston. London: Whiston, 1737. Online. https://penelope.uchicago.edu/josephus/index.html.

Jung, Carl. *The Archetypes and the Collective Unconscious*. Vol. 9. Translated by R. F. Hull. Princeton, NJ: Princeton University, 1981.

———. *Memories, Dreams, and Reflections*. London: Routledge & K. Paul, 1963.

Kallas, James. *The Real Satan: From Biblical Times to the Present*. Minneapolis: Augsburg Fortress, 1975.

Kant, Immanuel. *Religion within the Boundaries of Mere Reason*. Edited by Allen Wood and George di Giovanni. Cambridge: Cambridge University Press, 1998.

Kapelrud, A. S. "You Shall Surely Not Die." In *History and Traditions of Early Israel*, edited by André Lemaire and Benedikt Otzen, 50–61. Leiden: VTA, 1993.

Kasper, Walter. *Dogma unter dem Wort Gottes*. Mainz: Matthias Grünewald, 1965.

Kasper, Walter, and Karl Lehmann, eds. *Teufel, Dämonen, Besessenheit. Zur Wirklichkeit des Bösen*. Broschier: M. Grünewald, Mainz, 1983.

Kaufmann, Walter, ed. *Goethe's Faust: Part One and Sections from Part Two*. Garden City, NY: Doubleday, 1963.

Kearney, Richard. "Myth as the Bearer of Possible Worlds: An Interview with Paul Ricoeur." *The Crane Bag Journal of Irish Studies* 2 (1978) 112–18.

———. *A Passion for the Possible: Thinking with Paul Ricoeur*. New York: Fordham University Press, 2010.

Keller, Catherine. *Apocalypse Then and Now: A Feminist Guide to the End of the World*. Boston: Beacon, 1996.

Kelly, Henry Ansgar. "Adam Citings before the Intrusion of Satan: Recontextualizing Paul's Theology of Sin and Death." *Biblical Theology* 44.1 (2013) 176–79.

———. *Satan: A Biography*. New York: Cambridge University Press, 2006.

———. *Satan in the Bible, God's Minister of Justice*. Eugene, OR: Cascade, 2017.

Kelly, James. "The Hermeneutical Debate Within Modernism: Loisy, Blondel, and Von Hügel." *Irish Theological Quarterly* 71.3 (2006) 285–95.

Kendall, George A. "Existence and Revelation in the Theology of Paul Tillich." *Faith & Reason* (1990). Online. https://www.ewtn.com/catholicism/library/existence-and-revelation-in-the-theology-of-paul-tillich-10024.

Kent, John. "Review of H. D. McDonald *Theories of Revelation: An Historical Study, 1860–1960*." *The Journal of Ecclesiastical History* 18 (1967) 123–24.

Kermode, Mark. "Devilish Deceptions." *Fear Magazine* 24 (1990). Online. http://www.the-exorcist.co.uk/articles/deceptions.htm.

Kipling, Rudyard. "How the Leopard Got His Spots." In *Just So Stories*, by Rudyard Kipling, 30–46. Chapel Hill, NC: Yesterday's Classics, 2009.

Kittle, Gerhard, and Gerhard Friedrich. *Theological Dictionary of the New Testament*. Grand Rapids: Eerdmans, 1985.

Klutz, Todd. *The Exorcism Stories in Luke-Acts: A Sociostylistic Reading*. Cambridge: Cambridge University Press, 2004.

Knox, Jean. *Archetype, Attachment, Analysis: Jungian Psychology and the Emergent Mind*. New York: Brunner-Routledge, 2003.

Kronen, John, and Sandra Menssen. "The Defensibility of Zoroastrian Dualism." *Religious Studies* 46.2 (2010) 185–205.

Kuhn, Thomas. *The Structure of Scientific Revolutions*. Chicago: University of Chicago Press, 1962.

Laccino, Ludovicca. "Pope Francis Satan Talk 'Opens Doors to Superstition.'" In *International Business Times*, May 12, 2014. Online. https://www.ibtimes.co.uk/pope-francis-satan-talk-opens-doors-superstition-1448208.

Lane, Dermot. *The Experience of God: An Invitation to Do Theology*. New York: Paulist, 2003.

Lateran IV. "The Canons of the Fourth Lateran Council (1215)." In *Disciplinary Decrees of the General Councils: Text, Translation and Commentary*, edited by H. J. Schroeder, 236–96. St. Louis: Herder, 1937. Online. http://www.fordham.edu/halsall/basis/lateran4.asp.

Levenson, Jon. *Creation and the Persistence of Evil: The Jewish Drama of Divine Omnipotence*. San Francisco: Harper and Row, 1988.

Lévi-Strauss, Claude. *The Naked Man*. Chicago: University of Chicago Press, 1971.

———. "The Structural Study of Myth." In *Critical Theory Since 1965*, edited by H. Adams and L. Searle, 808–22. Tallahassee: Florida State University Press, 1986.

Lewis, C. S. *The Abolition of Man*. New York: MacMillan, 1944.

Lewis, James. "Diabolical Activity: Anton LaVey, the Satanic Bible and the Satanist Tradition." *Marburg Journal of Religion* 7 (2002) 1–16. Online. https://archive.org/details/TheAbolitionOfMan_229.

Lieber, Justin. "On What Sort of Speech Act Wittgenstein's *Investigations* Is and Why It Matters." *The Philosophical Forum* 28.3 (1997) 232–67.

Lincoln, Bruce. *Theorizing Myth: Narrative, Ideology, and Scholarship*. Chicago: University of Chicago Press, 1999.

Bibliography

Lindbeck, George. "How a Lutheran Saw It: A Different Kind of Reformation." *Commonweal* 129.20 (2002) 15–17.

———. *The Nature of Doctrine: Religion and Theology in a Postliberal Age*. Philadelphia: Westminster, 1984.

———. "Vision of a World Renewed." In *The Future of Roman Catholic Theology: Vatican II—Catalyst for Change*, by George A. Lindbeck, 1–18. Philadelphia: Fortress, 1970.

Link, Luther. *The Devil: A Mask without a Face*. London: Reaktion, 1995.

Loisy, Alfred Firmin. *The Birth of the Christian Religion*. Translated by L. P. Jacks. New Hyde Park, NY: University Books, 1962. Online. http://www.earlychristianwritings.com/loisy.

———. *The Gospel and the Church*. Edited by Bernard Scott. Translated by Christopher Home. New York: Scribner's, 1976.

———. "Le Développement Chrétien d'Après le Cardinal Newman." *Revue du clergé français* 17 (1898) 5–20.

———. *L'Evangile et L'Eglise*. Paris: Alphonse Picard, 1902.

Lonergan, Bernard. *Insight: A Study of Human Understanding*. San Francisco: Harper & Row, 1978.

Lubac, Henri de. *Athéisme et Sens de l'homme: Une Double Requête de Gaudium et spes*. Paris: Cerf, 1968.

———. *Mémoire sur l'occasion de mes écrits*. Namur: Culture et Verité, 1989.

Lyotard, Jean-François. *La Condition Postmoderne: Rapport Sur Le Savoir*. Paris: Minuit, 1979.

MacKenzie, R. A. F. "Job." In *The Jerome Biblical Commentary*, edited by Joseph Fiztmyer et al., 511–33. Englewood Cliffs: Prentice Hall, 1968.

Malachi, Martin. *Hostage to the Devil*. New York: Reader's Digest, 1976.

Malinowski, Bronislaw. *Magic, Science and Religion and Other Essays*. Edited by Robert Redfield. Glencoe, IL: Free Press, 1948.

Maly, Eugene. "The Book of Genesis." In *The Jerome Biblical Commentary*, edited by Raymond Brown et al., 1–46. Englewood Cliffs, NJ: Prentice-Hall, 1968.

Mann, Benjamin. "New Documents Reveal Inner Workings of Papal Birth Control Commission." *Catholic News Agency*, March 16, 2011. Online. http://www.catholicnewsagency.com/news/new-documents-reveal-inner-workings-of-papal-birth-control-commission.

Marion, Jean-Luc. "The Erotic Phenomenon." Translated by Stephen E. Lewis. *Ethics* 118.1 (2007) 164–68.

———. *God Without Being: Hors-Texte*. Translated by Thomas A. Carlson. Chicago: University of Chicago Press, 1991.

Mark, Johsua J. "Set (Egyptian God)." *Ancient History Encyclopedia*, March 7, 2016. Online. https://www.ancient.eu/Set_(Egyptian_God).

Martin, Ralph. "What Is the New Evangelization? Why Is It Important for Priestly Formation?" Paper presented at the Ninth Annual Symposium on the Spirituality and Identity of the Diocesan Priest, St. Paul Seminary School of Divinity, St. Paul, MN, March 11–14, 2010. Online. http://www.renewalministries.net/files/freeliterature/what_is_the_new_evangelization_ipf_symposium_2010_4_07_10.pdf.

May, Herbert, and Bruce Metzger, eds. *Oxford Annotated Bible with the Apocrypha, Revised Standard Version*. New York: Oxford University Press, 1977.

McBrien, Richard. *Catholicism*. New York: HarperCollins, 1994.
McCabe, Herbert. *God Still Matters*. London: Continuum, 2002.
McClarey, Donald. "Pope Paul VI and the Smoke of Satan." *Catholic Stand* (blog), January 29, 2013. Online. http://www.catholicstand.com/109.
McDonald, H. D. *Theories of Revelation: An Historical Study, 1860–1960*. London: Allen & Unwin, 1963.
McFarland, Ian. *In Adam's Fall: A Meditation on the Christian Doctrine of Original Sin*. Chichester: Wiley, 2010.
McGill, Alan. "Diagnosing Demons and Healing Humans: The Pastoral Implications of a Holistic View of Evil and Collusion between Its Forms." *New Theology Review* 27.2 (2015) 70–80.
———. "Envisaging Afterlife in Light of the Doctrine of Divinization and the Co-Presence of the Divine in and through All Things." *Modern Believing* 59.4 (2018) 339–52.
———. "In the Aftermath of a Synod: A Sacramental Argument for the Development of Doctrine." *New Theology Review* 29.1 (2016) 9–18.
———. "Reading the Bible through Stained Glass: Postmodern Resistance to the Historical-Critical Method as an Impediment to the Development of Doctrine." *New Theology Review* 30.2 (2018) 31–42.
———. "Tensions between the Catechism's Teachings on the Interpretation of Scripture versus its Exegesis of the Adamic Narrative: The Explicit and the Null Curriculum in an Evolving Tradition." *Journal of Religious Education* 65 (2018) 51–68.
———. "The Vassal's Lament: The Vocation of Humankind in the Adamic Myth and the Fall to Authoritarianism in Its Reception History." *Glossolalia* [Spring] (2011) 107–25.
McKenzie, John. "Aspects of Old Testament Thought." In *The Jerome Biblical Commentary*, edited by Raymond Brown et al., 736–67. Englewood Cliffs: Prentice Hall, 1968.
———. "The Gospel According to Matthew." In *The Jerome Biblical Commentary*, edited by Raymond Brown et al., 62–114. Englewood Cliffs, NJ: Prentice-Hall, 1968.
McLuhan, Marshsall. "The Medium is the Message." In *Understanding Media: The Extensions of Man*, by Marshall McLuhan, 7–21. New York: Signet, 1964.
Mele, Alfred. *Free Will and Good Luck*. Oxford: Oxford University Press, 2006.
Melvin, David. "Divine Mediation and the Rise of Civilization in Mesopotamian Literature and Genesis 1–11." *The Journal of Hebrew Scriptures* 10.17 (2010) 2–15.
Metz, Johann Baptist. *The Emergent Church*. New York: Crossroad, 1986.
Milton, John. *Paradise Lost: Complete Poems and Major Prose*. Edited by Merritt Y. Hughes. Indianapolis: Hackett, 1957.
Monaghan, John. "Fr. Pat Collins Links Persistent Suicidal Thoughts to Potentially Being 'Oppressed by an Evil Spirit.'" *Irish News*, February 18, 2019. Online. https://www.irishnews.com/news/northernirelandnews/2019/02/18/news/fr-pat-collins-criticised-for-linking-persistent-suicidal-thoughts-to-potentially-being-oppressed-by-an-evil-spirit--1553784.
Morrow, Jeffrey. "Alfred Loisy's Developmental Approach to Scripture: Reading the 'Firmin' Articles in the Context of Nineteenth- and Twentieth-Century Historical Biblical Criticism." *International Journal of Systematic Theology* 15.3 (2013) 324–44.

Morton, Michael. "Catholic Modernism (1896–1914)." *Sea of Faith Network*. Online. http://www.sofn.org.uk/doctrine/catholic_modernism.html.

Moss, Candida. "Roman Imperialism and the Political Context of the Early Christian Apocrypha." In *The Oxford Handbook of Early Christian Apocrypha*, edited by Andrew Gregory and Christopher Tuckett, 378–88. Oxford: Oxford University Press, 2013.

Mudge, Lewis. "Introduction." In *Essays on Biblical Interpretation*, by Paul Ricoeur. Edited by Lewis Mudge. Philadelphia: Fortress, 1980. Online. https://www.religion-online.org/book-chapter/introduction-by-lewis-s-mudge.

Mulholland, Seamus. "Incarnation in Franciscan Spirituality: Duns Scotus and the Meaning of Love." *Franciscan*, January 2001. Online. http://www.slr-ofs.org/uploads/9/5/5/8/9558460o/incarnation_in_franciscan_spirituality_-_scotus.pdf.

Murphy, F. X. *Vatican Council II*. New York: Farrar, Straus and Giroux, 1968.

Murray, Robert. "Further Reflection on Magisterium and 'Magisterium.'" In *Commentary on the Catechism of the Catholic Church*, edited by Michael Walsh, 34–35. Collegeville, MN: Liturgical, 1994.

Newman, John Henry. *An Essay on the Development of Christian Doctrine*. 6th ed. South Bend: University of Notre Dame Press, 1989.

———. "On the Inspiration of Scripture." *The Nineteenth Century* 15 (1884) 185–99.

Nichols, Sallie. *Jung and Tarot: An Archetypal Journey*. York Beach, ME: Weiser, 1980.

Nielson, Kirsten. *Satan, the Prodigal Son: A Family Problem in the Bible*. Sheffield: Sheffield Academic, 1991.

Nir, Rivka. "The Struggle between the 'Image of God' and Satan in the Greek Life of Adam and Eve." *Scottish Journal of Theology* 61.3 (2008) 327–39.

Obbink, H. "The Horns of the Altar in the Semitic World, Especially in Jahwism." *Journal of Biblical Literature* 56 (1937) 43–49

O'Connor, Flannery. *Mystery and Manners: Occasional Papers*. Edited by Sally Fitzgerald and Robert Fitzgerald. New York: Farrar, Straus and Giroux, 1957.

O'Connor, James T. "Von Balthasar and Salvation." *Homiletic & Pastoral Review* 89.10 (1989) 10–21. Online. http://www.catholicculture.org/culture/library/view.cfm?recnum=565.

O'Donovan, Leo. "Was Vatican II Evolutionary?" *Theological Studies* 36 (1975) 494–502. Online. http://www.ts.mu.edu/readers/content/pdf/36/36.3/36.3.5.pdf.

Oglesby, Les. *C. G. Jung and Hans Urs von Balthasar: God and Evil—A Critical Comparison*. New York: Routledge, 2014.

Oliver, Simon. "The Parallel Journey of Faith and Reason: Another Look via Aquinas's *De Veritate*." In *Faithful Reading: New Essays in Theology in Honour of Fergus Kerr*, edited by Simon Oliver et al., 113–30. London: T&T Clark, 2012.

Olson, Alan. "The Mythic Language of the Demonic." In *Disguises of the Demonic*, edited by Alan Olson, 9–16. New York: Association, 1975.

O'Malley, John W. "Vatican II: Did Anything Happen?" *Theological Studies* 67 (2006) 3–33. Online. http://www.ts.mu.edu/readers/content/pdf/67/67.1/67.1.1.pdf.

———. *What Happened at Vatican II*. Cambridge: Harvard University Press, 2008.

O'Meara, Thomas. "Vast Universe and Extraterrestrials: Threat or Mystery for the Christian Faith?" *New Theology Review* 27.1 (2014) 1–7. Online. http://newtheologyreview.org/index.php/ntr/article/view/1037.

Origen. *Commentary on the Gospel of Matthew*. Edited by Allan Menzies. Translated by John Patrick. Buffalo, NY: Christian Literature, 1896. Revised and edited for New Advent by Kevin Knight. Online. http://www.newadvent.org/fathers/1016.htm.

Orlov, Andrei. "The Watchers of Satanail: The Fallen Angels Traditions in 2 (Slavonic) Enoch." In *Selected Studies in the Slavonic Pseudepigrapha*, by Andrei Orlov, 133–64. Studia in Veteris Testamenti Pseudepigrapha 23. Leiden; Boston: Brill, 2009. Online. https://www.marquette.edu/maqom/select123.pdf.

Orr, James. "The Early Narratives of Genesis." In vol. 1 of *The Fundamentals: A Testimony to the Truth*, edited by R. A. Torrey, 228–40. Los Angeles: Bible Institute of Los Angeles, 1917. Online. https://online.flippingbook.com/view/359601/228.

Orsy, Ladislas. *Receiving the Council: Theological and Canonical Insights and Debates*. Collegeville, MN: Liturgical, 2009.

Osburne, Grant. *The Hermeneutical Spiral*. Downer's Grove, IL: InterVarsity, 1991.

Pagels, Elaine. *The Origin of Satan*. New York: Vintage, 1995.

Paul V. "De Exorcizandis Obsessis A Daemonio." In *Ritual Romanum*, 1614. Paris: J. Lecoffre et Socios, 1853. Online. http://www.saintsbooks.net/books/Rituale%20Romanum%20(1853).pdf.

Paul VI. "*Dei Verbum*: Dogmatic Constitution on Divine Revelation." November 18, 1965. Online. https://www.vatican.va/archive/hist_councils/ii_vatican_council/documents/vat-ii_const_19651118_dei-verbum_en.html.

———. "Deliver Us from Evil." November 15, 1972. *Papal Encyclical Online*. Online. https://www.papalencyclicals.net/paul06/p6devil.htm.

———. "*Gaudium et Spes*: Pastoral Constitution on the Church in the Modern World." December 7, 1965. Online. http://www.vatican.va/archive/hist_councils/ii_vatican_council/documents/vat-ii_cons_19651207_gaudium-et-spes_en.html.

———. "*Inter Mirifica*: Decree on the Media of Social Communications." December 4, 1963. Online. http://www.vatican.va/archive/hist_councils/ii_vatican_council/documents/vat-ii_decree_19631204_inter-mirifica_en.html.

———. "*Lumen Gentium*: Dogmatic Constitution on the Church." November 21, 1964. Online. https://www.vatican.va/archive/hist_councils/ii_vatican_council/documents/vat-ii_const_19641121_lumen-gentium_en.html.

———. "Mass on the Ninth Anniversary of the Crowning of His Holiness Paul VI on the Solemnity of the Apostles Peter and Paul." Homily given June 29, 1972. Online. http://www.vatican.va/content/paul-vi/it/homilies/1972/documents/hf_p-vi_hom_19720629.html.

———. "*Nostra Aetate*: Declaration on the Relation of the Church to Non-Christian Religions." October 28, 1965. Online. http://www.vatican.va/archive/hist_councils/ii_vatican_council/documents/vat-ii_decl_19651028_nostra-aetate_en.html.

———. "*Sacrosanctum Concilium*: Constitution on the Sacred Liturgy." December 4, 1963. Online. https://www.vatican.va/archive/hist_councils/ii_vatican_council/documents/vat-ii_const_19631204_sacrosanctum-concilium_en.html.

———. "*Unitatis Redintegratio*: Decree on Ecumenism." November 21, 1964. Online. https://www.vatican.va/archive/hist_councils/ii_vatican_council/documents/vat-ii_decree_19641121_unitatis-redintegratio_en.html.

Peck, Scott. *People of the Lie: The Hope for Healing Human Evil*. New York: Touchstone.

Perriman, Andrew. "Was Gehenna a Burning Rubbish Dump, and Does it Matter?" *P.OST* (blog), August 4, 2011. Online. https://www.postost.net/2015/11/was-gehenna-burning-rubbish-dump-does-it-matter.

Peterson, Jordan, et al. *Twelve Rules for Life: An Antidote to Chaos.* Toronto: Random Canada, 2018.

———. "Who Dares Say He Believes in God." Lecture presented at the International Convention Centre, Sydney, Australia, February 26, 2019. Audio recording. Online. https://www.jordanbpeterson.com/podcast/s2-e15-who-dares-say-he-believes-in-god.

Pius IX. "*Ineffabilis Deus.*" December 8, 1854. *Papal Encyclical Online.* Online. http://www.papalencyclicals.net/Pius09/p9ineff.htm.

———. "The Syllabus of Errors." December 8, 1864. *Papal Encyclical Online.* Online. http://www.papalencyclicals.net/Pius09/p9syll.htm.

Pius X. "*Lamentabili Sane Exitu.*" July 3, 1907. *Papal Encyclical Online.* Online. http://papalencyclicals.net/pius10/p10lamen.htm.

———. "*Pascendi Dominici Gregis.*" Encyclical given September 8, 1907. Online. http://w2.vatican.va/content/pius-x/en/encyclicals/documents/hf_p-x_enc_19070908_pascendi-dominici-gregis.html.

Pius XI. "*Casti Connubii.*" Encyclical given December 31, 1930. Online. http://www.vatican.va/content/pius-xi/en/encyclicals/documents/hf_p-xi_enc_19301231_casti-connubii.html.

Pius XII. "*Divino Afflante Spiritu.*" Encyclical given September 30, 1943. Online. vatican.va/content/pius-xii/en/encyclicals/documents/hf_p-xii_enc_30091943_divino-afflante-spiritu.html.

———. "*Humani Generis.*" Encyclical given December 8, 1950. Online. http://www.vatican.va/content/pius-xii/en/encyclicals/documents/hf_p-xii_enc_12081950_humani-generis.html.

Plantinga, Alvin. *The Analytic Theist.* Grand Rapids: Eerdmans, 1998.

Pontifical Biblical Commission (PBC). *Enchiridion Biblicum: documenta ecclesiastica Sacram Scripturam spectantia.* 2nd ed. Naples: D'Auria; Rome: A. Arnodo, 1954.

———. "The Interpretation of the Bible in the Church." April 23, 1993. Online. http://catholic-resources.org/ChurchDocs/PBC_Interp.htm.

———. "*Sancta Mater Ecclesiae*: Instruction Concerning the Historical Truth of the Gospels." Translated by Joseph A. Fitzmyer. *Theological Studies* 25 (1964) 402–8. Online. http://catholic-resources.org/churchdocs/pbc_histtruthfitzmyer.htm#pbctext.

Post, Laurens van der. *Jung and the Story of Our Time.* New York: Random, 1977.

Probst, Manfred, and Richter Klemens. *Exorzismus Oder Liturgie Zur Befreiung des Bösen.* Münster: Aschendorff, 2002.

Puthussery, Johnson. *Days of Man and God's Day.* Rome: Gregorian University, 2002.

Putz, Oliver. "'I Did Not Change, They Did!' Joseph Ratzinger, Karl Rahner, and the Second Vatican Council." *New Wineskins* 2.1 (2007) 11–30. Online. https://issuu.com/santaclarauniversity/docs/new-wineskins-spring-2007.

Pytches, David. *Come Holy Spirit.* London: Hodder and Stoughton, 1985.

Quay, Paul. "Angels and Demons: The Teaching of IV Lateran." *Theological Studies* 42.1 (1981) 20–45.

Rahner, Karl. "The Dignity and Freedom of Man." In *Man in the Church*, by Karl Rahner, 223–63. Vol. 2 of *Theological Investigations.* New York: Crossroad, 1982.

———. *Foundations of the Christian Faith: An Introduction to the Idea of Christianity.* Translated by William Dych. New York: Seabury, 1978.

———. "The Punishment of Sins." In *Sacramentum Mundi: An Encyclopedia of Theology* 6, edited by Karl Rahner et al., 92b–94b. New York: Herder & Herder, 1968.

———. *Spirit in the World*. New York: Herder & Herder, 1968.

———. "Theology of Freedom." In *Concerning Vatican II*, by Karl Rahner, 190–93. Vol. 6 of *Theological Investigations*. Baltimore: Helicon, 1969.

———. "Yesterday's History of Dogma and Theology for Tomorrow." In *God and Revelation*, by Karl Rahner, 11–12. Vol. 18 of *Theological Investigations*. New York: Crossroad, 1982.

Rand, Ayn. *For the New Intellectual: The Philosophy of Ayn Rand*. New York: New American Library, 1961.

Rapp, Christof. "Aristotle's Rhetoric." *Stanford Encyclopedia of Philosophy*, May 2, 2002. Revised February 1, 2010. Edited by Edward Zalta. Online. http://plato.stanford.edu/entries/aristotle-rhetoric.

Ratzinger, Joseph. "Abschied vom Teufel?" In *Dogma und Verkündigung*, by Joseph Ratzinger, 221–30. Translated by David Kirchhoffer. München/Freiburg: Wewel, 1973.

———. *Eschatology*. Washington, DC: Catholic University of America, 1977.

———. *The Ratzinger Reader: Mapping a Theological Journey*. Edited by Lieven Boeve and Gerard Mannion. London: T&T Clark, 2010.

———. "Relativism: The Central Problem for Faith Today." Address given at the meeting of the Congregation for the Doctrine of the Faith with the presidents of the Doctrinal Commissions of the Bishops' Conferences of Latin America, Guadalajara, Mexico, May 1996. Online. https://www.ewtn.com/catholicism/library/relativism-the-central-problem-for-faith-today-2470.

Renger, Almut-Barbara. "The Ambiguity of Judas: On the Mythicity of a New Testament Figure." *Literature and Theology* 27.1 (2013) 1–17.

Rensberger, David Johannine. *Faith and Liberating Community*. Philadelphia: Westminster, 1988.

Ricoeur, Paul. *Fallible Man*. Translated by Charles Kelbey. Chicago: Regnery, 1965.

———. *Figuring the Sacred: Religion, Narrative, and Imagination*. Translated by David Pellauer. Minneapolis, Fortress, 1995.

———. "Humanities between Science and Art." Speech given at the Humanities at the Turn of the Millennium Conference, University of Århus, Denmark, June 4, 1999. Online. http://www.hum.au.dk/ckulturf/pages/publications/pr/hbsa.htm.

———. "Preface to Bultmann." In *Essays on Biblical Interpretation*, edited by Lewis Mudge, 49–72. Translated by Peter McCormick. Philadelphia: Fortress, 1980. Online. https://www.religion-online.org/book-chapter/chapter-1-preface-to-bultmann.

———. *The Symbolism of Evil*. Translated by Emerson Buchanan. New York: Harper and Row, 1967.

———. "Toward a Hermeneutic of the Idea of Revelation." *The Harvard Theological Review* 70.1–2 (1977) 1–37.

Rigby, Paul, et al. "The Nature of Doctrine and Scientific Progress." *Theological Studies* 52 (1991) 669–88.

Roberts, J. M. M. "Myth versus History: Relaying the Comparative Functions." *Catholic Biblical Quarterly* 38 (1976) 1–13.

Robinson, G. D. "Paul Ricoeur and the Hermeneutics of Suspicion: A Brief Overview and Critique." *Premise* 2.8 (1995) 1–13.

Robinson, J. M. "Scripture and Theological Method: A Protestant Study in *Sensus Plenior*." *CBQ* 27 (1965) 6–27.
Rosica, Thomas. "Why Is Pope Francis So Obsessed with the Devil?" *CNN*, July 20, 2015. Online. https://www.cnn.com/2015/07/20/living/pope-francis-devil/index.html.
Ross, Colin. "Possession Experiences in Dissociative Identity Disorder: A Preliminary Study." *Journal of Trauma Dissociation* 12.4 (2011) 393–400.
Ross, Robert H., ed. *Alfred, Lord Tennyson: In Memoriam*. New York: Norton, 1973.
Russell, Jeffrey Burton. "The Early Christian Tradition." *Medieval Academy of America* 60.2 (1981) 458–61.
———. *Lucifer: The Devil in the Middle Ages*. Ithaca, NY: Cornell University Press, 1984.
———. *Satan: The Early Christian Tradition*. Ithaca, NY: Cornell University Press, 1981.
Rynne, Terrence. *Jesus Christ, Peacemaker: A New Theology of Peace*. Maryknoll, NY: Orbis, 2014.
Salisbury, Lee. "Eternity Explained." *Grow and Know* (blog), May 26, 2010. http://growandknow.blogspot.com/2010/05/eternity-explained-by-lee-salisbury.html.
SanMartín, Inés. "Modern Pope Wants Rosary Prayer to Protect Church from Devil's Turbulence." *Crux*, September 29, 2018. Online. https://cruxnow.com/vatican/2018/09/29/pope-wants-rosary-prayed-to-protect-church-from-devils-turbulence.
Sartre, Jean-Paul. *Being and Nothingness*. Translated by Hazel B. Barnes. New York: Washington Square, 1984.
Saunders, Daniel. "The Devil and the Divinity of Christ." *Theological Studies* 9.4 (1948) 536–53. Online. http://cdn.theologicalstudies.net/9/9.4/9.4.2.pdf.
Schaefer, Richard. "True and False Enlightenment: German Scholars and the Discourse of Catholicism in the Nineteenth Century." *The Catholic Historical Review* 97.1 (2011) 24–45.
Schaff, Philip. *Modern Christianity. The German Reformation*. Vol. 7 of *The History of the Christian Church*. 2nd ed. 1882. Reprint, Grand Rapids, MI: Christian Classics Ethereal Library, 2002. Online. http://www.ccel.org/ccel/schaff/hcc7.txt.
Schoonenberg, Piet. *Man and Sin*. Translated by Joseph Donceel. South Bend, IN: University of Notre Dame, 1965.
Schumpeter, Joseph. *Capitalism, Socialism and Democracy*. New York: Harper, 1975.
Schüssler Fiorenza, Francis. *Systematic Theology: Roman Catholic Perspectives*. New York: Fortress, 2011.
Schüssler Fiorenza, Francis, and John Galvin, eds. *Systematic Theology: Task and Method*. New York: Augsburg-Fortress, 1991. Online. http://www.augsburgfortress.org/media/downloads/0800662911chapter1.pdf
Segal, Robert. "Myth and Ritual." *The Routledge Companion to the Study of Religion*, edited by John R. Hinnells, 355–79. New York: Routledge, 2005.
Segundo, Juan Luis. *The Liberation of Theology*. Maryknoll, NY: Orbis, 1976.
Seidler, John, and Katherine Meyer. *Conflict and Change in the Catholic Church*. New Brunswick, NJ: Rutgers University Press, 1989.
Seiple, D., and Frederick Weidmann, eds. *Enigmas and Powers: Engaging the Work of Walter Wink for Classroom, Church and World*. Eugene, OR: Pickwick, 2008.

Sentes, Bryan, and Susan Palmer. "Presumed Immanent: The Raelians, UFO Religions, and the Postmodern Condition." *Novo Religio* 4.1 (2000) 86–105.
Seymour, Charles. "Hell, Justice and Freedom." *International Journal for Philosophy of Religion* 43 (1998) 69–86.
Shakespeare, William. *Othello*. Oxford: Clarendon, 1975.
———. *The Tempest*. Cambridge: Harvard University Press, 1958.
Shelburne, Walter. *Mythos and Logos in the Thought of Carl Jung*. Albany: State University of New York Press, 1988.
Simms, Karl. *Paul Ricoeur*. London: Routledge, 2003.
Spülbeck, Otto. "Fortschrittsglaube und Evolutionm." In *Der Fortschrittsglaube: Sinn und Gefahren*, edited by Ulrich Schöndorfer, 85–107. Graz: Verlag Styria, 1965.
———. "Teilhard de Chardin und die Pastoralkonstitution." In vol. 3 of *Die Autorität der Freiheit*, edited by Johann Christoph Hampe, 86–97. Munich: Kosel, 1967.
Spyridakis, S. "Zeus Is Dead: Euhemerus and Crete." *The Classical Journal* 63.8 (1968) 337–40.
Stewart, David. "The Hermeneutics of Suspicion." *Journal of Literature and Theology* 3 (1989) 293–307.
Storr, Anthony, ed. *The Essential Jung: A Compilation*. Princeton: Princeton University, 1983.
Stromer, Richard. "On Satan, Demons and Daimons: An Archetypal Exploration." *Soul Mentor—Guidance and Support for the Journey of Life*, n.d. Online. http://www.soulmyths.com/archetypalexploration.pdf.
Stuhlmueller, Carroll. "The Gospel According to Luke." In *The Jerome Biblical Commentary*, edited by Joseph Fitzmyer et al., 115–64. Englewood Cliffs, NJ: Prentice Hall, 1968.
Suchocki, Marjorie. *The Fall to Violence: Original Sin in Relational Theology*. New York: Continuum, 1994.
———. "Original Sin Revisited." *Process Studies* 20.4 (1991) 233–43.
Suenens, Leon-Joseph. *A New Pentecost?* New York: Seabury, 1974.
———. *Renewal and the Powers of Darkness*. London: Darton, Longman and Todd, 1983.
Sullivan, Francis. *Creative Fidelity: Weighing and Interpreting Documents of the Magisterium*. New York: Paulist, 1996.
———. *Magisterium. Teaching Authority in the Church*. New York: Paulist, 1983.
Talar, C. J. T., ed. *Prelude to the Modernist Crisis: The Firmin Articles of Alfred Loisy*. Translated by Christine Thirlway. New York: Oxford University Press, 2010.
Tertullian. *Adversus Marcionem*. Translated by Ernest Evans. London: Oxford University, 1972. Online. http://www.tertullian.org/articles/evans_marc/evans_marc_00index.htm.
Tillich, Paul. *Systematic Theology*. Vol. 1. Chicago: University of Chicago Press, 1957.
Tolkien, J. R. R. "Mythopoeia." In *Tree and Leaf*, by J. R. R. Tolkien, 83–90. London: HarperCollins, 2001. Online.
Tornielli, Andrea. "To What Extent Does the Pope Acknowledge the Devil?" *Vatican Insider*, August 20, 2013. Online. http://vaticaninsider.lastampa.it/en/the-vatican/detail/articolo/francesco-francis-francisco-27230.
Torre, Miguel de la, and Albert Hernandez. *The Quest for the Historical Satan*. Minneapolis: Fortress, 2011.

Tracy, David. *The Analogical Imagination: Christian Theology and the Culture of Pluralism*. New York: Crossroad.

———. "Fragments, the Spiritual Situation of Our Times." In *God, the Gift and Postmodernism*, edited by John Caputo and Michael Scanlon, 170–80. Bloomington: Indiana University Press, 1999.

———. "The Uneasy Alliance." *Theological Studies* 50 (1989) 548–70.

Trueman, Carl. "Traditional Troubles: A Review of Thomas Guarino, *Vincent of Lerins and the Development of Christian Doctrine*. New York: Baker, 2014." *First Things*, May 2014. Online. https://www.firstthings.com/article/2014/05/traditional-troubles.

Tuckett, Christopher. "Scripture in Q." In *The Scriptures in the Gospels*, edited by Christopher Tuckett, 3–26. Leuven: Leuven University Press, 1997.

Turvasi, Francesco. *The Condemnation of Alfred Loisy and the Historical Method*. Rome: Ediz. di Storia e Letteratura, 1979.

United States Conference of Catholic Bishops (USCCB). *Economic Justice for All*. Washington, DC: USCCB, 1996. Online. http://www.usccb.org/upload/economic_justice_for_all.pdf.

———. *Rebuking the Devil*. Washington, DC: USCCB, 2019.

———. "Responsibility, Rehabilitation, and Restoration: A Catholic Perspective on Crime and Criminal Justice." November 15, 2000. Online. http://www.usccb.org/issues-and-action/human-life-and-dignity/criminal-justice-restorative-justice/crime-and-criminal-justice.cfm.

Vaino, Ollie-Pekka. *Beyond Fideism: Negotiable Religious Identities*. New York: Routledge, 2010.

Vatican I. "*Dei Filius*: Dogmatic Constitution on the Catholic Faith." In *The Vatican Council and Its Definitions*, edited by Henry Edward Manning. New York: D. & J. Sadlier, 1871. Online. http://www.catholicplanet.org/councils/20-Dei-Filius.htm.

Vincent of Lerins. *The Commonitory*. Translated by T. Herbert Bindley. London: SPCK, 1914.

Viviano, Pauline. "Genesis." In *Collegeville Biblical Commentary*, edited by Diane Bergant and Robert Kallas, 35–78. Collegeville, MN: Liturgical, 1988.

Volz, Paul. *Das Daimonische in Jahwe [The Demonic in YHWH]*. Tübingen: Mohr, 1924.

Voogd, Stephanie de. *C. G. Jung: Psychologist of the Future, "Philosopher" of the Past*. New York: Spring, 1977.

Weigel, George. *Evangelical Catholicism: Deep Reform in the Twenty-First Century Church*. New York: Basic, 2013.

———. "The Making of a New Benedict." In *God's Choice: Pope Benedict XVI and the Future of the Catholic Church*, by George Weigel, 157–87. New York: HarperCollins, 2005. Online. https://www.catholiceducation.org/en/faith-and-character/faith-and-character/the-making-of-a-new-benedict.html.

White, Thomas Joseph. "The Tridentine Genius of Vatican II." *First Things*, November 2012. Online. https://www.firstthings.com/article/2012/11/the-tridentine-genius-of-vatican-ii.

Whitehead, Kenneth. "How Dissent Became Institutionalized in the Church in America." *Homiletic & Pastoral Review* 99.10 (1999) 20–28.

Wicks, Jared. "Six Texts by Prof. Joseph Ratzinger as *Peritus* Before and During Vatican Council II." *Gregorianum* 89 (2008) 233–311.

Wilkins, John. "Bishops or Branch Managers: Collegiality after the Council." *Commonweal*, October 12, 2012. Online. https://www.commonwealmagazine.org/bishops-or-branch-managers?key=31ae255b31eeba7b6de4731f5067009b.
Wills, Gary. *Papal Sin: Structures of Deceit*. New York: Doubleday, 2000.
Wink, Walter. *The Human Being: Jesus and the Son of Man*. Minneapolis: Fortress, 2002.
———. *Naming the Powers*. Philadelphia: Fortress, 1984.
———. *The Powers That Be: Theology for a New Millennium*. New York: Galilee Doubleday, 1993.
———. "Response to Luke Timothy Johnson's *The Real Jesus*." *Bulletin for Biblical Research* 7 (1997) 233–48.
Wittgenstein, Ludwig. *Tractatus Logico-Philosophicus*. London: Routledge & Kegan Paul, 1922.
Wolpe, David. "Angels in Jewish Tradition." *Beliefnet* (blog), April 2002. Online. https://www.beliefnet.com/faiths/judaism/2002/04/angels-in-jewish-tradition.aspx.
World Health Organization (WHO). "Trance and Possession Disorders." In *ICD-10 Classification of Mental and Behavioural Disorders: The Diagnostic Criteria for Research*, F44.3. Geneva: WHO, 2014. Online. https://www.who.int/classifications/icd/en/GRNBOOK.pdf.
Worthington, Everett, et al. "Interpersonal Forgiveness as an Example of Loving One's Enemies." *Journal of Psychology and Theology* 34 (2006) 32–42.
Wray, T. J., and Gregory Mobley. *The Birth of Satan: Tracing the Devil's Biblical Roots*. New York: Palgrave MacMillan, 2005.
Wright, N. T. *Jesus and the Victory of God*. Minneapolis: Fortress, 1996.
———. *Surprised by Hope: Rethinking Heaven, the Resurrection and the Mission of the Church*. New York: HarperCollins, 2008.

www.ingramcontent.com/pod-product-compliance
Lightning Source LLC
Chambersburg PA
CBHW050849230426
43667CB00012B/2208